Praise for Jeffrey Mayer

"The most tangible and immediate result of Mayer's work is a clean, organized desk where once there was a cluttered nightmare."
— Richard Roeper, *Chicago Sun-Times*

"Some people even give a session with the dean of the desk cleaners as a birthday gift for the CEOs in their lives."
— *People*

"Jeffrey Mayer is 'Mr. Neat the Clutterbuster.' He makes molehills out of messy mountains of paper."
—Jim Freschi, *USA Today*

"Jeffrey Mayer tells clients how to efficiently manage their time and their paperwork."
— Kevin McCormally, *Kiplinger's Personal Finance Magazine*

"Jeffrey Mayer is the messy manager's solution to piles of files."
— Annetta Miller, *Newsweek*

"Jeffrey Mayer describes his approach as a crash course in how to get organized."
— Thomas J. Brazaitis, *Cleveland Plain Dealer*

"Jeffrey Mayer helps business and professional people create order out of disorder."
— William Gruber, *Chicago Tribune*

"*If You Haven't Got the Time to Do It Right, When Will You Find the Time to Do It Over?* is filled with timesaving tips that Jeffrey Mayer has picked up from an obsession with doing things quickly."
— Alexa Bell, *Investor's Business Daily*

"Jeffrey Mayer can clean your desk and get you organized in just two hours."
— Ronald E. Yates, *Chicago Tribune*

"Jeffrey Mayer, author of *Winning the Fight Between You and Your Desk* receives about $1,000 for helping offices combat clutter."
— Lucinda Harper, *Wall Street Journal*

"Jeffrey Mayer's *Winning the Fight Between You and Your Desk* is a guide to the joys of personal computing."
— Mark Mehler, *Investors Business Daily*

"Jeffrey Mayer's *Winning the Fight Between You and Your Desk* tells you how to get organized at work with your computer. I need this one, even if you don't."
— Larry Shannon, *New York Times*

"Jeffrey Mayer's organizing strategy relies heavily on the use of two pieces of common office equipment — a wastebasket and a computer."
— Robert A. Devaney, *Washington Times*

"As companies move toward the paperless office, Jeffrey Mayer has begun encouraging executives to supplement clean desks with efficient computer usage."
— Mukul Pandya, *New York Times*

"Jeffrey Mayer's *Winning the Fight Between You and Your Desk* is concise, focused, well-organized, and easy to read — just as it should be from someone who is paid $1,000 to clean up an executive's desk."
— Scott Pendleton, *Christian Science Monitor*

"When I consulted with Jeffrey Mayer several years ago to improve the management of my time, I told him that the real test of his work would be measured by recidivism. In other words, how much would my behavior have changed a year or two later? Jeff's contribution passed with flying colors! His deceptively simple ideas and techniques have persisted and brought about a permanent improvement in how I handle paper flow, meetings, telephone calls, etc. I would recommend him to anyone as a time management consultant."
— David Shute, Senior Vice President, General Counsel, and Secretary; Sears, Roebuck and Co., Chicago, Illinois

"Jeffrey Mayer's *If You Haven't Got the Time to Do It Right, When Will You Find the Time to Do It Over?* is a *must* read. I've long been a proponent of a 'clean desk' and have kept one myself for more than 25 years. I'm a firm believer in the time management techniques that he espouses in his books, tapes, and seminars. He's got a lot of important things to say. His books should be required reading for anyone who wants to save time, be more productive, and make more money."
— Norman R. Bobins, President and Chief Executive Officer, LaSalle National Bank, Chicago, Illinois

"My professional relationship with Jeffrey Mayer dates back more than twenty years. I have found Jeffrey to be intelligent, articulate, detailed, and competent in all our dealings. He is an accomplished and successful author of many business books and does practice what he preaches."
— Howard S. Goss, President, Transco Inc., Chicago, Illinois

"Five years, ago, Jeffrey Mayer introduced me to a whole new way of staying organized and focused on both my personal and professional priorities. I'm still using the tips, techniques, and strategies he gave me. They really do work! Jeff is a wizard at helping people stay organized!"
— Richard W. Pehlke, Vice President and Treasurer, Ameritech, Chicago, Illinois

"Jeffrey Mayer is a talented writer who deals with complex business subjects in a very succinct, meaningful, and practical way. I highly recommend his books."
— Ronald J. Patten, Ph.D., C.P.A., Dean of the College of Commerce, DePaul University, Chicago, Illinois

"We liked Jeffrey Mayer's *If You Haven't Got the Time to Do It Right, When Will You Find the Time to Do It Over?* so much that we referenced it in our book."
— Paul & Sarah Edwards, Authors, *Working From Home*

"Jeffrey Mayer got me organized. His organizational tips and techniques have helped me to save time. His helpful hints for using ACT! for Windows have made me a much more proficient user. His knowledge and experience has provided me with many valuable tools for improving the management of my time."

> — Robert J. Winter, Jr., President, Stein & Company, Chicago, Illinois

"If your time is money, then you've got to read Jeffrey Mayer's *If You Haven't Got the Time to Do It Right, When Will You Find the Time to Do It Over?*. His ideas will save you at least an hour of time a day. He really knows his stuff!

> — Arthur S. Nicholas, President, The Antech Group, Chicago, Illinois

"It was my habit for too many years to creat piles of 'I Gottas' and 'I'm Gonnas.' Jeffrey Mayer came into my life and I had a huge pile of throwaways: papers, magazines, and books. And he left me with a clean desk, clean closet, clean book case, and a process to assure that the 'I Gottas' and 'I'm Gonnas' were controlled in the future."

> — Ben T. Nelson, Retired Executive Vice President,
> Harris Trust and Savings Bank, Chicago, Illinois

"Since working with Jeffrey Mayer I have totally revamped my personal workspace in line with his suggestions . . . out with the file folders, and away with the stacks of untended documents! Jeffrey's 'clean desk' approach to getting organized has convinced me that a fresh perspective can bring about positive changes. I leave my office each day with a feeling of accomplishment, and, more importantly arrive the next morning in a position of control. His system is simple, effective, and easy to keep moving.

> — Bill Jacobs, Chairman of the Board, Office Concepts, Inc.,
> Chicago, Illinois

"Jeffrey Mayer reminded me that it's important to manage the paper flow and not let the paper flow manage me. His timesaving tips are invaluable. My colleagues can't believe that my office has *stayed* organized."

> — Gregory A. Browne, ARM; Manager, Insurance Claims,
> GATX Corporation, Chicago, Illinois

"Just when all seemed hopeless and I was about to drown in a sea of paper and computer files, Jeffrey Mayer came along and *saved* me. What he offers can make the difference between success and failure in any field."

> — Michael Harrison, Editor and Publisher, *Talkers* Magazine,
> Longmeadow, Massachussets

"Jeffrey Mayer's approach is very straightforward. It employes common sense, purposefulness, and a range of techniques that can be of great value to anyone and everyone. Jeffrey Mayer has identified the secret of success: Use your time to your advantage."

> — James Paglia, President, Tassani & Paglia, Chicago, Illinois

"I'm really grateful to Jeffrey Mayer for the time he spent going over my organizational needs and prompting me to organize myself appropriately. I found that it most beneficial to have someone take a fresh look at my old habits to help me streamline my follow-up systems, making me more productive and efficient. As a consultant, time is money, and I feel the time spent with Jeffrey Mayer has enabled me to work at a higher level.

> — Gerri Hilt, Executive Recruiter, Chicago, Illinois

"Both my husband and I have known Jeffrey Mayer for nine years and are stagestruck with his abilities. He truly delivers what he promises with an incomparable wit. Indecision is an unknown to Jeff. He gets it done. His time management techniques have streamlined our business and personal affairs."

> — Ellie Thompson CTC, President, Brookshire Travel Services Inc., Chicago, Illinois

"Jeffrey Mayer's ideas for time management should be a basic primer for everyone entering the business world. His genius is in clearly describing a set of simple tools that provide immediate timesaving benefits no matter how organized or disorganized one may be. If you're sick and tired of stacks of paper, lost memos, missed deadlines, and a general state of administrative chaos, or if you're on the other extreme of time management and are looking for a way to wring out the last 2 percent of efficiency, you will find that Jeffrey Mayer's tools will help you accomplish your objectives."

> — J.E. Treadway, Vice President Human Resources, Metromail (An R.R. Donnelley & Sons Company), Lombard, Illinois

"Jeffrey Mayer does the impossible. He makes time management fun. Everyone knows in his or her heart of hearts that he or she is wasting time, and Jeff offers solid suggestions on how to get 65 minutes out of every hour.

> — George M. Taber, Editor and Publisher, New Jersey Business Newspapers, New Brunswick, New Jersey

"Jeffrey Mayer helped me to clean off my desk. The time he spent with me has helped me become much more efficient and productive. I've recommended his services to a number of my friends and associates."

> — Ronald N. Primack, Attorney, Lansing, Illinois

Praise for Jeffrey Mayer's Books

"Jeffrey Mayer's book *If You Haven't Got the Time to Do It Right, When Will You Find the Time to Do It Over?* has been invaluable to me. It has helped me accomplish more work in less time. Jeffrey Mayer's system and time management principals save me five to seven hours per week."

> — Jeffrey W. Durkee, Resident Vice President, Merrill Lynch, Century City, California

"Being able to keep my desk organized and uncluttered all the time is an intriguing prospect. I appreciate your perceptive note and look forward to reading your book, *If You Haven't Got the Time to Do It Right, When Will You Find the Time to Do It Over?*. I take some comfort in knowing that many others have been confronted with this problem — and have solved it."
> — Bill Bradley, United States Senator, Washington, D.C.

"I found Jeffrey Mayer's *If You Haven't Got the Time to Do It Right, When Will You Find the Time to Do It Over?* to be thoroughly enjoyable. It had numerous ideas and suggestions which could be readily absorbed into my short- and long-term activities. Furthermore, his book is now part of my team's reading list."
> — Chris Hutchinson, Product Development Manager,
> Fisher & Paykel Healthcare, Auckland, New Zealand

"When I discovered Jeffrey Mayer's book *If You Haven't Got the Time to Do It Right, When Will You Find the Time to Do It Over?* almost five years ago, my business life changed — dramatically — for the better. Since then I've used his system exclusively and find that time I was wasting shifting paper from one pile to another has been put to substantially more profitable use. I credit Jeffrey Mayer and his book with helping me and my company grow and prosper, I recommend it without reservation."
> — Chaz Cone, Chief Executive Officer, OPMS Software Manufacturing
> Group, Inc., Atlanta, Georgia

"Jeffrey Mayer's time management system is practical and more efficient than any other I have ever used. His easy-to-follow methods will help anyone become more organized and help them to better utilize their time. His book, *If You Haven't Got the Time to Do It Right, When Will You Find the Time to Do It Over?*, is a book that I've keep available for ready reference. Quite simply, Jeffrey Mayer's methods help me get things done!"
> — Mark Lawley, Photographer, Leeds, Alabama

"Jeffrey Mayer's book *If You Haven't Got the Time to Do It Right, When Will You Find the Time to Do It Over?* has immediate, simple and practical ideas to increase both personal and team productivity. I highly recommend it to anyone who wants to be more organized for maximum results with minimum effort!"
> — Shelly Espinosa, M.S.W., Executive Director, Working Solutions,
> Thornton, Colorado

"I loved Jeffrey Mayer's book *If You Haven't Got the Time to Do It Right, When Will You Find the Time to Do It Over?.*"
> — M. Bachammar, Stanel Corp., Paris, France

"I thoroughly enjoyed Jeffrey Mayer's *If You Haven't Got the Time to Do It Right, When Will You Find the Time to Do It Over?.*"
> — N.H. Atthreya Ph.D., Director, M M M School of Management,
> Bombay, India

"As a time management expert, I enjoyed Jeffrey Mayer's book *If You Haven't Got the Time to Do It Right, When Will You Find the Time to Do It Over?.*"
> — Sandra Woods, President, Up The Ladder, Toronto, Ontario

"I thoroughly enjoyed reading Jeffrey Mayer's *If You Haven't Got the Time to Do It Right, When Will You Find the Time to Do It Over?*. Many of the principals in his book are common sense, everyday principles that have been systematized for practical application for a clear way of action."

> — Khalid Al-Turki, Al Turki Trading, Contracting,
> Kingdom of Saudi Arabia

"I loved Jeffrey Mayer's book *If You Haven't Got the Time to Do It Right, When Will You Find the Time to Do It Over?* It's lively, fun to read, and full of good advice."

> — Sarah Hutter, Associate Editor, *Working Mother*,
> New York, New York

"Jeffrey Mayer's concise, user-friendly approach to time management is just what today's managers need. His book *If You Haven't Got the Time to Do It Right, When Will You Find the Time to Do It Over?* is must-reading for any manager."

> — Timothy S. Mescon, Ph.D., Dean of the Michael J. Coles School of
> Business, Kennesaw State College, Marietta, Georgia

"I loved Jeffrey Mayer's *Winning the Fight Between You and Your Desk*. I first read about him in *People* years ago and was so impressed with his ideas that I kept the article, and still have it."

> — Dennis Rahilly, Exact Hi-Tech Engineering Communications,
> Cambridge, Massachusetts

"Jeffrey Mayer's *Winning the Fight Between You and Your Desk* is loaded with excellent information and the format made it very easy to breeze through. Thanks for taking the time to write an informative book like this and presenting it in such a useable format."

> — Dr. Scott R. Fladland, Chicago, Illinois

"Thanks for writing *Winning the Fight Between You and Your Desk*."

> — Samuel R. Phillips, Consulting Engineer, Portola Valley, California

"Jeffrey Mayer has many good ideas in *Winning the Fight Between You and Your Desk*."

> — Robert B. Mellman, Attorney, Montclair, New Jersey

 ™

References for the Rest of Us™

BUSINESS BOOK SERIES FROM IDG

Are you intimidated and confused by personal finance and business issues? Do you find that traditional books are overloaded with technical details and advice that you'll never use? Do you postpone important financial decisions because you just don't want to deal with them? Then our ...*For Dummies™* business book series is for you.

...*For Dummies™* business books are written for those frustrated and hard-working souls who know they aren't really dumb but find that that the myriad of personal finance and business issues and the accompanying horror stories make them feel helpless. ...*For Dummies™* books use a lighthearted approach, a down-to-earth style, and even cartoons and humorous icons to diffuse fears and build confidence. Lighthearted but not lightweight, these books are perfect survival guides to solve your personal finance and business problems.

> ## "More than a publishing phenomenon, 'Dummies' is a sign of the times."
> ### — The New York Times

> ## "... you won't go wrong buying them."
> ### — Walter Mossberg, Wall Street Journal, on IDG's ...For Dummies™ books

> ## "This is the best book ever written for a beginner."
> ### — Clarence Petersen, Chicago Tribune, on DOS For Dummies ®

Already, hundreds of thousands of satisfied readers agree. They have made ...*For Dummies™* the #1 introductory level computer book series and a best selling business book series. They have written asking for more. So if you're looking for the best and easiest way to learn about personal finance and business, look to ...*For Dummies™* to give you a helping hand.

TIME MANAGEMENT FOR DUMMIES™

by Jeffrey J. Mayer

IDG
BOOKS

IDG Books Worldwide, Inc.
An International Data Group Company

Foster City, CA ♦ Chicago, IL ♦ Indianapolis, IN ♦ Braintree, MA ♦ Dallas, TX

Time Management For Dummies™

Published by
IDG Books Worldwide, Inc.
An International Data Group Company
919 E. Hillsdale Blvd.
Suite 400
Foster City, CA 94404

Library of Congress Catalog Card No.: 95-75882

ISBN: 1-56884-360-7

Printed in the United States of America

10 9 8 7 6 5 4 3 2

1B/RQ/QU/ZV

3 9082 06059107 3

Distributed in the United States by IDG Books Worldwide, Inc.

Distributed by Macmillan Canada for Canada; by Computer and Technical Books for the Caribbean Basin; by Contemporanea de Ediciones for Venezuela; by Distribuidora Cuspide for Argentina; by CITEC for Brazil; by Ediciones ZETA S.C.R. Ltda. for Peru; by Editorial Limusa SA for Mexico; by Transworld Publishers Limited in the United Kingdom and Europe; by Al-Maiman Publishers & Distributors for Saudi Arabia; by Simron Pty. Ltd. for South Africa; by IDG Communications (HK) Ltd. for Hong Kong; by Toppan Company Ltd. for Japan; by Addison Wesley Publishing Company for Korea; by Longman Singapore Publishers Ltd. for Singapore, Malaysia, Thailand, and Indonesia; by Unalis Corporation for Taiwan; by WS Computer Publishing Company, Inc. for the Philippines; by WoodsLane Pty. Ltd. for Australia; by WoodsLane Enterprises Ltd. for New Zealand.

For general information on IDG Books in the U.S., including information on discounts and premiums, contact IDG Books at 800-434-3422 or 415-655-3000.

For information on where to purchase IDG Books outside the U.S., contact IDG Books International at 415-655-3021 or fax 415-655-3295.

For information on translations, contact Marc Jeffrey Mikulich, Director, Foreign & Subsidiary Rights, at IDG Books Worldwide, 415-655-3018 or fax 415-655-3295.

For sales inquiries and special prices for bulk quantities, write to the address above or call IDG Books Worldwide at 415-655-3000.

For information on using IDG Books in the classroom or ordering examination copies, contact Jim Kelly at 800-434-2086.

For authorization to photocopy items for corporate, personal, or educational use, please contact Copyright Clearance Center, 222 Rosewood Drive, Danvers, MA 01923, or fax 508-750-4470.

 is a trademark under exclusive license to IDG Books Worldwide, Inc., from International Data Group, Inc.

About the Author

Photo Credit: Roger Lewin

Jeffrey Mayer is one of the country's foremost authorities on time management. For a living he helps busy people get organized, save time, and become more productive. Jeff's claim to fame is his *clean desk* approach to time management. *USA Today* dubbed him "Mr. Neat, the Clutterbuster," and *People* called him "The Dean of the Desk Cleaners."

He walks into an office, one that looks like a toxic waste dump — with piles of paper, and everything else you can imagine, strewn all over the place — and in two hours the desktop looks like the flight-deck of an aircraft carrier. So much has been thrown away that the wastebasket is filled to the brim, overflowing, and spilling onto the floor. All that remains are a handful of file folders, a pad of paper, and a telephone. Everything else is neatly filed away.

Long ago, Jeff realized that if everybody was better organized, they could take more control over their day and would have more time to focus on their most important work. Once they were done, then they could leave the office, go home, and spend more time with their family and friends.

Today, Jeff is paid more than a $1,000 for each desk he overhauls. But he's not paid all this money because his clients want to have a nice, neat, orderly desk. The desk is secondary — he's paid all of this money because his clients realize that time is money. And Jeff's able to help them convert time that's wasted during the course of a normal business day into time that can be used more efficiently, effectively, and profitably. Jeff's specialty is in teaching people how to improve their follow-up systems. With a good follow-up system, people are able to spend more time working on the things that are important, instead of the things that keep them busy.

Since the founding of his Chicago, Illinois based consulting firm, Mayer Enterprises, he has helped more than a 1,500 men and women get organized and learn how to use their time more effectively. Many of his clients are top executives at Fortune 500 Companies. His corporate clients include Ameritech, Commonwealth Edison, Harris Bank and Trust Company, LaSalle National Bank, R.R. Donnelley & Sons Company, and Sears, Roebuck & Co., just to name a few.

Jeff has been interviewed by almost every major newspaper and magazine in the United States, including the *Wall Street Journal*, the *New York Times*, the *Chicago Tribune*, the *Los Angeles Times*, *USA Today*, *People*, *Newsweek*, *Forbes*, *Business Week*, and *Fortune*. And he has been interviewed on hundreds of radio and television programs across the United States, including the *Today Show*, *American Journal*, CNN, CNBC and ABC News. Jeff lives with his family in Chicago, Illinois.

Speeches and seminars

Jeff would be delighted to speak at your next business meeting, conference, or convention. For date availability he can be reached at: Mayer Enterprises, 50 East Bellevue Place, Suite 305, Chicago IL 60611. His e-mail address on CompuServe is 74552,157@compuserve.com.

Thoughts and comments

If you would like to offer your thoughts or comments about this book, please send them to the above address.

Other Books by Jeffrey J. Mayer

If You Haven't Got the Time to Do It Right, When Will You Find the Time to Do It Over?

Find the Job You've Always Wanted in Half the Time with Half the Effort

Winning the Fight Between You and Your Desk

ABOUT IDG BOOKS WORLDWIDE

WINNER
Eighth Annual
Computer Press
Awards ≥ 1992

WINNER
Ninth Annual
Computer Press
Awards ≥ 1993

IDG BOOKS

Welcome to the world of IDG Books Worldwide.

IDG Books Worldwide, Inc., is a subsidiary of International Data Group, the world's largest publisher of computer-related information and the leading global provider of information services on information technology. IDG was founded more than 25 years ago and now employs more than 7,200 people worldwide. IDG publishes more than 233 computer publications in 65 countries (see listing below). More than sixty million people read one or more IDG publications each month.

Launched in 1990, IDG Books Worldwide is today the #1 publisher of best-selling computer books in the United States. We are proud to have received 3 awards from the Computer Press Association in recognition of editorial excellence, and our best-selling ...*For Dummies*™ series has more than 12 million copies in print with translations in 25 languages. IDG Books, through a recent joint venture with IDG's Hi-Tech Beijing, became the first U.S. publisher to publish a computer book in the People's Republic of China. In record time, IDG Books has become the first choice for millions of readers around the world who want to learn how to better manage their businesses.

Our mission is simple: Every IDG book is designed to bring extra value and skill-building instructions to the reader. Our books are written by experts who understand and care about our readers. The knowledge base of our editorial staff comes from years of experience in publishing, education, and journalism — experience which we use to produce books for the '90s. In short, we care about books, so we attract the best people. We devote special attention to details such as audience, interior design, use of icons, and illustrations. And because we use an efficient process of authoring, editing, and desktop publishing our books electronically, we can spend more time ensuring superior content and spend less time on the technicalities of making books.

You can count on our commitment to deliver high-quality books at competitive prices on topics consumers want to read about. At IDG, we value quality, and we have been delivering quality for more than 25 years. You'll find no better book on a subject than an IDG book.

John J. Kilcullen

John Kilcullen
President and CEO
IDG Books Worldwide, Inc.

IDG Books Worldwide, Inc., is a subsidiary of International Data Group, the world's largest publisher of computer-related information and the leading global provider of information services on information technology. International Data Group publishes over 220 computer publications in 65 countries. More than fifty million people read one or more International Data Group publications each month. The officers are Patrick J. McGovern, Founder and Board Chairman; Kelly Conlin, President; Jim Casella, Chief Operating Officer. International Data Group's publications include: **ARGENTINA'S** Computerworld Argentina, Infoworld Argentina; **AUSTRALIA'S** Computerworld Australia, Computer Living, Australian PC World, Australian Macworld, Network World, Mobile Business Australia, Publish!, Reseller, IDG Sources; **AUSTRIA'S** Computerwelt Oesterreich, PC Test; **BELGIUM'S** Data News (CW); **BOLIVIA'S** Computerworld; **BRAZIL'S** Computerworld, Connections, Game Power, Mundo Unix, PC World, Publish, Super Game; **BULGARIA'S** Computerworld Bulgaria, PC & Mac World Bulgaria, Network World Bulgaria; **CANADA'S** CIO Canada, Computerworld Canada, InfoCanada, Network World Canada, Reseller; **CHILE'S** Computerworld Chile, Informatica; **COLOMBIA'S** Computerworld Colombia, PC World; **COSTA RICA'S** PC World; **CZECH REPUBLIC'S** Computerworld, Elektronika, PC World; **DENMARK'S** Communications World, Computerworld Danmark, Computerworld Focus, Macintosh Produktkatalog, Macworld Danmark, PC World Danmark, PC Produktguide, Tech World, Windows World; **ECUADOR'S** PC World Ecuador; **EGYPT'S** Computerworld (CW) Middle East, PC World Middle East; **FINLAND'S** MikroPC, Tietoviikko, Tietoverkko; **FRANCE'S** Distributique, GOLDEN MAC, InfoPC, Le Guide du Monde Informatique, Le Monde Informatique, Telecoms & Reseaux; **GERMANY'S** Computerwoche, Computerwoche Focus, Computerwoche Extra, Electronic Entertainment, Gamepro, Information Management, Macwelt, Netzwelt, PC Welt, Publish, Publish; **GREECE'S** Publish & Macworld; **HONG KONG'S** Computerworld Hong Kong, PC World Hong Kong; **HUNGARY'S** Computerworld SZT, PC World; **INDIA'S** Computers & Communications; **INDONESIA'S** Info Komputer; **IRELAND'S** ComputerScope; **ISRAEL'S** Beyond Windows, Computerworld Israel, Multimedia, PC World Israel; **ITALY'S** Computerworld Italia, Lotus Magazine, Macworld Italia, Networking Italia, PC Shopping Italy, PC World Italia; **JAPAN'S** Computerworld Today, Information Systems World, Macworld Japan, Nikkei Personal Computing, SunWorld Japan, Windows World; **KENYA'S** East African Computer News; **KOREA'S** Computerworld Korea, Macworld Korea, PC World Korea; **LATIN AMERICA'S** GamePro; **MALAYSIA'S** Computerworld Malaysia, PC World Malaysia; **MEXICO'S** Compu Edicion, Compu Manufactura, Computacion/Punto de Venta, Computerworld Mexico, MacWorld, Mundo Unix, PC World, Windows; **THE NETHERLANDS'** Computer! Totaal, Computable (CW), LAN Magazine, Lotus Magazine, MacWorld; **NEW ZEALAND'S** Computer Buyer, Computerworld New Zealand, Network World, New Zealand PC World; **NIGERIA'S** PC World Africa; **NORWAY'S** Computerworld Norge, Lotusworld Norge, Macworld Norge, Maxi Data, Networld, PC World Ekspress, PC World Nettverk, PC World Norge, PC World's Produktguide, Publish& Multimedia World, Student Data, Unix World, Windowsworld; **PAKISTAN'S** PC World Pakistan; **PANAMA'S** PC World Panama; **PERU'S** Computerworld Peru, PC World; **PEOPLE'S REPUBLIC OF CHINA'S** China Computerworld, China Infoworld, China PC Info Magazine, Computer Fan, PC World China, Electronics International, Electronics Today/Multimedia World, Electronic Product World, China Network World, Software World Magazine, Telecom Product World; **PHILIPPINES'** Computerworld Philippines, PC Digest (PCW); **POLAND'S** Computerworld Poland, Computerworld Special Report, Networld, PC World/Komputer, Sunworld; **PORTUGAL'S** Cerebro/PC World, Correio Informatico/Computerworld, MacIn; **ROMANIA'S** Computerworld, PC World, Telecom Romania; **RUSSIA'S** Computerworld-Moscow, Mir - PK (PCW), Sety (Networks); **SINGAPORE'S** Computerworld Southeast Asia, PC World Singapore; **SLOVENIA'S** Monitor Magazine; **SOUTH AFRICA'S** Computer Mail (CIO),Computing S.A.,Network World S.A., Software World; **SPAIN'S** Advanced Systems, Amiga World, Computerworld Espana, Communicaciones World, Macworld Espana, Macworld Espana, NeXTWORLD, Super Juegos Magazine (GamePro), PC World Espana, Publish; **SWEDEN'S** Attack, ComputerSweden, Corporate Computing, Macworld, Mikrodatorn, Natverk & Kommunikation, PC World, CAP & Design, Datalngenjoren, Maxi Data,Windows World; **SWITZERLAND'S** Computerworld Schweiz, Macworld Schweiz, PC Tip; **TAIWAN'S** Computerworld Taiwan, PC World Taiwan; **THAILAND'S** Thai Computerworld; **TURKEY'S** Computerworld Monitor, Macworld Turkiye, PC World Turkiye; **UKRAINE'S** Computerworld, Computers+Software Magazine; **UNITED KINGDOM'S** Computing /Computerworld, Connexion/Network World, Lotus Magazine, Macworld, Open Computing/Sunworld; **UNITED STATES'** Advanced Systems, AmigaWorld, Cable in the Classroom, CD Review, CIO, Computerworld, Computerworld Client/Server Journal, Digital Video, DOS World, Electronic Entertainment Magazine (E2), Federal Computer Week, Game Hits, GamePro, IDG Books, Infoworld, Laser Event, Macworld, Maximize, Multimedia World, Network World, PC Letter, PC World, Publish, SWATPro, Video Event; **URUGUAY'S** PC World Uruguay; **VENEZUELA'S** Computerworld Venezuela, PC World; **VIETNAM'S** PC World Vietnam.   02/28/95

Acknowledgments

A big thank you goes to my publisher, editor, and good friend, Kathy Welton, for all she's done in helping me put *Time Management For Dummies* together.

I would also like to thank project editor, Tim Gallan, for all of his editorial help, support, and encouragement in writing *Time Management For Dummies*. Tim, it would have been impossible to do this without you.

Another thank you goes to Greg Robertson, my other editor, who offered many great editorial tips that helped to turn this manuscript into a lively, easy to read book; and to Corbin Collins, another IDG Books project editor, for teaching me about the Internet.

And a special thank you goes out to Stacy Collins, Brand Manager, Kathy Day, Publicity and Events Manager, and Polly Papsadore, Director of Marketing, who did just a marvelous job of marketing and promoting *Time Management For Dummies*.

And I can't forget the Production people who put this book together, so thanks to Valery Bourke, Linda Boyer, Chris Collins, and Carla Radzikinas for making the pages look so good.

And finally, I would like to say thank you to my good friend and computer guru extraordinaire Rich Barkoff, the owner of Ernie's Office Machines in Chicago, for the many hours he's spent over the past several years helping me solve my computer problems and teaching me how to make my computer work.

(The publisher would like to give special thanks to Patrick J. McGovern and Bill Murphy, without whom this book would not have been possible.)

Dedication

To the important women in my life: my mother, Estelle Mayer Loeb; my grand-mother, Ida Cohn; two very close friends, Eleanor Brennecke and Magnolia Monroe; two close friends who have recently passed away, Clara Siegel Ehrlich and Pauline Novak; and to my closest friends of all, my wife Mitzi and my daughter DeLaine.

I love you all.

Credits

VP & Publisher
Kathleen A. Welton

Brand Manager
Stacy S. Collins

Production Director
Beth Jenkins

**Supervisor of
Project Coordination**
Cindy L. Phipps

Project Coordinator
Valery Bourke

Pre-Press Coordinator
Steve Peake

Associate Pre-Press Coordinator
Tony Augsburger

Editorial Assistants
Kevin Spencer
Tamara S. Castleman
Stacey Holden Prince

Associate Project Editor
A. Timothy Gallan

Copy Editor
Greg Robertson

Production Staff
Paul Belcastro
Linda M. Boyer
Chris Collins
Dominique DeFelice
Sherry Gomoll
Drew R. Moore
Carla C. Radzikinas
Dwight Ramsey
Patricia R. Reynolds
Gina Scott

Proofreader
Kathleen Prata

Indexer
Sharon Hilgenberg

Cover Design
Kavish + Kavish

Contents at a Glance

Cartoons at a Glance

By Rich Tennant

Table of Contents

Introduction

Time Management in the 90s

1 f you're like most people, you never have enough time to get everything done at the office. You're working harder and you're working longer, but you still don't feel as though you're making any headway. So you come in early; you stay late; you work weekends; and when you finally get home at the end of a long day, you're so worn out that you don't have any time or energy left for yourself, your friends, or your family. The time management techniques that worked so well for you in the 80s just don't work anymore. Because the world around us has changed in so many ways, they've become obsolete.

The 5th Wave   **By Rich Tennant**

"WHO'S BEEN COMPLAINING ABOUT HAVING NOTHING TO DO?"

- ✔ We used to believe that we could get our work done if we could just "handle a piece of paper only once!" Today we've still got the papers, and we've got e-mail, voice mail, and wireless communications systems. On our desktops are super-fast computers that are all networked together. And we're all communicating with each other via the Internet and on-line services like CompuServe, Prodigy, and America Online.

- ✔ We were once thrilled when we could send a letter via FedEx and get it to someone by 10:30 the next morning. Today, you just fax it from your computer directly to another computer. And if you want to send someone a document, you just attach it to an e-mail message.

- ✔ Secretaries and administrative assistants used to sit at their desks typing letters, memos, reports, presentations, and other documents on their IBM Selectric electronic typewriters at 60 words per minute. Today most of the secretaries are gone, and in their place is a blazingly fast PC that we use to write our own letters, memos, reports, and presentations. Then we use our spell checkers and grammar checkers to correct our mistakes.

- ✔ To create complex documents, presentations, and reports, we used to have to get together for long, drawn out meetings in the company's conference room. Today, our computers are all networked together and with the new groupware products, a group of people — in different cities — can now work together at the same time to create documents, presentations, and reports.

We aren't handling paper any more! We're handling information. And the time frames we have to make decisions continue to shrink.

To succeed in the 90s, you've got to do more than just "get organized." You've got to do a better job of staying on top of all of your unfinished work, tasks, and projects, and you accomplish this goal by improving your follow-up systems. With an efficient and effective follow-up system, you can convert the time that's wasted during the course of a normal business day into time that can be used more efficiently, effectively, and profitably.

I call this *addition by subtraction.* By eliminating the wasted time, you'll have more time to spend on the things that are most important to you. Then you can get your work done, leave the office at a reasonable hour, and spend the rest of the day with your family and friends doing the things that you enjoy.

It's the Quality, Not the Quantity, of the Hours You Work

With workloads that have become swollen by the downsizing fervor, we're all working harder than ever. We're coming into our offices earlier each morning. We're staying later in the evening. And though we're putting in all of these extra hours, we aren't getting to our important projects, let alone the routine correspondence and the other miscellaneous things that have accumulated in piles on our desk, in our in-boxes, on the credenza, and on the floor. These things wait until Saturday, when we *hope* to have some uninterrupted time so that we can actually get something done.

So what are we doing during our eight-, ten-, or twelve-hour days? I haven't got the slightest idea, and I'll bet that you don't either. That's probably why you're reading this book at this very moment. And on the following pages, you'll learn some wonderful timesaving tips, techniques, ideas, and strategies that will help you get your work done faster and better, and give you more time to spend with your family and friends.

Become More Productive, Efficient, and Effective — Not Just Busy

In today's highly competitive business environment, working additional hours doesn't guarantee that your business will be more successful or that your career will prosper. The only way that you can be successful today is to become more productive, efficient, and effective, not just busy. When productivity increases, the quality of your work improves, you get things done on time, and best of all, you accomplish more tasks with less effort. The company makes money, and so do you.

You must remember that you're getting paid for your results, not the number of hours you work. We all have encountered coworkers who try to impress us by bragging about how many hours they work. They wear their 70- or 80-hour work weeks as a badge of honor, believing that the extra hours show dedication to company and career. In many instances, though, the overtime is a smoke screen that covers up inefficiencies and poor work habits. If you analyze the quality of these people's work, the volume of work produced, and the timeliness for completing it, you discover that they really aren't superstars; in fact, they're just barely getting by. They rarely get their work done on time, and the quality of that work is just OK. Considering the number of hours they actually work, they're getting a very poor return on their investment.

ANECDOTE

Time utilization analysis

While I was meeting with the division manager of a large public company, he showed me a copy of a time utilization survey that his firm had recently conducted. The survey showed that the employees were spending the majority of their time on tasks not directly related to serving their clients' needs. The employees were spending most of their time doing routine office work, shuffling papers back and forth, attending meetings, and answering electronic- and voice-mail messages. The breakdown is as follows:

Time spent doing office work and attending meetings	25 percent
Time spent responding to electronic- and voice-mail messages	15 percent
Time spent on the telephone	15 percent
Time spent in face-to-face meetings with clients	20 percent
Time spent in preparation for those meetings	25 percent

Upon analysis, it became apparent that many of the company's employees were devoting most of their time to activities unrelated to their clients' needs. Management has now set an overall goal of increasing their employees' client meeting/client preparation time to at least 60 percent of each employees work week, thus reducing the time spent on administrative activities to 40 percent.

You've Got to Pace Yourself

Many people don't realize that there's a big difference between working hard and working smart — between being busy and being productive. For most of us, a career will span 30 to 40 years. If you think of a career as if it were a marathon, you realize the necessity to pace yourself over the course of the race. Sure, there are times when you need to pick up the pace, and then you need to slow down again to catch your breath. Your goal should be to use *and* conserve energy so that you don't burn out or become exhausted long before crossing the finish line.

The people who work 50, 60, or 70 hours per week are pacing themselves through a 100-yard sprint when they're really in a marathon. They're working as hard as they can, for as long as they can, in the hope of crossing the finish line *before* they collapse. They look at the completion of the next project or task as the finish line, and they look no further. As soon as they have another project to work on, they soon find themselves running another race.

Until recently, most employers didn't care how many hours it took for an employee to get a particular job done. Productivity and efficiency weren't that important because the extra costs could always be passed along to the customer.

That approach doesn't work any longer. The competition is just too fierce. As a result, corporate America's been forced to find ways to cut expenses, increase employee productivity, and improve the quality of their products or services. These goals can't be achieved by asking employees to work longer and harder. Employees need to be taught to work more efficiently and effectively.

For one thing, working longer hours doesn't necessarily make an employee more productive. Every person has a limit, and there's a point of diminishing returns where additional hours of work don't result in a measurable increase in the quality or the quantity of the work produced. In fact, when a person's putting in too many hours, the probability of making an error or mistake dramatically increases, and history has shown that these kinds of mistakes can be very costly in time and in money both to the company and to the employee. Studies have also shown that working long hours leads to burnout, increased stress and tension on the job, and additional pressures at home. Today, people need to measure and balance the requirements at work with those of their personal and family life.

ANECDOTE

All work and no play *almost* makes Frank a dead man

Early in my career, I knew a man who worked in sales for a major life insurance company. As a new agent, he sold a phenomenal amount of life insurance and was held up as the model agent that everybody else was supposed to emulate. It shouldn't surprise anyone that the managers in the office were only looking at his end results — the volume of life insurance sold — not the daily activities that produced the sales. When I analyzed his daily activity, I found that he wasn't working a regular 40 hour work week. He was working more than 80 hours.

This was a typical workday for Frank: Each morning he would get up at 5:00 a.m. and have one or maybe two appointments before he got to the office. Then he would work a full day, and after dinner, he would have one or two additional appointments. Many evenings he didn't get home before midnight. He followed this work schedule Monday through Friday, week-in and week-out, for years. He even worked on weekends, with several appointments on Saturdays and occasional appointments on Sundays.

Yes, he was achieving fabulous results in comparison to his colleagues, but he was doing it because he was more or less working two jobs. His performance wasn't that of a super salesman; he was merely a man who chose to put all of his time, energy, effort, and his life into selling. He never had any time for his wife or children, and he couldn't even enjoy the things that his money could purchase.

One day, the results of this man's work habits finally caught up to him. He was giving a speech to a group of fellow life insurance agents — telling them what a great salesman he had become — and collapsed in front of the audience. He was rushed to the hospital and spent the next week under his doctor's care. The doctor's diagnosis was that he was suffering from exhaustion. At the time, he was still months away from his 35th birthday. Frank learned the hard lesson that when you burn the candle from both ends, sooner or later the candle may burn out.

Testing Your Time Management Savvy

We're all looking for ways in which we can do our work quicker, faster, and better. Now if you want to learn how to manage your time better, you've got to become aware of how you're spending your time during a typical business day. So before you dive into this book, I would like to ask you some questions:

1. How long does it take you to find important papers — like that report your boss wants in the next sixty seconds — that are buried in piles on the top of your desk? See Chapter 1 to learn how to transform a desk that looks like a toxic waste dump into one that resembles the flight deck of an aircraft carrier.

2. How many times have you been put into Voice Mail Jail? To get out of Voice Mail Jail, read Chapter 10.

3. Do you find yourself playing endless games of telephone tag with your most important clients? To quickly win the game, turn to Chapter 9.

4. Do you spend your day putting out fires while your important tasks just seem to fall through the cracks? See Chapter 5 for help.

5. Would you like to spend less time responding to your e-mail messages and more time doing important work? If so, see Chapter 12.

6. Do you find that you don't get to your important tasks until the very last minute? Then check out Chapter 2 for tips on getting the most out of your Master List.

7. Would you like to get your appointment book, calendar, Rolodex file, and things-to-do list off your desk and inside your computer? Then read Chapter 4 to learn how you can use ACT! to take control of your day.

8. Would you like to do a better job of promoting your company and yourself? Then see Chapter 14.

9. Do you spend too many hours each week sitting in meetings that don't accomplish much and leave important issues unresolved? Then read Chapter 5 for help.

10. Would you like to have more time for yourself, your family, and your friends? If so, you should sit yourself down and read this book cover to cover. It's packed with so many timesaving tips, techniques, ideas, and strategies that you'll quickly find yourself doing better work, completing it on time, with less pressure and strain. The time you wasted during a normal business day will be used much more productively and efficiently. And as a result, you'll be spending less time at work and more time with your family and friends. Now that's being productive!

So What's Exactly in This Book?

In Part I, I'll show you how to get organized and help you develop an efficient follow-up system.

In Part II, I'll talk about how you can plan your days, manage your meetings, maintain control of the flow of a conversation, and help people make better decisions.

And in Part III, I'll talk about how you can improve your ability to communicate information by using the telephone, electronic mail, and voice mail.

In Part IV, I'll show you how to make presentations to groups of people, how to promote yourself, how to set goals for yourself, and how to go through life as a winner.

And in Part V, the Part of Tens, I'll throw in a bunch of top-ten lists to inform you, entertain you, and increase the page count of this book to meet my contractual obligation to IDG Books Worldwide.

Icons Used in This Book

The Tip icon flags a juicy, bite-size bit of information guaranteed to make your life easier.

The Timesaving Tip icon points out the kind of tip that's going to save you gobs of time and add years to your life.

I stuck the Remember icon next to stuff you ought not forget lest a terrible curse befall thee.

The Technical Stuff icon serves two purposes: For people who like fancy-shmancy computer jargon, this icon lets you know where to look. For people who get nervous seeing a digital clock, this icon lets you know that there's stuff you don't want to read nearby.

The Anecdote icon lets you know that I'm about to tell some sort of story, usually a story with a point, but not always.

Part I
Improve Your Time Management System

The 5th Wave   By Rich Tennant

"I DON'T CARE HOW FAR YOU TRAVELED, I'M NOT SCHEDULED TO MEET WITH YOU UNTIL NEXT TUESDAY."

In this part . . .

A less inviting title for this part might be "Clean Up That Mess!" Before you're ever going to be more productive, you need to get organized, and that's what this first part is all about. After a brief overview, I help you clean up your office. Then I show you how to create a Master List so that you can get your work in order. After that, I cover how you can make the most of your daily planner. And last but not least, I discuss the benefits of using ACT!, a computer application that will make any person's life more organized.

Chapter 1

Getting and Staying Organized

You Can Save Yourself an Hour a Day If You Get Organized

You probably don't realize it, but most people waste almost an hour a day looking for papers that are lost on the top of their desks — 60 percent of which aren't needed anyway. So that's where I think we should start: with the top of the desk.

Let me describe a typical office: There are piles of paper everywhere — on the desk, the credenza, the chair, and the floor. Next to the phone there's a pile of pink phone slips; the lights on the phone itself are blinking so fast that one would think the phone's about to explode because of all of the new voice-mail messages; on the wall there are so many sticky notes that they could be mistaken for a swarm of butterflies; and off in a corner there are piles of unread newspapers, magazines, and trade journals. Somewhere in all of this mess is a calendar, appointment book, and to-do list. Sound familiar?

Well, you're going to get rid of all of those piles of paper on the desk. In just a few hours, you can take a desk that looks like a toxic waste dump — with piles of papers everywhere — and transform it into a desk that looks like the flight deck of an aircraft carrier. You'll throw away so much that your waste basket (or recycling bin) will be filled to the brim, overflowing and spilling onto the floor. All that remains on the desktop will be a telephone and a pad of paper.

Your goal isn't to have a nice, neat, orderly desk. The desk is secondary. Your goal is to get organized so that you can convert time that's wasted during the course of a normal business day into time that can be used more efficiently and effectively.

With a neat, orderly desk, you'll improve your follow-up systems so that you can do a better job of staying on top of all of your unfinished work. And when you can spend your time working on the things that are important and will make you money, instead of the things that keep you busy, the quality of your work will improve. A clean desk is the place where it all begins. So let's get started.

On the next few pages, I'm going to show you my fun and easy process for getting, and staying, organized. You should be able to organize your desk in about two hours time, so turn off the phone and close the door — if you're lucky enough to have one — so that you won't be interrupted, and don't forget to bring a dumpster. As I said before, you'll find that at least 60 percent of the papers on your desk can be tossed, and when you start working on the drawers inside your desk, as well as your file drawers, you'll discover that at least 80 percent of those papers can go.

Separate the Wheat from the Chaff (or Is It the Pigs from the Cows?)

The first step in getting organized is to separate the wheat from the chaff. So go through all of the papers on your desk, one piece at a time. If a paper is important, put it in a keeper pile for the time being. If a paper belongs to someone else, create a pile of things to give to your colleagues or co-workers. If you don't need a paper any longer, put it in the recycling bin or throw it away! In the span of 20 to 30 minutes, you should be able to lighten your paper overload by more than half, and your waste basket will soon be filled to the brim.

If you're finding it difficult to part with some of your files or other papers at this time, just take them off your desk and put them in one of the drawers in your filing cabinet. This way, you've got the best of both worlds. If you need the materials at some future time, you know where to find them, and if you find that you don't need them, then you can throw them out in six months.

Organize your keeper pile

Now go through your keeper pile one piece of paper at a time. If there's work to do, note it on your Master List, which is a things to-do list that's written on a big piece of paper. (I'll be describing how you can use your Master List to take control of your workload and workday in Chapter 2.) If you no longer need that particular piece of paper, throw it away. If you do need it, put it in a properly labeled file folder and file it away. If a folder doesn't exist, create one. I'll talk about filing in a few moments.

File the important stuff

If you have papers or files you wish to keep but don't really need right now, file them away. There's no reason to leave them on the top of your desk any longer.

Sort through all those other piles of paper in your office

Now that you've gone through everything on your desk, continue the same process by going through the piles that have accumulated on your credenza, floor, and everywhere else. If there's work to do, note it on your Master List. If you need to keep a document, file it away; and if you don't need it any longer, throw it away!

Don't reminisce or interrupt yourself

While you're going through these papers, your objective is to sift, sort, and catalog each and every one of them. Don't allow yourself to get sidetracked from the task at hand. When you come across a note for a phone call that you were supposed to have returned sometime last week, don't drop everything to make that call. Just note it on your Master List and keep going. Or, when you find a memo that outlined a project you were supposed to be working on for the past few days but haven't yet begun, don't start now. And when you discover a copy of a letter that you recently sent to a client, customer, or prospect — that's been sitting on your desk for a month — just note on your Master List that you've got to make a phone call, and keep sifting and sorting. These documents are the items of business that you're looking for. You're going through your piles, one piece of paper at a time, so that you can create a list of everything that you need to do!

While You're at It, Remove the Sticky Notes from the Wall

Many of us use sticky notes in much the same way as we use our piles. They allow us to see what it is that we've got to do. When we need to remind ourselves that we've got something to do — like write a letter, work on a proposal, or return a telephone call — we jot down a brief note on this small piece of paper and stick it on the wall, computer, telephone, or anything else on which it may adhere. The problem with this system is that many of us fail to notice, or do anything about, the notes that we've written. The next few paragraphs outline a better way to take down notes.

Write everything down — on big pieces of paper

The habit of jotting down a thought on a piece of paper is a very efficient way of remembering that you've got something to do. Putting things down on paper frees you from having to try to remember what those things are. Now you can use your wonderful brain power for something that is considerably more important.

But when you write notes to yourself on small pieces of paper and then stick them on the wall, you begin to create problems. After you post more than a few of them, you tend to stop paying attention to any of them, and none of them appears to be of much importance. As a result, you ignore the note and forget the task. Even though you see these notes throughout the day, day after day, simply seeing the note doesn't provide you with the necessary motivation to do the task. So the notes remain attached to the wall, the work remains undone, and everything begins to back up.

When there's work to do, such as making a phone call, writing a letter, or following-up on something, you should note it on your Master List instead of a sticky note. A single piece of letter-sized paper, with about 25 lines, can hold the information of 25 sticky notes.

Don't forget to file your notes

The practice of taking detailed notes — especially of your telephone conversations and meetings — is a very good one, but when you don't place your notes inside a file folder along with all the other material on a specific subject or topic, there's the possibility that when you've got to make a business decision, you may not remember that you have this information. So when you take notes, place the paper in the appropriate file so that you can find it when you need it, and if there's work to do, note it on your Master List.

 Always date your papers. Every time you write something on a piece of paper, you should always put a date on it. This way you can see where things fell chronologically. Records of phone conversations and meetings become useless when you can't remember when they took place.

Dealing with Piles of Newspapers, Magazines, and Trade Journals

Every day, we get stacks of newspapers, magazines, and trade journals, many of which we never even look at, let alone read. Many of us have piled up so much reading material that we wouldn't get through it all if we spent an entire workday just reading.

So what do we do with all of this material? We stick it in a "reading" pile that's never looked at again. Isn't it ironic that we end up feeling guilty because we didn't get around to reading these things, even though our world didn't come to an end simply because we never read that stack of magazines. We just find it hard to admit that the majority of the information that crosses our desk isn't necessary, and somehow, we get along very well without the information we didn't know we were missing.

So the most important thing you can do when these reading materials cross your desk is to decide what you want to do with them. If you've got newspapers that are more than a few days old, throw them away (or recycle them). If your magazines are more than a week or two old (if a magazine's a monthly, two months old), get rid of them, too. Chances are that the information's already out of date, and for most of us, we have many ways of obtaining important information even if we missed it the first time around.

Instead of allowing yourself to feel guilty because you didn't get your reading done, you should focus all of your energies on getting your important work done, done well, and completed on time. You should never lose sleep because you didn't have time to read the latest newspaper or magazine.

Set Up a Reading File

As an alternative to having stacks of newspapers, magazines, and trade journals laying around, why don't you set up a reading file for yourself? When you receive a magazine, quickly skim the table of contents, and if you see an article that you think may be of interest, rip the pages out of the magazine and throw the rest of it away. Then just put the article in a reading file that you can take with you on your next business trip.

If you don't want to rip up the magazine, then you should circle the page number of the article you wish to read in the table of contents or put a Post-it Note on the page where the article starts; otherwise, you'll never remember why in the world you saved the magazine in the first place. Dealing with reading material in this way will save you a lot of time because you won't have to thumb through an entire magazine to try find that article that you wanted to read when you had a bit more time.

Do the same thing with your newspapers. Scan the paper quickly, and if you find an article that's of interest, rip out the page, put the article in a reading file, and throw the rest of the paper away.

And whenever you're reading anything — a letter, report, memo, newspaper, or magazine, always have a pen nearby so that you can circle or highlight any words, sentences, or phrases that you find of interest. You may also find it very helpful to write any thoughts, comments, or questions you may have in the margins. This way, you won't have to reread the material when you pick it up a week, a month, or a year later. With the important information highlighted, you'll know in an instant what it was that caught your eye at the very moment you read the material.

Clean Out Your Desk Drawers

After you've cleaned off the top of your desk, you may want to tackle the drawers inside your desk. This task would include both the drawer that's designed to store your files, the smaller drawers, and the lap drawer. You'll find that at least 80 percent of the papers in your file drawer can be tossed. That's because your working papers and to-do items have been sitting in piles on the top of your desk. In some of the offices that I've helped get organized, I've found that the file drawers were actually empty. And in others, the drawers contained files that belonged to the previous occupant of the office.

Since most of the papers in these drawers haven't been looked at in quite a while, it should be easy for you to go through them and toss the papers and files you no longer need. If you want to keep some papers and the file's beat up, make a new folder.

Use Expandable File Pockets Instead of Hanging Files

If you find that the files inside your file drawer aren't easy to work with, one of the reasons may be because you're using hanging files to keep your manila folders from falling over. The hanging files themselves can often take up 40 percent of the space of a file drawer — when it's empty.

So as an alternative to using hanging files, you can use expandable file pockets instead. You put your file folders inside the file pockets and then place them inside the file drawer. The file pockets come in various widths, from one and a half inches to five inches. In most cases, I've found the pockets that expand to three and a half inches to be the most convenient to use.

What's Your Briefcase Look Like?

And finally, once you've organized your office, why not organize your briefcase? Over the years, I've met many people who have a briefcase that they keep filled with work, reading materials, and other things that they never look at. Each night they lug this briefcase home so that they can do some work after dinner. And each morning they bring it back to the office, without ever having opened it.

So take a few minutes and go through all of the *stuff* that's in your briefcase. If there's work to do, note it on your Master List and plan to do it during regular business hours. If you need to keep something, file it away. The rest should be pitched.

Hard Drive House Cleaning Anyone?

I know that I started this chapter with a discussion on how to get organized and clean off all the stuff that's accumulated on the top of your desk, but you can't forget about cleaning up the stuff that's inside your computer. (If you don't use a computer, you can skip these next few pages and learn how to create an effective follow-up system in Chapter 2.) You see, a hard drive is nothing more than an electronic filing cabinet. And no matter how large a hard drive you've got, if you continue to add more and more files and software programs, without deleting the ones you no longer need or use, the drive, like the file drawers in your office, will eventually become stuffed beyond capacity. Until you actually start getting rid of your old computer files and unused programs, you won't realize how much space is being wasted.

Tips for Mac users

If you're a Windows user, skip to the next section. It's easy to delete files on a Mac. Just select the files or folders you don't want to keep and drag them to the Trash. Then choose the Empty Trash command from the Special menu.

To determine which files you ought to delete, view a given folder by date. The files within the folder will dispay from newest to oldest. Chances are you'll want to trash the oldest files.

Tips for DOS/Windows users

The next few paragraphs will help DOS and Windows users get rid of unneeded files that are on their hard drives.

Delete your automatic backup files

When cleaning up your hard drive, the first thing you should do is delete your automatic backup files. Many programs, such as your word processor and spreadsheet program, have a feature that automatically backs up a file. You can recognize this type of file because it has the extension *.BK!. or *.BAK.

Now before I continue, I want to take a moment to explain how a computer creates automatic backup files. Let's say you create a document — a letter to a friend — whose file name is C:\LETTER. A little while later, you decide to make a change to the letter, so you open the file, make your changes, and then save it. Well here's what your automatic backup program does. The original version of C:\LETTER becomes C:\LETTER.BAK, and the revised version become C:\LETTER.

You can always tell which version of a file is older by looking at the date and time it was last saved.

So you can see that if you've been writing a lot of letters, memos, presentations, and reports, and you have been using your programs' automatic backup features, you may have an awful lot of backup files. And these backup files are certainly taking up valuable space on your hard drive. It's very easy to get rid of your backup files. First you open your File Manager and select a directory. All the files within the directory will be displayed. Then sort the files in the directory by extension.

In the Windows File Manager, select View, Sort by Type, and the directory will be sorted by the type of file.

Then scroll through the list of files for the ones that have the *.BAK extension. You can then delete the files one at a time. Or, if you hold down the Shift key while clicking your mouse, you can select a group of files and delete them all at once.

To select files that are not next to each other, hold down the Ctrl button while you select the individual files with your mouse.

Delete unneeded files

After you get rid of your backup files, you should delete old files that you no longer need. And if you're like me, I'm sure you've got plenty of them. You can delete files in one of two ways — from the File Manager or from within the program that created the file, such as your word processor.

Select a directory and browse through the files, one at a time. If you no longer need a file, delete it. If you're not sure at this particular moment whether or not you should keep a specific file, create an archive directory where you can store these old files and get them out of the way. At a future time, you can go in and delete the files you no longer need.

Create a permanent archive directory for unused computer files you wish to keep

If you have files that you wish to keep on your hard drive but don't need to access very often, create a permanent archive directory (a folder on a Mac) where you can move them just to get them out of the way.

Copy unneeded files to floppy disks

If you want to keep specific files but don't need to store them on your hard drive, then copy the files to a floppy disk and keep it in a safe place.

When you save files onto a floppy disk, be sure to write a label for the floppy disk that properly describes each of the files. Then print a hard copy of the disk's directories and subdirectories, fold the piece of paper until it's about the same size as the disk, and use a rubber band to keep it securely attached. Now you'll always know what files are on the disk — even if you don't look at it for a year. And if you want to make some additional notations as to the nature of these files, you can write them on the piece of paper.

Did you inherit someone else's old computer files?

Did you ever move into someone's office and discover that you had inherited all of that person's old files? You know, the ones that had been sitting in a desk drawer or filing cabinet and hadn't been looked at in years? Today, the same thing's probably happening when you move into someone's old office and inherit his or her computer. You not only have the old paper files to deal with, but the old computer files as well.

So if you've got a computer that's filled with someone else's old files, it's time to go through them and delete the ones you don't need. Here are some tips on how to do some hard drive house cleaning:

- Check the dates of the files to determine how old they are. You want to be sure you're looking at data files and not your program or system files. If you delete any program or system files, you'll be in big trouble. When you look at these files, you'll quickly see that some of them are so old there can't possibly be any reason to keep them.

- Before you delete any files, you should view them — one by one — to determine if there is anything important in the files. If you find an important file, either (1) print it out, file the hard copy away, and delete the file, or (2) if you want to keep the computer file, move it to one of the directories you've created. If there's nothing of importance in the file, delete it.

- If you want to keep some or all of the files (just to be sure that you don't get rid of something important), you have two choices. You can leave them alone for the time being and make a note that sometime in the future the files should be purged, or you can save the files to a floppy disk, put it in a safe place, and get it off your computer.

Do you need two versions of the same files

If you've got print-outs of your computer files, do you need to keep both the hard copy and the computer file? Keeping both is often redundant. So would you rather throw away the papers or delete the computer file?

Copy the computer file onto a floppy disk, label it appropriately, put it into the proper file, and throw away the hard copy.

How many programs do you have on your computer that you don't use?

We've all got programs that we no longer use. Maybe you still have the DOS version of a program even though you've been using the Windows version for years. Or maybe you replaced one program with a better one but never got rid of the old one. And we've all installed software that we tried for a few days or weeks, found that we didn't like it, and never used it again. But for some strange reason, we never get around to removing these unused programs from our hard drives.

- ✔ On a Mac, simply drag old programs to the Trash and choose the Empty Trash command from the Special menu.

- ✔ Deleting a DOS program is easy because all you've got to do is open the File Manager, go to the directory that contains the program's files, mark the files, and press the delete key.

- ✔ Deleting a Windows program can be tricky because Windows programs are a lot more complicated than DOS programs. The first time I tried to delete a Windows program, I just deleted the program's icon in the Program Manager. Little did I know that I had only deleted the symbol that turned the program on. The program files were still on my hard drive.

- ✔ What the *&@#%@ are INI files? In Windows, you can't just get rid of a program by deleting the program's files. There are some additional files that also need to be deleted. These files are called *initialization* files and are easily identified because they have the *.INI extension. These files make each specific application work within the Windows operating environment, and every Windows application has its own *.INI file. And if that isn't complicated enough, there's a master file in the Windows directory, WIN.INI — some people pronounce WIN.INI as "winnie," as in Winnie the Pooh; others pronounce it "weeny," as in "itsy, bitsy, teeny, weeny, yellow polka dot bikini" — that has additional information about every program that's been installed. Needless to say, you shouldn't try to delete any of these files, and you should NEVER delete the WIN.INI file unless you really know what you're doing.

Uninstall your Windows programs

I wouldn't recommend that you try to delete any of the specific lines from the WIN.INI file, or even the *.INI files, because the task can be rather tricky and complicated, especially if you're not an experienced computer user. So instead of trying to delete all these program files, icons, and lines of *.INI text yourself — and possibly delete something that you shouldn't — you can use a utility program that's designed to uninstall your unused Windows programs. Here are two programs that work very well:

- ✔ UnInstaller; MicroHelp, Inc., 439 Shallowford Industrial Parkway, Marietta, GA 30066, 800-922-3383.

- ✔ Clean Sweep; Quarterdeck Office Systems, Inc., 150 Pico Boulevard, Santa Monica, CA 90405, 310-392-9851.

Work at Staying Organized

Once you get organized, it's easy to stay organized, but it's going to take some work on your part. There's no avoiding the fact that every day you're going to continue to receive several inches of mail, e-mail messages, voice-mail messages, and a handful of faxes. However, you don't have to allow yourself to lose control of your daily work plan. All you've got to do is continue to add new items of business to your Master List (discussed in detail in Chapter 2).

I'm sure you've often been told that "You should only handle a piece of paper once." In theory, this advice sounds great, but in reality, it doesn't work! You may in fact have to handle a piece of paper many times, and your goal shouldn't be to try to get rid of those papers as soon as they cross your desk. Your goal should be to complete your important work.

So when something comes into your office, don't drop everything so that you can deal with it at that very moment. Instead, you should just add it to your Master List and plan to get to it at some time in the near future.

If there's work to do, you add it to your Master List. If you need to keep the piece of paper, you file it, and if you don't need it any longer, you throw it away, pass it on, or recycle it.

Clean Up Before You Go Home at the End of the Day

Before you go home at the end of the day, you should spend a few minutes getting organized. Go through your stack of mail, listen to your voice-mail messages, and scan your e-mail to see what items of business need to be added to your Master List. Papers you need to keep should be filed appropriately or thrown away. You should then review your Master List so that you can select the specific work, tasks, or projects that you feel are the most important and then plan to work on them tomorrow morning.

Get into the habit of going through all of the things that have accumulated on your desk during the course of a typical business day, and you'll find that it's relatively easy to stay organized. Should you find that after a few busy or hectic days that things have backed up and stacked up on you, then just stop cold. Take a half hour to get yourself cleaned up and organized again.

Now it's going to take you a bit of time to get organized. It's not going to happen overnight, but if you do a little bit at a time and stick with it, you'll see amazing results. You'll find that you're able to do a better job of staying on top of your important work, tasks, and projects. You'll feel that you've got much more control over your work and your day. And when you leave the office at the end of the day, you'll pat yourself on the back and congratulate yourself for a job well done.

Your goal is to complete as much work as possible done during normal business hours. When you go home at the end of the day, you've earned the right to relax and spend some quiet time with your family, your friends, and yourself.

Chapter 2

The World's Most Effective Follow-Up System: The Master List

. . . .

In This Chapter

▶ Creating a follow-up system

▶ What is a Master List?

▶ Using a Master List

. . . .

*W*hat does the top of your desk look like? Do you have piles of *stuff* everywhere? Well, if you're trying to stay on top of all of your unfinished work, tasks, projects, and telephone calls and you're doing it by leaving everything out on the top of your desk, then you're flirting with disaster. It's just impossible to keep on top of everything, or anything, when your office looks as if a tornado has gone through it. Important things get lost, misplaced, or are soon forgotten, and at the very least it takes a lot of time — wasted time — to find that letter, memo, file, or report when you need it. And why did you begin to look for it in the first place? Because your boss just asked for it, and he or she is standing at your doorway; or someone just called and is waiting patiently, or impatiently, on hold while you frantically search through the stacks of papers on your desk.

You may not be aware of this fact, but most people waste at least an hour a day looking for papers that are *lost* on the top of their desk. By getting organized, you can convert the time that's usually wasted during the course of a normal business day into time that can be used more productively and efficiently.

With piles of papers everywhere it does become very difficult, if not impossible to stay on top of the important things in your life.

In my best-selling book, *If You Haven't Got the Time to Do It Right, When Will You Find the Time to Do It Over?*, I described how to get organized and get rid of the piles of papers on your desk top. Some of that information is summarized in Chapter 1, so if your desk is a mess, go back and read Chapter 1 for the help you'll need to get your office organized. Then come back this chapter to develop a better follow-up system.

The first few pages of this chapter are meant to convince you that using piles of papers is an inefficient follow-up system. After I get you to agree that you need to change your evil ways, I'll show you how a Master List is a better follow-up system.

Oh Where Did I Put My Calendar?

I know that you've never given this much thought, but many of the things that remain on the top of the desk are left out as reminders of things to do. We think that by seeing a piece of unfinished business, it will remind us to write that letter or make that call, and we'll do it. In theory, this may sound great; in practice, it just doesn't work! Yes, you do get things done, and you often, but not always, meet your deadlines, but you're paying a price: It takes a lot more effort and exertion on your part to get the work done, usually because you start working on a project when there's no lead time left. So your stress level is higher than it should be, and I would venture to say that the quality of your work isn't *always* at the highest level that you're capable of producing.

One of the main causes of efficiency problems is the piles themselves. The piles of papers are supposed to remind a person of the tasks he or she is supposed to do, but the person never gets to these tasks until the last minute because the papers were put aside and forgotten within the piles. And the person doesn't start work on the task or project until someone calls to ask, "Where is it?" Now this person has to drop everything to do something that's been sitting around for a month.

I'll get to it later...

Do you ever go through your in-box and look at the pile of letters, memos, and reports that have accumulated, and just put them aside in an "I'll get to it later" pile? Well, you're not alone because almost everybody else is doing it too. But when you put things aside in this manner, you're going to create problems for yourself because once you get into the habit of leaving piles of paper everywhere, too many things end up in the "I'll get to it later" pile. And later never comes.

Over the years I've had many people say to me, "I put things aside, and if I don't get a follow-up call or additional correspondence, I'll eventually throw it away." This system may be an easy way to get through the day, but it isn't necessarily the best way to take *control* of the things that are going on in your business life, and it certainly isn't an efficient way to manage all of the papers that come cross your desk. When you just put things aside, you're putting yourself in the position of waiting for things to happen, and then you're forced to react to them. You're no longer making your own decisions, and you've lost control of your daily business affairs.

But I Know Where Everything Is

Now I know you're going to tell me that you know where everything is, and I'm sure that you do, but the question isn't "Do you know where everything is?" The *real* question is: "Do you know what work, tasks, and projects you have to do, and when you have to do them?"

- ✔ Who do you have to call?
- ✔ From whom are you awaiting a telephone call?
- ✔ Who are you supposed to be sending a letter, memo, presentation, proposal, or other piece of information to?
- ✔ Who is supposed to be sending you a letter, memo, presentation, proposal, or other piece of information?

The answer to these questions has nothing to do with whether or not you know that a particular piece of paper is sitting three inches from the top of one pile, or two inches from the bottom of another.

Just because you *think* you know where something is has nothing to do with your ability to get your work done, get it done on time, or even done well. Many times the work will remain undone until someone asks for it, and it's at this time that you must drop everything so you can complete a task that should have been done days ago. Now you have another fire to put out; your whole day is going up in smoke; and you don't even realize that you're guilty of arson.

So instead of leaving things out in piles, you'll find that you can be much more efficient and productive when you keep a list of all of your tasks, projects, and other items of business on what I call a *Master List,* which is a things to-do list that's written on a large piece of paper. By writing everything down on your Master List, you give yourself the ability to maintain complete and total control over everything that's going on in both your business and your personal life.

An Efficient Follow-Up System Is the Key to Being Successful

I know that you work hard, that you put in a lot of hours on the job, and that you're dedicated to your company. But hard work and dedication can only take you so far, and after a while there just aren't any more hours left in the work day or the work week. So if you want to become more efficient and effective; improve your ability to stay on top of all of their unfinished work, tasks, projects, and correspondences; and be able to do your work faster and better, then all you've got to do is improve your follow-up systems. Here are some of the things that an efficient follow-up system will do for you:

✔ It will help you get your work done well and done on time.

✔ It will help you improve the quality of your work.

✔ It will give you the opportunity to start your important projects while you've got plenty of lead time.

✔ It will help you remember who you're supposed to call and when you're supposed to call.

✔ It will give you complete control of your business affairs.

✔ You will be able to stay on top of the work you've delegated to others.

✔ It will allow you to compress the amount of time it takes to make decisions.

✔ You won't have to spend so much time putting out fires because fewer fires will start.

✔ It will give you the ability to juggle lots of balls at once — without dropping any of them — thus avoiding the time consuming and costly process of dealing with emergencies that could easily have been avoided.

✔ You will have complete control over your schedule, your day, and yourself.

✔ At the end of the day, you will be able to say to yourself, "I *really* got a lot done today."

✔ You will be able to get a good night's sleep.

✔ You will get to stay home on the weekends.

✔ You will have more time to spend with your friends and family, doing the things that *you* enjoy.

With an effective follow-up system, things just don't slip through the cracks. You're able to stay on top of your most important work, tasks, and projects. You get your work done on time, and you do it well, and you make it home for dinner.

Now that you're aware of the importance of having a good and thorough follow-up system, sit back and relax as you read the next few pages because I'm going to explain how easy it is to setup an efficient follow-up system. I start by showing you how to make a Master List of all your things to-do. In Chapter 3, I explain how to get the most out of your daily planner. And in Chapter 4, you'll learn how easy it is to put your daily planner inside your computer with the ACT! contact management program.

ANECDOTE

My own follow-up system

As an author, I represent myself as my own literary agent, and in selling my books, follow-up is of prime importance. After I send a proposal, I make it a point to find out if it has been received (I usually call within 2 days if I used FedEx or a within a week if I used Priority Mail). After I'm told that my proposal was received, I ask the editor how long it will be before the publisher and acquisitions people expect to get around to looking at my proposal. And after they've had a chance to look at it, how long will it take them to decide whether or not they want to make me an offer to publish my book.

By making these phone calls, I learn a lot about the people I'm dealing with. Some answer their own phone, and others have their calls screened by an assistant or secretary. And a small handful actually return my calls. Once I have the opportunity to speak with them, I can get a pretty good idea of their interest just by the tone of their voice as they talk to me. Some are friendly and cordial and are happy to hear from me; and others are short and curt and speak to me as if I was a nuisance to them.

Based on these conversations, it is easy for me to identify the both people I should continue following up with and the people who have already decided to turn me down. Most important, by calling, I know who's interested and who isn't. And with this information I can continue to move forward. (I was once told that "If you're not being rejected, you're not trying hard enough.")

I've learned that if I contact enough people, sooner or later I will find someone who not only likes my books, but wants to buy them. That's how I sold my first three books, and that's how I sold the book you presently hold in your hands.

What Is a Master List?

The basic concept behind using a Master List is that by writing everything down in an orderly, meticulous way, you can do a better job of staying on top of all of your unfinished work, tasks, projects, and correspondences. When you put things down on paper, you don't have to remember as many things.

Now I know that you've been writing things down for years, but you just haven't been doing it methodically. You've been writing names, addresses, and phone numbers on sticky notes and sticking them onto the wall; you've been keeping to-do lists on the backs of envelopes, and you've been scribbling notes to yourself on any piece of paper that you can get your hands on. So yes, you've been in the habit of writing things down, but the manner in which you've been doing it isn't a very efficient or effective way of staying on top of all of your unfinished work. By using a Master List to keep an itemized inventory of your unfinished work, you will have an organized and systematic format for maintaining control of your workload and your workday.

Shouldn't I only handle a piece of paper once?

I know that you've heard the old adage: "You should only handle a piece of paper once," but that advice just doesn't work in the high-pressure business world of the 90s. And besides, we're not only dealing with paper, but we've got voice mail, e-mail, and all kinds of computer files. So you shouldn't be concerned if you handle a piece of paper once, twice, or a dozen times. The number of times you handle a piece of paper isn't important; what is important is that you make a decision about what you're going to do with that piece of paper.

When something crosses your desk, make a decision — *now* — instead of waiting to see what happens next. If there's work to do, it should be noted on your Master List. If you need to keep it, file it away. And if you don't need it any longer, pass it on to someone else, put it in the recycling bin, or throw it away.

You shouldn't keep unneeded or unnecessary papers in a pile on the top of your desk for the next six months.

Getting the Most out of Your Master List

Over the next several pages, I provide advice on setting up and using a Master List. Much of the information might sound like common sense, but you'd be surprised how many people don't practice the simple techniques I illustrate here. So read it carefully.

Use a big piece of paper

It's my suggestion that you keep your Master List on a big piece of paper. That way, you've got 25 lines on a page with which to list your projects, tasks, and the other items of business that you must do or follow up on. And because you're using a big piece of paper instead of a sticky note or the back of an envelope, you've got enough space to not only include such information as names and phone numbers, but you can also include things like the purpose of a phone call and any other pertinent information. If necessary, you can even write this additional information on a second or a third line.

Don't skip lines. When you're adding items of business to your Master List, make it a point to use every line so that you can get 25 items listed on a page instead of 12.

Write everything down

The key to making your Master List work for you is to make sure that you write everything down. The more tasks, projects, calls, and other to-do items that you put down on paper, the greater your ability to control the events that are taking place during the workday.

Add additional pages to your Master List

When you've used up all of the lines on the first page, don't be afraid to start a second one. It's common for most people to have a Master List that's one or two pages in length.

Cross off completed tasks

When you've completed a task, project, or other item of business, give yourself the pleasure of crossing it off of your list. Don't just place a check mark in the margin; it's not gratifying enough. You should draw a line through it instead

Transfer unfinished items and consolidate the pages of your Master List

The key to making your Master List work for you is to transfer and consolidate the unfinished items of business from the older pages to the newest ones. As a general rule, when 50 percent of the items on a particular page have been completed, transfer the unfinished items — one at a time — to the newest page, and cross them off the old page. After you've rewritten the unfinished items onto the newest page, take one last look at the old page, just to see if you've missed anything, before you throw it away.

If you feel that it's important to keep your old Master Lists so that you've got a record of what you've accomplished, make a file and label it "Old Lists."

Get your work done

Throughout the day, you should scan the items on your Master List to determine which item of business is the most important so you can determine which task you need to work on next. If you have a project that will take time, schedule a block of uninterrupted time on your calendar and think of it as an appointment with the boss or your most important client — because it is!

If you've only got 15 minutes between meetings, use this time to make or return a few phone calls. Or pick off a few of the smaller, less time-consuming tasks so that you can get rid of them.

Review your Master List before you go home

Before you go home at night, take a few minutes to review your Master List to determine which items of business are most important so that you can plan to do them tomorrow. You can also use this time as an opportunity to plan your work for the future. What do you have to during the next few days? Next week? Next month? Your objective is to produce the highest quality work that you're capable of. When you give yourself more time to do your work, you don't have to worry about whether the first draft is good enough because you've got the time to revise it. And in the end, the *finished* product will be great. So when you give yourself plenty of time to think about and plan your work, the work itself is much easier.

Use your Master List as a planning tool so you can start on all of your work, tasks, and projects while you've got sufficient lead time.

Schedule your important work for the first thing in the morning

When you schedule your work, try to tackle your most important tasks as soon as you arrive in the morning, when you're fresh, alert, and energetic. You'll be amazed at how much you can accomplish when you get into the habit of working on your most important projects early in the day before the inevitable fires flare up.

If you give yourself the first two hours of the workday — no meetings, no phone calls, and no interruptions — you'll find that you're able to complete twice as much work, in half the time, with half the effort.

Don't rewrite your Master List every day

Some people make it a point to rewrite their things to-do list every morning so that the most important items are at the top of the list. I think that this system is not only a waste of time, it's a waste of effort. You're in the business of doing your work, not rewriting your lists.

You're not going to get to everything

You must also realize that you're not going to be completing each and every item on your Master List every day. Your goal is to get to your important work, do it well, and get it done on time. Your Master List is the tool that will help you stay focused on your most important tasks and projects and keep you in complete and total control.

Unfortunately, Your Master List Can't Do Everything

The Master List is great for initially getting organized, but as you use it, you'll find that it has some shortcomings, the biggest of which is that it doesn't integrate with a calendar. Let me give you a few examples.

It's not easy to keep track of future follow-up's

Let's say you have an item on your list to call Jim Smith. So you make the call and are told that Jim is not going to be in the office until Wednesday of next week. The Master List doesn't offer an efficient way to keep track of when you need to make this next call. You can write down the date on which you plan to make this call in the margin next to the original entry (or somewhere else on the line which notes the item), perhaps using a red pen. But things get more complicated when you call again and are told that Jim will be out of town for another ten days. Now you've got to cross out the original follow-up date and replace it with a new one. Or maybe you rewrite the entire entry, or perhaps you just forget about it and hope that you'll remember to call Jim at some future date.

As you can see, the more times that you have to reschedule the follow-up date of a to-do item, the more complicated the process becomes, and your Master List gets messier and messier. A daily planner is better suited to dealing with this type of situation because you can write a person's name onto the day of the calendar that you plan to call.

How do you remember to call someone six months from now?

Another ticklish problem arises when a person asks you to follow-up in six or eight months, or for that matter, any time in the future. Your Master List is designed to help you stay on top of your daily work, not the things you may need to do in the coming months. One possible way to deal with this situation is to create a Master List that's designed solely for your long-range projects, tasks, and calls. On this Master List, you keep track of things by date. But for most people, this follow-up process can become rather cumbersome, and in the end, some important things may slip through the cracks. A daily planner can also solve this problem because you can write information down on any future date in the book.

How do you remember to start on a project six weeks from now?

Here's another problem that highlights the shortcomings of using a Master List: You've got a task or project that needs to be completed at some point in the not-so-distant future, but you don't plan to start working on it for several days, or even several weeks. Once again, a daily planner solves this problem. You just write down when you want to start on the project on a specific future date in the daily planner.

What about names, addresses, and phone numbers?

And finally, what do you do with the names, addresses, phone numbers, and notes of conversations that may have become part of your Master List? How do you keep this valuable information if you're in the habit of throwing the pages of your Master List away after the list of unfinished tasks has been transferred to another page? A daily planner gives you the ability to maintain access to this valuable information because you don't throw the old pages away. They're still in the book and are available for future reference.

Always write a person's name and phone number in your name and address book or Rolodex file so that you can find it when you need it.

It is for these, and many other, reasons that many people have found daily planners to be so useful when it comes to helping them take control of their daily activities and affairs. A daily planner is designed to integrate your calendar, things-to-do list, call list, meetings, and appointments, into one book that can help you to stay on top of all of your unfinished work, tasks, and projects.

So What Now?

Using a Master List is a great way to keep track of your daily work, but as the preceding section illustrates, you need to supplement your Master List with a daily planner, which is a topic I cover in detail in Chapter 3.

Chapter 3

Take Control: Use Your Daily Planner

....

....

For years, people have been keeping track of meetings, appointments, telephone calls, and unfinished work by using daily planning books — Day Timers, Day Runners, Filofaxes, and Franklin Planners. These leather bound personal organizers have been wonderful productivity-improvement tools. They've helped us set our priorities, organize and coordinate our important long-term projects, keep track of our delegated work, and establish and set our goals. We've also used them to jot down notes or background information about our business meetings and phone conversations, keep track of miscellaneous ideas and thoughts, and record our tax deductible or reimbursable expenses.

In addition to helping us keep track of what we need to do and when we need to do it, we use the phone book section to store the names, addresses, and phone numbers of our family, friends, customers, clients, and other important people in our lives.

We use these books to not only keep track of our daily activities but to keep our lives in order. For some of us, these books play such an important part of our lives that we won't go any place without them. We even use them to carry our check books and credit cards.

It's a To-Do List, a Calendar, and a Dessert Topping

The basic concept behind the daily planner is that you use it to coordinate your list of things to do (your Master List), your list of people to call, and your meetings and appointments with your calendar. You're no longer writing these lists of your unfinished work, tasks, and projects on a things-to-do list; you're writing them on a specific date in the daily planning book — a date when you think you can get to them. The integration of your things-to-do list with your calendar gives you the flexibility to schedule future tasks on a date when you plan to start working on them, which in many cases will not be the date on which you wrote the item down in the book.

You Can Schedule To-Do Items on Future Days

Have you ever been given an assignment by your boss that was due in, let's say, two weeks? The boss walks into your office on Monday morning, hands you a piece of paper that outlines the project, and tells you that it has to be completed by a week from Friday. As you look at your calendar, you realize that this week is shot because of all of the other appointments and commitments you made, so you schedule this project for Tuesday of next week. And now you're assured that you can work it into your schedule and finish it without being rushed. That's what the daily planner is designed to do.

I used a guy named Jim Smith as an example in Chapter 2, so I might as well use him again for another example here. Let's say that on Monday of this week you decide that you want to call Jim to discuss the benefits of the new product that your company's about to introduce. But in looking at your calendar, you realize that you're all booked up until Thursday, which will be your first full day in the office. So instead of writing your note to call Jim on Monday's page, you enter it in your book on the day you actually will be able to make the call, which would be Thursday.

You Have More Control of Your Scheduling

In scheduling our daily activities, we all need to have some flexibility, and with a daily planner, we've got a lot of flexibility because we're able to associate specific tasks with certain days of the week. So when someone asks you to call him or her a week from Thursday, all you've got to do is write it down on Thursday's page, and it's done. And if you're asked to follow up with someone in six months, you just select a date six months in the future, write down the person's name and the purpose or nature of the call on that page, and when that date arrives, six months from now, you'll find that person's name with your note to give him or her a call.

A daily planner also gives you flexibility in planning your schedule and work flow. With a Master List, you're always looking at a list of *everything* you need to do — things that need to be done today, as well as those tasks that need to be done in the future. When you're using a daily planner, you don't need to list all of your to-do's, calls, and other tasks on a single day. You can spread them out, so you'll do some of the work today, some tomorrow, and the rest on the following day. And if you find that you're not going to be able to get to certain tasks because of your other commitments, you can write down those tasks on days on which you know that you can get to them.

When you use your daily planner, instead of a piece of paper, to list of all of the tasks you need to complete, the projects you need to begin working on, the letters or memo's you've got to write, and the other items of business you ought to follow-up on, then you have much more control of your day. You have control because you're able to associate an unfinished task or other item of business with a specific date on the calendar

Making Your Daily Planner Work for You

If you've been keeping track of all of your unfinished work, tasks, calls, and projects on a Master List, the first thing you'll have to do is transfer the items onto the pages of your daily planner. If you haven't been keeping track of things with a Master List, it's about time you started writing everything down and getting yourself organized. So if you haven't done so already, please read Chapter 1 on getting your office cleaned up and Chapter 2 on developing a Master List.

Transfer your to-do items to your daily planner

As you review your Master List, ask yourself when you plan to get to each specific task and write it down on the day you *expect* to be able to get to it, start it, or complete it. Don't write things down on a day when you already know that you're going to be tied up in meetings or out of town. As you transfer each item to your daily planner, draw a line through it to ensure that you don't miss anything. When each item on your Master List has been transferred, you can throw the list away.

Add new items of business to your daily planner

Throughout the day, new items of business will come up, and they should be entered immediately in your book on the day that you plan to do them. Just because you were assigned a project this morning doesn't mean that it has to be entered on today's page of your daily planner. Maybe it should be entered on tomorrow's page, or one day next week. By writing things down immediately, they won't get buried in a pile and easily lost or forgotten.

Cross off completed items of business

As you complete a task or project, you should draw a line through it. (A check just isn't gratifying enough.) The line is your way of knowing that the task was in fact completed.

Move each unfinished piece of business to a future day, one item at a time

The single most important part of keeping your daily planner up-to-date comes when you move the unfinished work from one day to another. Many times, when a day has ended, a person just turns the page of his or her daily planner without checking to make sure that everything that had been entered on that day had actually been done. In most cases, there are at least one or two items, sometimes many more, that remain undone. Because the person hasn't moved these items forward, the person must continually flip through the daily planner to see which items of business weren't completed. This method of organization guarantees that something will slip through the cracks.

Draw a line through each item as you transfer it and then draw a big X across the page

To guarantee that nothing slips through the cracks, at the end of each day, go through the to-do items, one at a time, and move them to a future day. You can move them to tomorrow, later in the week, or some other date in the future. After you move each item, you should draw a line through it, and when all of the items have been moved, you should draw a big **X** across the page. By drawing a line from one corner of the page to the other, you know that everything on that page has either been completed or moved forward. And when you see that **X**, you know that you never have to refer to that page again.

Use a pencil to schedule appointments

When you schedule your meetings or appointments, write them into your daily planner with a pencil because half of all the appointments that you schedule will be rescheduled or postponed. By using a pencil, you can erase the meeting from your daily planner. If you use a pen, you have to scratch it out.

Write your to-do and call items with a pen

Use a pen to write your to-do items and follow-ups into your book. Pencils tend to smudge, and since you won't be erasing these items, you'll have a more permanent record of the things that you did or need to do.

Write your phone numbers in your Rolodex file or in your name and address book

If you're in the habit of writing people's names, phone numbers, or other information on the pages of your daily planner, you *must* transfer that information to your name and address book, Rolodex file, or database file. Otherwise, you may not be able to find a piece of information when you need it, or at the very least, it won't be at your fingertips. Should you need this information after the end of the current calendar year, when you're using a new daily planner, you may never be able to locate that information again.

Block out vacation time for yourself

Most of us are spending too many hours at the office and not enough time with our family and friends. So go through your daily planner and decide when you want to take a vacation. If you don't block out time for yourself, there won't be any.

At the beginning of each year, a friend of mine, who is the vice-chairman and chief financial officer of a Fortune 500 company and on the board of directors of several public companies, asks for a list of all the various meetings that he is expected to attend during the coming year. After he enters these meetings into his daily planner, he then decides when he wants to take his vacations and also enters those dates. He knows that if he didn't block out some time for himself, there wouldn't be any.

Add birthdays and anniversaries

Add the birthdays and anniversaries of your family, friends, relatives, and important customers or clients to your daily planner so that you'll remember to send them a card, buy them a present, or invite them out to celebrate that special day.

Make the entry into your daily planner at least two weeks in advance of that special day so that you'll have plenty of time to go out and buy a card or gift.

Daily Planners Do Have Limitations

You will find that there are some limitations to using a daily planner, based upon the simple fact that you're using a pencil and paper. I'm going to point out these shortcomings now because in the next chapter, I'm going to explain why I think you should replace your paper-based personal organizer with a computerized contact manager.

Today, it's easy to harness the power of your computer to help you stay on top of every task and project that crosses your desk. With a computerized contact manager, it's no longer necessary to write and rewrite the same information over and over again. You can spend your time doing your work, instead of *planning to do* your work. The rest of this section shows some examples of what I mean.

It's not easy to keep your to-do list up to date

As I've described previously, it takes a lot of work to keep a list of things to-do up to date. We meticulously write down the names of various tasks, projects, or other items of business that need to be done on a specific day's page in our daily planning book. But if that item isn't done on the day it was entered, it must be moved to a future day. And if it's not moved, we run the risk of forgetting about it.

A computerized contact manager solves this problem because an unfinished task is automatically moved forward at the beginning of each day.

Moving or changing to-do items can be a lot of work

I'll use the Jim Smith example again. Suppose you have a to-do item that says: Call Jim Smith to set up a luncheon appointment. In all likelihood, you'll have to move this item around several times before you're able to schedule the appointment. On Monday, you call and learn that he's out until Friday. When you call on Friday, you're told that he's in meetings all day and won't be in the office again until the following Thursday. And when you call on Thursday, you finally get through and set up your luncheon meeting for the following Wednesday.

Now look at what you did physically to schedule this appointment. First you wrote down the item: "Call Jim Smith to set up luncheon appointment." Then you wrote it a second time when you moved it to Friday, and you wrote it a third time when you moved it to the following Thursday. When you scheduled the luncheon appointment for Wednesday, you wrote the item a fourth time as you entered the luncheon appointment on your calendar.

And if you weren't in the habit of moving items of business from one page to another in your daily planner, it's quite likely that you would never have gotten around to scheduling the appointment in the first place because you would have forgotten about it. (This is a perfect example of how easy it is for a person to lose track of things by not continually writing things down.)

A computerized contact manager, on the other hand, can automate this task for you. For starters, you only have to enter the item on your to-do list once. Thereafter, you only have to change the date. When you were told on Monday that Jim was out till Friday, you just clicked on the pop-up calendar, double-clicked on Friday's date, and the item was moved electronically. When you called on Friday and were told that he's out until Thursday, you clicked on the pop-up calendar again, double-clicked on Thursday's date, and the to-do item was once again moved electronically.

When you turned on your computer on Thursday morning, the item that said "Call Jim Smith to set up luncheon appointment" was at the top of your list of things to-do. And when you spoke to Jim on Thursday and scheduled the luncheon appointment for Wednesday, all you had to do was change the "to-do" item to a "meeting," change the date to Wednesday, and select the time.

With a contact manager, it's easy to move items from your to-do list to your appointment calendar and back again because it's all done electronically. With just a few clicks of the mouse, you have complete control of everything that's going on in your business life.

Do you like to carry your calendar around with you?

Many people have more than one calendar. They keep a calendar on their desk and carry a pocket calendar with them when they travel or are out of the office. And secretaries or administrative assistants often keep a third calendar so that additional appointments can be scheduled while people are away from the office. But when people keep more than one calendar, eventually they're going to experience scheduling problems.

"He who has two calendars never knows his true appointment schedule."

And the same goes for the "Shes" out there.

A computerized calendar guarantees that you'll always have a true picture of your daily activities — appointments, calls, and to-dos — because it's always up to date. Your assistant can have a printed copy of it on his or her desk, and when you leave the office, you take a printed copy with you. If your assistant has access to your computer, he or she can make changes to your calendar. If you're on a network, your assistant can access your calendar from another computer.

It takes a lot of effort to keep track of the important people in your life

In today's fast-paced world, it's not easy to keep a person's vital information up to date. Everybody has a direct phone number and fax number. Then there's a number for the beeper, the car phone, mobile telephone, and home phone. To make this record keeping more complicated, most people will probably change jobs, positions, or cities every few years, which means that you need to constantly update the information. How do you do it? You have three real choices: Rolodex cards, a name and address book, or a computerized contact manager. (You also have a fourth choice, which is to not bother trying to keep track of any of these people. But if you go this route, your career will be brief.)

Let's look at the shortcomings of using either a Rolodex card file or a name and address book.

- **Rolodex cards quickly become unreadable.** How much information can you really store on a 2" × 4" or 3" × 5" card? If you're writing the names, addresses and phone numbers by hand, it won't take very long before the cards become beat-up, dog-eared and dirty, especially if you're using them every day. And what happens to a card when you learn that something has changed in a person's life? You scratch out the old information and start scribbling the person's new company, address, and phone number on the card. To say the least, it soon becomes unreadable.

- **Name and address books quickly get beat-up.** Keeping a name and address book can cause you even bigger problems. For starters, you must write each name, address and phone number by hand, which can be an enormous waste of time. And after a couple of months of continuous use, a name and address book can get pretty beat-up and messy — because old numbers have been scratched out and replaced with the current numbers. It doesn't take very long before you've got a really big mess.

One day my wife, Mitzi, and I were at a nearby park with our daughter DeLaine. While we were there, we watched a woman who was sitting on a park bench rewrite the list of names that were in her old address book into the new address book that she had just purchased. As Mitzi and I watched her we said to each other, "Doesn't she have something more important to do?"

Put your names and addresses inside your computer

When you keep your list of name and addresses inside your computer, it's easy to keep everything up to date. Whenever a number changes, you just make the change to the person's record. And with just a few clicks of the mouse you can add additional people to your contact manager or remove them from the program. Once the names are inside your computer, you can use them for your mailing lists, phone lists, or even your Rolodex cards. Chapter 4 tells you all about it.

Chapter 4

ACT!ing Lessons, or Learn How to Put Your Daily Planner Inside Your Computer

· ·

In This Chapter

▶ Why I like ACT!

▶ Put your Rolodex inside your computer

▶ Write notes and letters

▶ Create reports

· ·

*I*f you would really like to improve your daily productivity and take control of all of your daily activities — your telephone calls, to-dos, meetings, and appointments — start using a contact manager and put your daily planner inside your computer. The whole idea of using a computer is to help you get more work done in less time. And with a contact manager you can coordinate the basic components of your planner with a single software program. These components include your

- ✔ Calendar
- ✔ Appointment book
- ✔ To-do list
- ✔ Name and address book

There are many good contact management programs available today, but I've found the ACT! contact management program to be the best at keeping me on top of everything that's going on in both my business and personal life.

On the following pages, I'm going to tell you how ACT! can help you to organize your day. If you're not presently using a contact management program, it's my suggestion that you go out and purchase a copy of ACT! today. If you're using a different contact manager I still think it would be worth your while to take a look at ACT!

ACT! is made by Symantec Corporation, 10201 Torre Avenue, Cupertino, CA 95014, 800-441-7234. (If you shop around you should be able to purchase it for about $200.) It's available in DOS, Windows, and Macintosh versions.

By the way, I would like to mention that I don't work for Symantec, and I don't own stock in the company. I'm just an everyday user who thinks ACT! is a very good productivity improving tool. Well, to be honest, I'll be writing *ACT! For Dummies* for publication in late summer, 1995, so I'm more than an everyday user.

Why I Chose ACT! for My Contact Management Program

In my most recent book, *Winning the Fight Between You and Your Desk,* I reviewed several dozen contact management programs. I found the majority of them to be very powerful, and most were easy to use, but when I had finished writing my manuscript, I found myself faced with an unusual dilemma: Which contact management program should I use for myself? There were so many good ones to choose from.

One of the programs I had previously evaluated was ACT!, which was, and still is, one of the most popular contact managers available. At the time I evaluated it, it's cumulative sales were more than 500,000 copies (today it's sales exceeds 750,000). I decided to reinstall it on my computer and give it another try. After I played around with it for a few days, I discovered that it had the majority of the features that I would want in a computerized appointment book/calendar/to-do list program if I, as a time management expert, were to write such a program myself.

Today, I use ACT! all day long. It's the main reason why I turn on my computer early in the morning, and ACT! is the last thing I turn off at the end of the day. ACT! does a wonderful job of keeping me on time and on top of everything that's going on in my life, both personally and professionally.

ACT! has a feature that will allow you to import all of the names, addresses, and phone numbers that you've already entered into your current contact manager, personal information manager, computerized name and address book, or word processing merge file. This feature will save you the time and effort of reentering the same information a second time.

What ACT! Can Do for You

If you're like most people, I'm sure that you do several different things during the course of a normal business day:

- ✔ You schedule appointments with many different people.

- ✔ You have follow-up work to do.

- ✔ You have joint projects that you're working on with other people.

- ✔ You keep detailed notes of your telephone conversations and/or face-to-face meetings (or at least you're supposed to).

- ✔ You spend a lot of time on the phone.

- ✔ You send out letters, faxes, proposals, and other correspondence throughout the day.

Now you can manage all of these activities and tasks, and more, from inside your computer. You no longer need a Master List, a daily planner, and a calendar to stay organized. Any piece of information about a person, project, or task that you used to keep as a note in a file folder, as a scrap of paper on your desk, or as a mental note in your head can now be kept in one place, inside ACT!. ACT! gives you a place to store the names, addresses, phone numbers, and lots of other information about your business and personal contacts, and ACT! integrates that information with your list of things to-do, your list of people to call, and your appointment calendar. Once you start using ACT!, you'll find that fewer things slip through the cracks because everything's at your fingertips. Figures 4-1 and 4-2 show you the front and back of an ACT! contact record.

Improve your business relationships, lose weight, make friends, and influence people

Day in and day out, you're working and interacting with many people — customers, clients, prospects, as well as your coworkers and colleagues — and you need to be able to stay on top of everything that's going on between you and them. With ACT!, you've got the tools you need to do a more thorough job of keeping track of all of the information that's associated with those projects, tasks, and your other daily activities.

And ACT! will also help you to develop and strengthen your long term relationships — which is the key to being successful in business — because it's designed to help a person get to know the important people in his or her life on a more personal basis. ACT! gives you a place to store a lot of important information about a person and have it available at your fingertips.

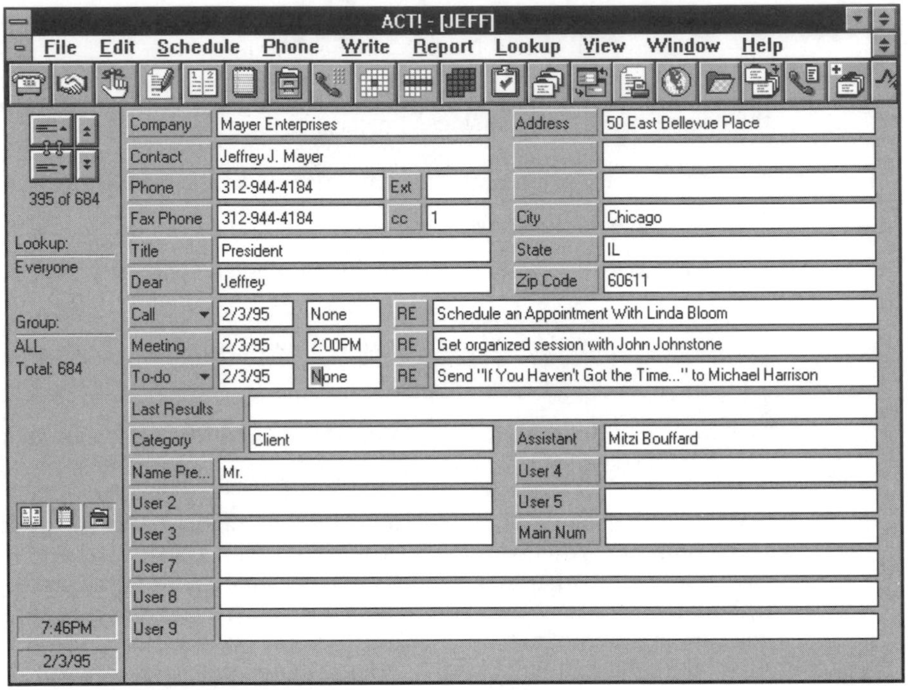

Figure 4-1:
The front side of an ACT! contact record.

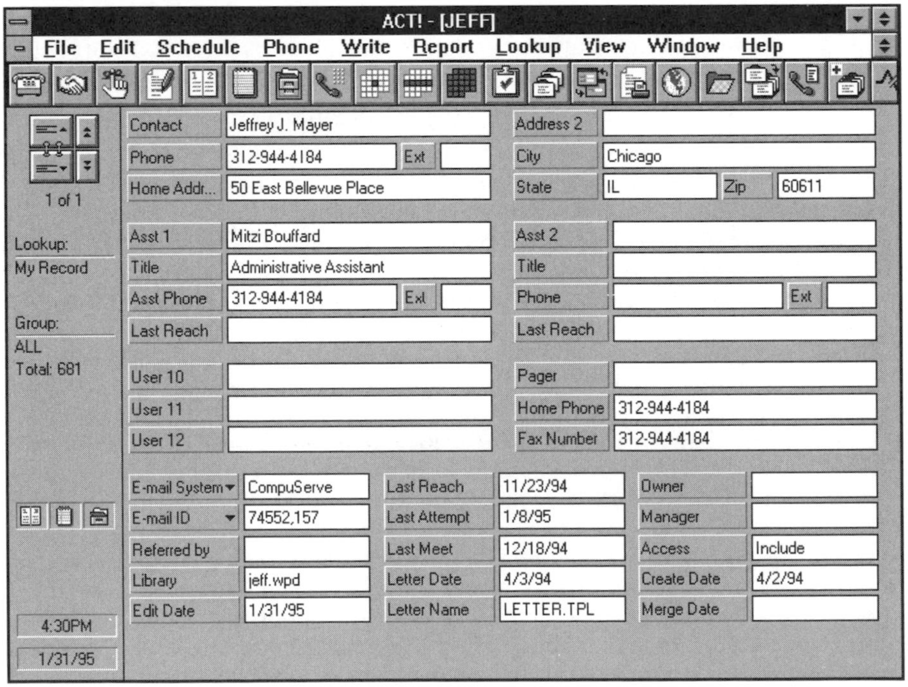

Figure 4-2:
The back side of an ACT! contact record.

You can use ACT! to store such pieces of Information as the names of a person's spouse and children and the dates of their birthdays and anniversaries. And you can even use ACT! to take note of their hobbies, outside interests, favorite restaurants, and most recent vacations. You can store this information in addition to their many addresses and phone numbers (work, home, fax, car, and mobile) and the names and numbers of their assistants.

With ACT! you've a place to routinely store little tidbits of miscellaneous information that you would otherwise forget.

Store and find names, addresses, and phone numbers

Whenever you speak with people, either on the phone or in person, you should always add their names to ACT! This practice will give you the ability to create an electronic Rolodex file so that you can keep in touch with hundreds, or thousands, of people easily and effortlessly. And because the information is stored in your computer, you're able to find any person's name and/or phone number in a fraction of a second with ACT!'s very powerful Lookup feature, shown in Figure 4-3.

How a beer can collection helped me sell some life insurance

When I started my business career as the Special Agent with Northwestern Mutual twenty-some years ago, I was taught to ask people a lot of questions about their personal, business, and financial situations. And during these interviews, I always made it a point to inquire about their outside interests and hobbies. One day, I was meeting with the treasurer of a large public com-pany, and during the course of the conversation he mentioned that his son had a beer can collec-tion, which I dutifully noted on my fact-finding form. When I came back a week later with my estate planning presentation, he was so moved by the fact that I had remembered to make men-tion of the beer can collection that he bought a very large life insurance policy from me.

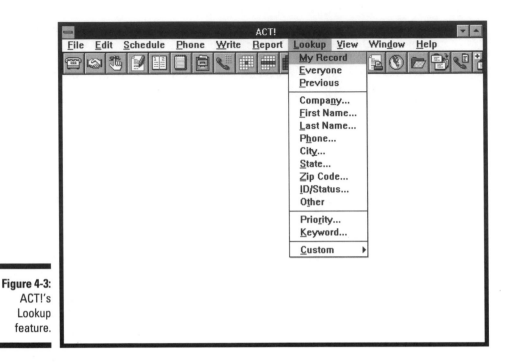

Figure 4-3:
ACT!'s
Lookup
feature.

I think the Lookup feature is one of the most important features in ACT! All you have to do is click Lookup with your mouse, select which criteria you want to lookup (company, first name, last name, etc.), type the first few letters of the name, and the results of the search are displayed before you can blink your eyes. This sure beats trying to find someone's name in an ancient Rolodex file or an old, beat-up name and address book.

So go through those business cards that have been gathering dust in the lap drawer of your desk and put the information inside ACT!. Now you'll have a way to find these people when you need them.

You can also use the Lookup feature to help you plan your business trips. When traveling, do a lookup for the names of people you know in the cities you're visiting so that you can schedule some additional meetings. You can also use ACT! to store the names of your favorite hotels and restaurants.

With all of this information at your fingertips, what could be easier? Needless to say, trying to find all of this information in your Rolodex file or name and address book is such a boring, laborious, and time consuming process that you probably wouldn't do it.

With CardScan from Corex Technologies, you can scan your business cards directly into ACT!, thus eliminating the biggest hurdle we all have for getting this important information into your computer — typing it. Cardscan, Corex Technologies Corp., 233 Harvard St., Brookline, MA 02146, 800-942-6739.

You can interface your ACT! database with Caller-ID with The Bridge to Caller-ID. After the first or second ring of your phone, The Bridge will identify who is calling, trigger your ACT! database, and display the person's record. For more information, contact The Bridge to Caller-ID, Postek Inc., 1857 Technology, Troy, MI 48083, 800-POSTEK-1.

Keep detailed notes of all of your conversations with the notepad

Each person in ACT! has his or her own notepad on which you can keep detailed notes of your telephone conversations and face-to-face meetings, eliminating the need to write notes to yourself on sticky notes or little pieces of paper. Each time you open the notepad, the current date is automatically entered in the left-hand margin. All you have to do is type in the notes to yourself and in just a few moments you're onto your next task. For ease of viewing, your previous entries are displayed in reverse chronological order. The notepad is shown in Figure 4-4.

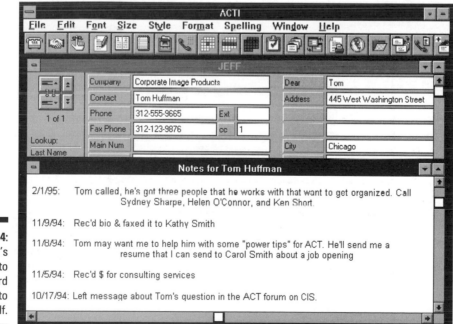

Figure 4-4:
Use ACT!'s notepad to record notes to yourself.

ACT! in action

As I was writing the section on ACT!'s notepad in WordPerfect for Windows, the phone rang. It was my friend John in Los Angeles who was returning my call from earlier in the week. While John and I were exchanging greetings, I toggled over to ACT!, did a lookup of his last name, found his record, and opened the notepad. With the information therein, I was able to remind myself why I had called, check the date when we last spoke, and read what we spoke about. It took me no more than four seconds to do the whole process. While we were talking, he asked me to fax him a copy of a recent article about me that had appeared in the *New York Times*, so I clicked on ACT!'s To-Do icon, selected today's date, and typed in "Fax NYT article." When the conversation ended, I wrote a few brief notes to myself in the notepad and went back to work on this book.

Scheduling activities — calls, meetings, and to-dos — is a breeze

You can use ACT! to keep track of everything that you need to do. ACT! makes scheduling activities — calls, meetings, or to-dos — easy because you hardly need to use the keyboard to enter any information; you can do almost all of it with just a few clicks of the mouse (see Figure 4-5).

Figure 4-5:
ACT!'s
Schedule an
Activity pop-
up box

Schedule an Activity	
Contact: Jeffrey J. Mayer	Type: To-do ▼
	Call
Date: 1/31/95	Duration: Meeting / To-do
Time: None	Lead Time: 0 min
Regarding: Send "If You Haven't Got the Time..." to Michael Har
Priority: Low ▼ ☐ Set Alarm ☐ Send E-mail ☐ Public
Contact... Recurring... OK Cancel

Whenever you've got to schedule a task, the first thing you do is use the Lookup feature to find the person's record. (In ACT!, each task — a call, meeting, or to-do — is associated with a specific person; it's not itemized on a list.) Then you decide which type of activity you want to schedule and click on the appropriate icon. Once you click the icon, a pop-up monthly calendar appears (shown in Figure 4-6) where you select a date. A mini-day calendar pops up (shown in Figure 4-7) where you can select the activity's starting time and duration. Then you can enter a brief description for this activity from the keyboard in the "Regarding" field or select an item — send proposal, send quote, send follow-up letter, confirm meeting, schedule lunch, and so on — from the pop-up box which contains frequently used phrases or terms that describe the specific nature of your daily activities. You can assign priority levels to each activity, and if you want to be reminded of an activity, you can set the alarm.

Figure 4-6:
ACT!'s pop-up monthly calendar.

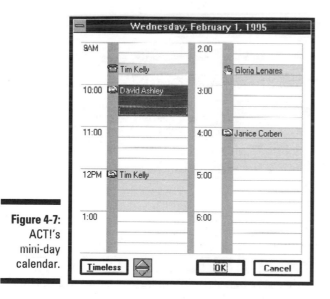

Figure 4-7:
ACT!'s mini-day calendar.

An alarming ACT!

I once called someone who said to me, "I can't talk to you right now. Would you call me back in 20 minutes?" In the past, I would have put this person's file aside and promptly forgotten about him. But this afternoon I came up with what I thought was a great idea: Why not use ACT!'s alarm to remind me of the call? So I clicked on the Call icon, set the alarm, and 20 minutes later I made the call.

View your meetings and appointments

With a single click of the mouse you can see your appointment calendar in a daily, weekly, or monthly format so that you can have a "picture" of what your future time commitments look like. You can change from one view to another by just clicking an icon. And you can schedule new appointments, modify existing appointments, or clear appointments. Figures 4-8, 4-9, and 4-10 show the daily, monthly, and weekly calendars, respectively.

Figure 4-8: ACT!'s daily calendar.

	Wednesday, February 1, 1995	
9AM	✉ Tim Kelly - 214-357-4909: Schedule an Appoin...	**Timeless Activities**
10:00	📧 David Ashley: Discuss Prices for cover stock	✉ David Rechs - 214-452-6281: Confirm shipment
11:00		✉ Gloria Lenares - 214-667-9090: Request updated catalog
		✉ Greg Thomas - 214-344-5577: Left message for me to ca
12PM	📧 Tim Kelly: Lunch - Empire Restaurant	✉ Janice Corben - 212-345-6756: Set up meeting
		✉ Jean Willis - 214-234-0098: FAX paper
1:00		✉ Jeff Nelson - 214-324-0023: Verify address
		✉ Jeffrey J. Mayer - 312-944-4184: Order Flowers for Mitzi's
2:00		✉ Tyler Stephens - 214-556-3421:
	🖐 Gloria Lenares. Prepare new price list	✉ Tyler Stephens - 214-556-3421: Envelopes and formal ca
3:00		🖐 David Rechs: Follow up on delivery
		🖐 Gloria Lenares: Call traffic about distribution
4:00	📧 Janice Corben: Discuss travel arrangements	🖐 Greg Thomas: Prepare presentation for 3rd quarter
5:00		🖐 Greg Thomas: Verify the cover stock prices from list
6:00		🖐 Jean Willis: Assemble catalogs

☒ Timeless
☐ All Public

Schedule... | Clear... | Lookup | OK

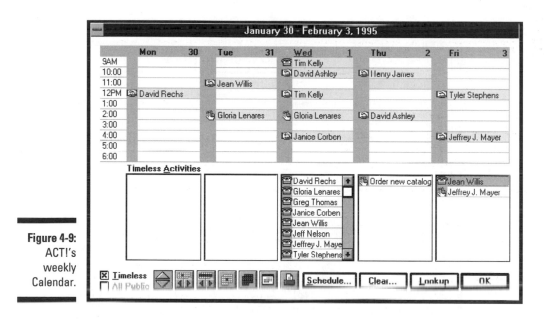

Figure 4-9:
ACT!'s
weekly
Calendar.

Figure 4-10:
ACT!'s
monthly
calendar.

In addition to viewing your activities in a calendar format, you also have the ability to view all of your tasks — calls, meetings, and to-dos — on a single list that's conveniently called the Task List. (Creative people, those software designers.) Just push a button or click an icon with your mouse, and your list of current tasks appears. And with another click of your mouse you can see a list of all your past, present, or future calls, meetings, or to-dos. Figure 4-11 shows the ACT! Task List.

All Dates					

Time Period
○ Today ○ T_o_morrow ○ _P_ast ● _A_ll ○ Date _R_ange

Priority
☒ Lo_w_ ☒ M_e_dium ☒ _H_igh

☒ Ca_l_ls: 10	Date	Time	Regarding	Duration	Priority
Tim Kelly	2/1/95	9:30AM	Schedule an Appointment	0 min	High
Jean Willis	2/1/95	None	FAX paper	0 min	Low
Janice Corben	2/1/95	None	Set up meeting	0 min	Low
Tyler Stephens	2/1/95	None	Envelopes and formal card stock	0 min	Low
Tyler Stephens	2/1/95	None		0 min	Low

☒ _M_eetings: 7	Date	Time	Regarding	Duration	Priority
David Ashley	2/1/95	10:00AM	Discuss Prices for cover stock	45 min	Low
Tim Kelly	2/1/95	12:00PM	Lunch - Empire Restaurant	1 hr	Low
Janice Corben	2/1/95	4:00PM	Discuss travel arrangements	1 hr	Low
Henry James	2/2/95	10:00AM	Follow-up presentation	1 hr 15 min	Low
David Ashley	2/2/95	2:00PM	Conference Call	45 min	Low

☒ _T_o-dos: 7	Date	Time	Regarding	Duration	Priority
Gloria Lenares	2/1/95	2:30PM	Prepare new price list	30 min	Low
Tom Huffman	2/1/95	None	Prepare presentation for 3rd quar...	0 min	Low
Tom Huffman	2/1/95	None	Order new catalog from National	0 min	Low
Jean Willis	2/1/95	None	Assemble catalogs	0 min	Low
David Rechs	2/1/95	None	Follow up on delivery	0 min	Low

☐ Show All Pu_b_lic Activities   [🖶]   [_M_odify...] [_C_lear...] [Loo_k_up] [OK]

Figure 4-11:
ACT!'s
Task List.

Enter information easily

One of the time consuming parts of entering information about people into a computer database is that much of the same information that must be entered is repetitive. It gets really boring typing "CHICAGO, IL 60611" over and over again. ACT! has a simple way of dealing with that problem. It uses pop-up dialog boxes.

A pop-up dialog box is a box that pops-up when the cursor is moved onto a specific field. The box can be set up so that it pops-up automatically or on request (by pressing F2). In a pop-up dialog box, you can select an item from a list that will be automatically inserted into the field. Any field in ACT! can be designated an automatic pop-up field. To enter the information in the City field, for example, you just use your cursor to select the city you want, or you can just type a letter: Type **C** for Chicago, **N** for New York, **L** for Los Angeles, and so on; then press Enter and the city's name is automatically inserted. Figure 4-12 shows a dialog box for cities, and Figure 4-13 shows a dialog box for states.

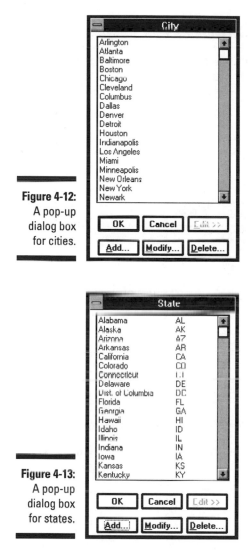

Figure 4-12:
A pop-up
dialog box
for cities.

Figure 4-13:
A pop-up
dialog box
for states.

Every field in ACT! can have a pop-up dialog box that can be customized to display the specific words or phrases that you use to describe your daily business activities.

Store and dial phone numbers

ACT! is designed to store all of a person's telephone numbers, including a number at a main office, a phone number at a second or third location, as well as a home number, beeper number, e-mail address, and fax number. ACT! can also store the secretary or assistant's name and phone numbers.

When you want to place a call, all you have to do is click on the Phone icon, and a list of all of the person's numbers displays in a pop-up dialog box, as shown in Figure 4-14.

Figure 4-14: The Telephone pop-up dialog box.

Fred Jones	
EMS	312-944-8321
Fax Phone	312-944-8845
Fred Jones	312-944-8321
Evelyn Smith - Secretary	312-944-8371
Main Num	312-944-8300
Car Phone	312-983-7548
Pager	312-791-6734

◉ Local ○ Long Distance ○ International ○ Alternate

Enter manually : 312-944-8321

[OK] [Cancel]

If your computer and your telephone share the same line, you can use the computer to dial the phone, and once the call goes through, all you have to do is pick up the receiver and begin your conversation. If your computer doesn't have a modem or it's not connected to your voice telephone line, you just click on the phone list, select the number you wish to call, and dial it manually. This method sure beats trying to find a number in an old, beat up Rolodex file.

Unlimited Systems makes a little black box, called Konnex, that allows you to connect your computer's fax/modem to a digital, PBX, or multiline phone system so that you can take advantage of ACT!'s autodialing capability. (Konnex, Unlimited Systems, 8586 Miramar Place, San Diego, CA 92121, 800-275-6354.)

Use categories to find selected groups of people

One of the features that makes ACT! so powerful is it's capability to group people in different categories based upon their business, profession, or any other criteria you might select. You can then do a lookup of this group, and in a few moments, you have a complete listing of everybody in that particular group. The Category pop-up dialog box it makes it very easy to enter this information (see Figure 4-15).

Figure 4-15:
The
Category
pop-up
dialog box.

I left my Rolodex in San Francisco

I do all of my own publicity and have set up categories for newspaper, magazine, radio, television, and so on. To date, I've stored the names of more than a thousand newspaper, magazine, radio, television, and other media people in my database. With the Lookup feature, I can do some amazing things with all this information. For example, in just a few seconds, I can create a list of the people who work for a radio station in Dallas and write for a newspaper in San Francisco. How long would it take you to gather such information with your Rolodex file? This example illustrates how ACT! puts the power of your computer at your fingertips.

Use ACT!'s word processor to write letters

ACT! has a built-in word processor that makes it easy for you to write letters, e-mail, memos, and faxes. Just select the person to whom you want to send a letter and then click the Letter icon. The basic format of the letter will be created in an instant. This format includes the date, the person's name and address, salutation, and your closing. All you have to do is write the text. You can then print the letter, fax the letter (ACT! works with WinFax Pro), or send it as electronic mail.

If you have some form letters that you send our regularly, you can use ACT!'s mail-merge feature to merge the form letter template with a single person or group of people. ACT! comes with predesigned letter templates that can be easily modified so that you can create your own customized letters, memos, and faxes. You can also print the information you've stored in ACT! as a telephone directory, mailing labels, envelopes, or Rolodex cards.

Use ACT! to create your reports

One of the biggest timesaving features of ACT! is its capability to take any of the different pieces of information that you have about each of the people in your database and use that information to create reports. You can generate reports of all your daily activities (your calls, meetings, and to-dos) and include any notes you may have taken about the various people in your file. You can display a history of what you've done with those people in the past and create a detailed list of the a calls, meetings, and to-dos that you have scheduled with them in the future. These reports can be created for a single individual or a group of people.

If ACT!'s report-generating capabilities aren't powerful enough for you, you may want to give Crystal Reports a try. With Crystal Reports, you can create personalized management reports, lead lists, forecast reports, statistical summaries, mailing labels, and much more. Crystal Reports, Crystal Services, 1050 West Pender Street, Suite 2200, Vancouver, B.C., Canada V6E 3S7, 800-877-2340 (US).

ANECDOTE

Use ACT!; save money

Several years ago, I was having some difficulty getting reimbursed for the telephone expenses I incurred as part of the ongoing publicity for one of my books. One day I got a letter from my publisher's publicity department stating that they would be happy to reimburse me for those expenses, but I would have to provide them with the names of everybody I spoke with, the dates we spoke, and the current status of the publicity that was being generated. They thought they were being cute because nobody could possibly create such a list without spending hours trying to put it together. But they didn't know what ACT! was capable of doing. I just printed a contact report for my entire "media" database — which had more than a thousand people in it — and put the 400-page report in the mail. Two weeks later, I received my check for almost 2,000 dollars.

Share your ACT! database with your coworkers

One of the extremely powerful features of ACT! is that it is network compatible. This feature allows you to share a common database and have access to another person's database.

Leaving the office? Print your calendar and take it with you

If you love your daily planner and can't live without it, you can print information from any part of ACT! (on a variety of paper sizes), insert the pages in your favorite daily planner, and take it with you as you walk out the door. This feature allows you to have the best of both worlds: a computer program that keeps you on top of everything that's going on in your life and a paper-based program that you can take with you when you're away from your office.

Part II
Taking Care of
Business

The 5th Wave   By Rich Tennant

"NO THANKS. BUT I WOULD LIKE TO CALL THE OFFICE AND LET THEM KNOW THAT I MIGHT BE LATE FOR THE NEXT BUDGET MEETING."

In this part . . .

The chapters in this part all focus on one goal: taking control. Your workday shouldn't run you ragged; you should be the one dictating what goes on and when.

Chapter 5 helps you plan the daily routine of getting your important work done. In Chapter 6, I share some tips on making the most of your business appointments. In Chapter 7, I show how you can be a more effective speaker. And in Chapter 8, I provide you with all you need to know about getting people to make the decisions that you want them to make.

Chapter 5

Do the Right Job at the Right Time

In This Chapter

▶ Planning your work day

▶ Planning your appointments

▶ Planning your travel

1 f you're like most of the people who are working in corporate America, you've probably got too much to do and don't have enough time to get it all done. But as you look at your Master List, I'm sure you'll see that some jobs are more important than others, and it's usually the important ones that are going to take up most of your time. So if you want to get ahead in today's fast paced world, you've got to be aware of which job you're doing and when you're doing it. It's just not enough that you're doing a particular job right. You've got to be sure that you're doing the right job at the right time, and that you're doing it right! It's not very difficult to stay focused, especially if you're using your Master List or ACT! to stay organized.

✔ First off, you need to sit down and analyze all the things you've got to do — your unfinished tasks, projects, and telephone calls.

✔ Then all you' have to do is make sure that you're spending your time on those activities that are of the highest priority, the ones that will have the biggest payoff for you and your company. The other tasks can wait until later.

And that's the beauty of this system. Because you're able to spend your time working on your most important tasks, you're able to take control of your work and your workday — it's no longer controlling *you*. You're able to see what's important and can set your own agenda. You're the one who is *making* things happen, and you're no longer just *reacting* to events as they occur. And after you've taken control of the tasks and projects that need your attention today, you're in a position to begin planning for tomorrow and beyond as you look at those tasks and projects that will need your attention in the days and weeks ahead.

Plan Your Activities

If you're not in the habit of *planning* your day, don't be alarmed, because it's really easy to do. You see, planning is nothing more than identifying, organizing, and scheduling your work. And that's what this whole book is about, helping you to take control of your day so you can get your work done, leave the office, and spend more time with your family and friends. Common sense tells us that we should spend the majority of our time working on our high-priority work, and put aside the lower-priority work until later.

But for most of us — me included — that's not what we usually do. It's just too easy to get distracted. So we end up spending the majority of our time doing things that aren't very high on the priority list, like reading the mail, answering e-mail, talking on the phone, or trying to solve someone else's problem, while our high-priority, big-ticket, big-payoff projects wait for us. Then when we finally *do* get around to working on them, we've got to rush through them because we've blown all of our lead time.

Now, you may be one of those people who feels that you're able to produce high-quality work under pressure, but even if that's the case, try to imagine how much better that work would be if you actually gave yourself the opportunity to put it aside for a while and then come back and make some additions, changes, or corrections. And for the rest of us, we should all be able to improve on that first draft if we leave ourselves enough time to go through it a second or a third time.

Did you know that in a recent time-management study the researchers found that most people spend only 20 percent of their time working on the handful of important tasks and projects that yield 80 percent of their positive results? This only confirms what I've long believed: That most people are spending the majority of their time — 80 percent — doing all sorts of things that keep them busy. And when they've finished doing all these miscellaneous things, they finally start working on their important and meaningful tasks and projects.

But by keeping your Master List up to date, you're able to keep track of all of the things you've got to do. As a result, you'll see a dramatic increase in your daily productivity. That's why it's so important for you to get organized because it's impossible for anyone to stay on top of unfinished work, projects, and tasks when so many piles of *stuff* are lying on top of the desk that no one even remembers whether the desktop is made of wood, glass, or Formica. (If you're not familiar with the concept of how to use a Master List, you can learn about it in Chapter 2.)

Get your ACT! together

With ACT! you can always see what it is you need to, whom you need to do it for, and when you need to do it. All you need to do is click the Task List and you can view a detailed list of everything you need to do today, tomorrow, or any day in the future. Then you decide which task you want to do, and you do it.

When you've completed the task, you just repeat the process and decide which item of business you want to tackle next. What could be easier?

Well, I can think of a lot of things that would be easier, especially if ACT! could do the work for me, but it can't. So I've got to sit down and do it myself. Life's hard! But there's a pot of gold at the end of this rainbow. After you start working on that task or project that you've been putting off, you'll find that it wasn't so bad after all. And when you're finished, you'll not only have the pleasure of crossing it off your Master List or clearing it from ACT!'s Task List, but you'll have that feeling of satisfaction that comes from knowing that you've done your job well. (For a more detailed description about how the ACT! contact management program can help you automate the process of staying organized, refer to Chapter 4.)

All Dates

Time Period: ○ Today ○ Tomorrow ○ Past ● All ○ Date Range

Priority: ☒ Low ☒ Medium ☒ High

☒ Calls: 10	Date	Time	Regarding	Duration	Priority
Tim Kelly	2/1/95	9:30AM	Schedule an Appointment	0 min	High
Jean Willis	2/1/95	None	FAX paper	0 min	Low
Janice Corben	2/1/95	None	Set up meeting	0 min	Low
Tyler Stephens	2/1/95	None	Envelopes and formal card stock	0 min	Low
Tyler Stephens	2/1/95	None		0 min	Low

☒ Meetings: 7	Date	Time	Regarding	Duration	Priority
David Ashley	2/1/95	10:00AM	Discuss Prices for cover stock	45 min	Low
Tim Kelly	2/1/95	12:00PM	Lunch - Empire Restaurant	1 hr	Low
Janice Corben	2/1/95	4:00PM	Discuss travel arrangements	1 hr	Low
Henry James	2/2/95	10:00AM	Follow-up presentation	1 hr 15 min	Low
David Ashley	2/2/95	2:00PM	Conference Call	45 min	Low

☒ To-dos: 7	Date	Time	Regarding	Duration	Priority
Gloria Lenares	2/1/95	2:30PM	Prepare new price list	30 min	Low
Tom Huffman	2/1/95	None	Prepare presentation for 3rd quar...	0 min	Low
Tom Huffman	2/1/95	None	Order new catalog from National	0 min	Low
Jean Willis	2/1/95	None	Assemble catalogs	0 min	Low
David Rechs	2/1/95	None	Follow up on delivery	0 min	Low

☐ Show All Public Activities   [Modify...] [Clear...] [Lookup] [OK]

Work on your important tasks first

Have you ever come into the office with the intention of working on one specific project and then discovered that the whole day had come and gone and you never got to it? This used to happen to me on a regular basis, and then one day

I realized that my focus was wrong and that I had my priorities backwards. I was trying to complete all the unimportant tasks and projects on my to-do list — those "B," "C," "D," and "E," items, the items that take up more of one's time than one's creative energies. I felt that once I could get them out of the way I would be able to start working on my "A" items — the *important* work.

You see, we get paid to complete our "A," #1, big-ticket, high-priority items. And nobody really cares if, or when, the other stuff gets done. But this important stuff, if it's done right, can mean big bucks to the company, and for you, it can mean raises, bonuses, and promotions at the end of the year.

That's why I believe it's so important to focus your time and energy in the right places. If you're spending the majority of your valuable time working on unimportant tasks and projects, there won't be enough time left to work on those *really* important high-priority ones. And it's these projects that we need to give our time and attention to because that's where the money is.

So don't spend your time trying to complete all the easy things first, just so you can get them out of the way. If you do, you won't have enough time or energy left to work on the harder projects, the ones that will take time, thought, and consideration. And since most of our important projects or tasks can't be completed in one sitting, you'll make your life so much easier and reduce your stress level when you can start working on them while you've got plenty of lead time. You do a little bit now and a little bit later, and before you know it, you're finished.

Review your things to-do list throughout the day

Have you ever been sitting at your desk and been unable to decide what it was that you wanted to do next? You looked at one pile, then another, and then another, and the more you looked, the more depressed you got — because those piles represented an awful lot of *unfinished* work. So you shuffled some papers back and forth for a few minutes, looked at the clock, and then went out to get a cup of coffee.

If you keep your Master List on the top of your desk, you can guarantee that it'll never happen again! Whenever you complete a task, look at your Master List, scan it from top to bottom, and ask yourself: "What should I be working on next?" And if you're like me, you may grumble a bit because it's not a task you were looking forward to doing, but you should just stop thinking about it and do it anyway.

When I was playing ball in college, a teammate of mine would say, "Jeff, stop thinking! It hurts the ball club." It was almost 20 years before I understood what he meant. Just do what comes naturally, and don't give yourself the opportunity to talk yourself out of doing it.

This is another area where you'll find ACT! to be a tremendous productivity-improving tool. See the sidebar in this chapter, "Get your ACT! together," for more info.

Review tomorrow's agenda before you leave in the evening

I like the idea of separating thinking and planning from doing. And the more time you can spend thinking and planning your work, the easier it will be to do. So, as part of your daily planning, you should make it a point at the end of the day to review your Master List to see what's on your agenda. Whom do you have to call, what projects or tasks need to be done, whom do you have meetings with, and where will they be held. By reviewing your Master List in this manner, you can get an overview of all the things that need to be done and identify the most important tasks or projects that you'll need to work on.

You may even want to pull out the project's file, just to refresh your memory about what's got to be done, and to put yourself in the right frame of mind so that when you arrive in the morning, you'll know exactly what you need to do. After you've taken the time to determine whichever task is most important, you may not realize it, but you've already made a commitment to start working on it. When you arrive in the morning, you'll be ready to go to work.

ACT! makes it a breeze to keep your daily plan current and up to date because you're able to use the power of your computer, instead of a pencil and paper, to keep you organized. This allows you to spend your time working on your important tasks and projects — the ones that will make you money — instead of *wasting* time making up a new daily plan or rewriting your to-do list so that the highest priority items are at the top of the list.

You should also make it a point to sit down with your secretary, administrative assistant, or the other members of your organization for a few moments at the end of the day so that they know exactly what things they should be working on when they arrive in the morning.

Get the most out of the first two hours of the day

Have you ever felt like Snoopy as he's trying to write his first novel and always gets stumped after he writes *It was a dark and stormy night . . .*? What probably happened is that you tried to start this difficult, time-consuming project and you didn't have enough mental or physical energy left to move forward. It's late in the day, you've gone from one meeting to the next, and now that you're sitting at your desk so exhausted that you can't write, you can't think, and nothing's happening.

You probably never gave this much thought before, but have you ever noticed that there's a time of day when you have the most energy and enthusiasm, and your ability to concentrate is very high? I call it Prime Time, the time of day when you're at your best. And if you're like most of us, you're probably at your best the first thing in the morning. You're bright, alert, and ready to go. That's why you may even call yourself a "morning person."

Here's a nifty idea: Tackle your most important work at the time of day that you have the most energy and enthusiasm. When you're able to complete your important work early in the day, it's much easier to deal with the inevitable fires that flare up.

If you're really adventurous and want to try something new, try this: Give yourself the first two hours of the workday and actually block it out on your calendar. Then when you come into the office, close the door, turn off the telephone, and don't allow yourself to be interrupted. You'll quickly discover that you're able to complete twice as much work in half the time with half the effort.

Schedule an appointment with yourself

Have you ever thought of scheduling an appointment with yourself? I'm serious. You schedule appointments with everybody else — your boss, your customers, your clients, your coworkers. Well, why not schedule an appointment with yourself so that you can get some of your important work done?

For instance, let's look at that big file that's been sitting on the corner of your desk for a week. If I were to guess, I'd say it's there because you have to do some work on it. Well if you want to guarantee that it gets done, why don't you schedule an appointment with yourself to do the work? Yes, actually write it down on your calendar and think of it as an appointment with your boss or most important client. Because in a way, it is. Your boss gave you the assignment but doesn't want to sit at your desk and watch you do the work. Your boss has other things to do, and besides, that's why he or she hired you in the first place.

 When you've got an important project or task that you need to work on, schedule an appointment with yourself and write it on the calendar. When it's time for your appointment, close the door and turn off the telephone so that you won't be disturbed. Then go to work. After you get started, you'll find that this dreadful project wasn't so bad after all, and when it's done, you'll experience the feeling of satisfaction that comes from doing a job well, and you will have a big smile on your face as you cross the item off your to-do list.

Give yourself more time than you think you'll need

Have you ever started a project, and just as you were getting to the good stuff, you ran out of time and had to go to a meeting? Then when you got back to your office, you found that it was difficult to get started again. Well, this happens to almost everybody because most of us aren't very good at estimating time. We usually underestimate the amount of time it will take to complete a difficult project, and then we overestimate the amount of time it will take to complete an easy one.

 When you start working on a task, ask yourself how long you think it will take and then expand that amount by at least 50 percent. (If you think you need an hour, give yourself 90 minutes. If you need two hours, give yourself three.) This will help to ensure that once you start working on a project, you'll have enough time to complete it.

Solve your problems before they become problems

Someone once told me that there are three kinds of problems: Those that solve themselves, those that will wait for you, and those that need your immediate attention and force you to drop whatever you're doing. But as I thought about what he said, I eventually came to the conclusion that most problems could be avoided in the first place if the work had been done the right way the first time. And those little problems that eventually grow into BIG problems won't *become* BIG problems if they're addressed while they're still little ones. In fact, even the most insignificant things can become a major headache if they're aren't addressed in a reasonable period of time.

Leave yourself some time to deal with unexpected problems

I have a friend who would plan his day as if nothing unexpected would come up, and then he would become very upset and frazzled because whenever things went wrong, he was forced to stop whatever he was doing to help solve a problem. After we talked about it for a while, we came up with a unique idea: Plan for those unexpected problems and actually allocate time to solve them on your daily calendar.

Get your important work done early in the morning, before the inevitable fires flare up, and then you can spend the rest of the day putting out those fires. As you begin to take more control over your daily affairs, you'll find that you have fewer fires to put out because the situations that previously would have become a three-alarm blaze had been dealt with long before being ignited.

And while we're on the subject of fires, you don't have to accept the fact that putting out fires is just an unavoidable part of your daily life. If you're coming into work each morning with the expectation that you're going to have to spend a major part of your day firefighting, you've got a problem: You've been putting out fires — usually started by other people — for so long that it has become a part of business as usual for you. Just because it's someone else's fire, however, doesn't mean that it has to be *your* fire. But never fear, because it's a problem that's easily solved.

Nowhere does it say that *you* have to drop everything because someone else has a problem. So the next time people walk into your office, ask them what they would do if you were on vacation — on a beach in the Caribbean would be nice — and weren't available at this very moment. Then tell them that you're too busy doing your own work and that they should figure out a way to solve their problem all buy themselves. Of course, you may not be able to say it quite so tactfully.

Meet your deadlines

When you were in school, did you have any friends who never opened a book, and then when it was time to prepare for a test, they would stay up all night and try to memorize enough material to pass the exam? I had a few friends who liked to "pull all-nighters," and I even tried it myself a few times, but I eventually came to the conclusion that nothing was worth losing a night's sleep over.

Well, many people in business pull the equivalent of all-nighters when they let an assignment sit, and sit, and sit, and when they finally begin to work on it, it's the fifty-ninth minute of the eleventh hour and they haven't left themselves enough time to even proofread their work for spelling or grammatical errors.

Maybe the work is satisfactory, but more often than not, it leaves something to be desired. If this approach isn't for you, I can show you a better way to get your work done, meet your deadlines, and get a good night's sleep. Just start on the project as soon as it's assigned. This way, you can do a little bit at a time and think about what you're doing; the more time you're able to put into it, the better it will be.

This is another way in which ACT! can help you get your work done on time because you can use it to schedule your tasks and projects as soon as they are assigned to you. Then you can start working on them long before you need to be concerned about an approaching deadline. The goal is to have a great finished product, not a great first draft. So the more time you can spend thinking about and planning what it is that you have to do — *before* you begin doing it — the easier the work becomes.

Don't use the arrival of the daily mail, an e-mail message, or voice mail as an excuse for interrupting yourself

Most of us require some motivation to get started on a project, but after we *do* get started, we begin to develop some momentum as we become more engrossed in the work. And after you get into the mood, the last thing you want to do is interrupt the flow of things by allowing yourself to be interrupted.

Just do it! But keep it short

Abe Lincoln once said, "I would have written a shorter letter, but I didn't have the time." It's easy to write a letter, memo, report, or presentation that's 5, 10, or 20 pages in length. But it becomes much more difficult, and it takes a lot more time, as you try to make it shorter, more concise, and to the point. How many months do you think it took to come up with Nike's slogan: "Just Do It!"?

Try to give yourself plenty of time to write, rewrite, edit, and think about your work. And after you've written, rewritten, and edited something — two, three, or even five times — you will finally reach the point where you feel satisfied with the quality of the work you produced. You can now pat yourself on the back and congratulate yourself for "a job well done." Then you can move on to your next project.

Don't use the arrival of the daily mail, e-mail messages, or a voice-mail message as an excuse for taking a break. By interrupting yourself and losing your flow, rhythm, and momentum, you'll find that it's twice as difficult to resume your work. So don't drop everything just because the mail's arrived, the lights on your telephone are flashing, or your computer is beeping. Instead, you should ignore these interruptions and continue working. When you've completed your task, you can see what new things need your attention.

When you go through your mail, e-mail, and voice mail, look for things that need your immediate attention and add them to your Master List at once so that you won't forget about them. You can get to the other things that you need to read, look at, or review later in the day.

When you open an envelope, don't look at the contents and then place them back inside the envelope. Take the papers out, unfold the paper, use a paper clip to group the papers together, and throw the envelope away.

How to get back to work after a marvelous vacation

My editor asked me to offer a couple of thoughts on how to get organized when you return from a vacation or a couple of days out of the office. I didn't quite know where to put this tip, so I figured that this spot was as good as any.

I don't know about you, but when I return from a vacation, or if I've been away from the office for a few days, my desk looks like a disaster site. There are piles of letters, memos, and reports, a stack of phone calls to return, and a list of people who want to see me that's two pages long. So here are a few thoughts on how you can go about cleaning up the mess.

✔ First off, before you even leave town, you should start planning for your return by blocking out some time on your calendar to get organized.

✔ Plan to leave open the morning of your first day back in the office. Then when you arrive, you should give yourself some quiet time, without any interruptions or phone calls, to go through the piles of things that have accumulated so that you can see what's important and what's not.

✔ If there's work to do, just note it on your Master List or add it to ACT!.

✔ If you need to keep something, put it into a file folder.

✔ And if you don't need it any longer, throw it away.

It's just that simple!

Plan Your Meetings, Your Appointments, and Your Day

One part of our daily planning that most of us don't spend enough time thinking about is how we go about scheduling our meetings, appointments, and our day. So I would like to ask you a few questions. Don't worry, you're not going to be quizzed; you don't have to write your answers out on a piece of paper and mail them to me for grading. All you've got to do is ponder the enormity and importance of these questions, for perhaps five to ten seconds. So think about these for a few moments:

- ✔ How much time do you spend planning your appointment schedule?
- ✔ How much thought do you give to the number of appointments you schedule during the course of a normal business day?
- ✔ How much thought do you give to where the appointments are located geographically?
- ✔ How much thought do you give to the amount of time it will take to get from one appointment to another?

If you're like most people, you don't give much thought to any of these questions. In fact, you're probably so excited that you were able to schedule that appointment in the first place that you would be happy to meet them at their office at 5:00 p.m. on Super Bowl Sunday. But unless you spend more time planning your appointment schedule, you'll find that it's very easy to waste a lot of time going back and forth, and before you know it, you've completely lost control of your workday.

Don't schedule appointments for early in the morning

It's been my experience that most people are capable of doing their best work during the early-morning hours. They've got a lot of energy, and their ability to concentrate is very good.

If that's true for you, then you should try your best to keep the early morning hours open so that you can get some of your important work done, and then you can schedule your meetings and appointments for later in the day. (If, on the other hand, you find that you do your most productive work during the early afternoon, late afternoon, after dinner, or in the middle of the night, make it a point to block out that time for you, and schedule your appointments around it.)

Don't be in a hurry to schedule appointments for 8:30 or 9:15 a.m. When someone asks if you're available at that time, just say that you've got a conflict and suggest that you meet later in the morning, or perhaps after lunch. Ninety-nine times out of a hundred, the other person will say OK. It's my suggestion that you try to keep the morning open until at least 10:30 or 11:00 a.m.

Actually block out the first two hours of the workday for yourself and write it on your calendar.

Give yourself breathing room between appointments

Have you ever had an appointment with your doctor and then discovered after you got there that the doctor was running two hours late? That's happened to me on too many occasions, and now I always schedule my appointments so that I'm his first patient. And I even make it a point to call his office just before I'm about to leave to see whether the doctor is going to be on time or is running late. This way, I don't waste too much time sitting in the waiting room.

Whoops! I don't know how I got sidetracked, but I'm the author, so I can get away with it. So let's get back to the subject at hand: Keeping you from booking so many appointments that when the first one runs late, all the others run late, and your day collapses around you like a falling stack of dominos.

Let's start with a basic premise: One of the easiest ways you can throw your daily schedule off track is to schedule your appointments back-to-back-to-back. Instead, you should always assume that a meeting will start late and take longer than you had anticipated.

How many times has this happened to you? The meeting that was supposed to start at 9:30 and end by 10:00 didn't start till 9:45 and didn't breakup until 10:25. Once in your lifetime? Twice in your lifetime? Or several times per day? Well, it can only happen once for the 9:30 a.m. meeting, but it can happen again, and again, and again to the other meetings you've scheduled. And once your 9:30 a.m. meeting runs long, what happens to the quality of the meeting that you've got scheduled with the person who has been waiting for you in the reception area since 9:55 and it's now 10:25?

As you plan your day, you should assume that every meeting will take at least 50 percent longer than you expect. Block out that additional time on your calendar.

> ✔ For a 30-minute meeting, you should allow 45 minutes.
>
> ✔ For an hour meeting, give yourself 90 minutes.

Always give yourself at least a 15-minute cushion between your meetings. This guarantees that you'll have at least a moment or two to catch your breath, return a few calls, and look at the mail before the next meeting starts — if this first meeting should end on time, and if it doesn't, maybe you won't be too late for your next one.

Group your appointments together

I have a friend, perhaps you know him — well, you probably don't, but you've certainly seen how he goes about scheduling his meetings and appointments. He'll come into the office and go out to a meeting, and then he'll return, and a little while later will leave the office for a second one. And after he returns, he'll come back, sit at his desk, read the mail for a few minutes, return some phone calls, and then go out for a third appointment. Apparently, it never dawned on him that he's wasting a lot of time — usually sitting in traffic — going back and forth from his office to a meeting and then returning.

If you want to have more time during the course of your day, look for ways in which you can eliminate the wasted commuting time. I call this *Addition by Subtraction.*

If you will be out of the office, try your best to group your appointments together to eliminate the time spent driving or walking from one person's office to another. You may also want to try to schedule appointments so that you can stop on your way into the office in the morning or on your way home in the afternoon.

If you need to travel through areas where traffic is heavy or the roadway is under construction, take this extra commuting time into consideration when you're setting up your appointments and meetings.

This is another way that ACT! can help you to use your time more effectively. With ACT!'s Lookup feature, you can look up people by city, ZIP code, or even telephone number. If, for example, you find that you've got to drive a long distance for an appointment, you can search your ACT! database to see who else you may know in that community that you could set up a meeting with. As long as you have to drive out there, you may as well try to see some additional people.

ACT! does my out-of-town meetings

ACT! helps me schedule my out-of-town meetings. I recently scheduled a trip to Los Angeles, and after I had scheduled my main appointment, I did a lookup of all the people I knew in L.A. and was able to schedule several additional appointments while I was in town. After I had scheduled these appointments, I booked my airline and hotel reservations.

If time is money, why do you spend so much of it sitting in traffic?

Have you ever thought about how much time you spend in your car? (I know that some of you may take public transportation — a bus or a train — to work, but the same thought applies here too.) At a minimum, you go to work and, at the end of the day, you return home. And if you're in your car driving to other places during the day, that's just more time that you're going to be stuck in traffic.

But if you're spending several hours per day in your car, it may be costing you a lot more of your valuable time and money than you might think. Yes, I know that you can make or return some phone calls and may even have a fax in your car, but trying to run a business from behind the wheel of your car just isn't the same as running your business from behind your desk.

Before you read any further, why don't you make a few copies of the Travel Analysis Form (Figure 5-1) and keep track of how many hours you spend commuting for two weeks. You may discover that you're spending much more time commuting to and from work than you thought.

After you've accumulated this information, why don't you try leaving your home at a different time in the morning, or your office at a different time in the evening. For illustrative purposes, how much would you shorten your travel time if you were to change the time you left your home by 30 minutes? What if you were to change the time you leave your home by 60 minutes?

Now I'm not trying to get you to spend more hours working — but if the time savings were large enough, perhaps you could work out an arrangement with your employer to change the starting and ending time of your workday. But by leaving earlier in the morning and earlier or later in the evening — to avoid the rush-hour traffic — you may be able to convert some of the time that's wasted sitting in traffic to time you can use more productively in the office.

Travel Time Analysis

	Monday	Tuesday	Wednesday	Thursday	Friday	Total Travel Time
Time you leave your home						
Time you arrive at the office						
Travel time						

Time you leave the office						
Time you arrive at your home						
Travel time						

Figure 5-1:
Travel
Analysis
Form.

Total weekly travel time						

I got tired of commuting, so I quit!

In the mid-seventies, when I lived in the Chicago suburb of Evanston, I discovered that if I left the house just before 7:00 a.m., I could cut my commuting time to my office from almost an hour to about twenty-five minutes. But with the passage of time, I became more and more disenchanted with sitting in traffic, so I moved into the city and cut my commuting time to under fifteen minutes. Eventually, I decided to eliminate commuting entirely and started working from home.

And while you're taking the time to analyze how much time you spending going to and from work, you should think about how much time you spend driving from one appointment to another. Whenever you schedule an appointment, you should always ask yourself if you could group this appointment together with any of your other appointments. And at the same time, you should see whether it would be possible to schedule your appointments for the beginning or end of your workday to combine your driving to or from work with an appointment.

The next time you schedule a business meeting or appointment, ask the person to come to your office. This way, you can eliminate the need to travel. If that's not possible, perhaps you can meet somewhere in the middle to reduce your total driving time.

What does it cost to operate your car?

The time spent commuting is one thing, but what' does it cost you to own and operate your car? When you add up the cost for auto insurance, gas, oil, regular maintenance, and wear and tear on your car, it may end up costing you 40 cents per mile to drive your car.

I thought it would be helpful for you to see how expensive it is to own and operate a car. So in the Annual Mileage Expense Chart (Figure 5-2), I used my super-duper spreadsheet program to work out these sophisticated mathmatical calculations. It only took me four hours to write the formulas. (I would have used my calculator, but my daughter had been playing with it and I couldn't find it.)

In Your Annual Auto Expense Chart (Figure 5-3), I included the major expenses that most people incur in operating a car. You're going to have to fill in the blanks yourself.

ANNUAL MILEAGE EXPENSE CHART		
Total Miles Driven	Cost per Mile	Total Cost to Operate Your Car
10,000	$.30/mile	$3,000
10,000	$.40/mile	$4,000
10,000	$.45/mile	$4,500
15,000	$.30/mile	$4,500
15,000	$.40/mile	$6,000
15,000	$.45/mile	$6,750

Figure 5-2:
Annual
Mileage
Expense
Chart.

Take a few moments and add up your total operating costs and then divide that number by the total number of miles you drive each year. If you're able to reduce your operating costs, you'll have more money left over that you can spend on yourself.

YOUR ANNUAL AUTO EXPENSE	
Auto insurance	$
Gasoline	$
Oil	$
Regular maintenance	$
Emergency maintenance	$
Miscellaneous auto expenses	$
Depreciation	$
Total annual cost	$

Figure 5-3:
Your Annual
Auto
Expense
Chart.

Manage your out-of-town travel

It's one thing to be losing valuable and precious time while you're sitting in
traffic, but it's even easier to lose a lot of hours, if not days, sitting on an
airplane. Over the years, I've heard many people brag about how much they fly.

They feel important because they're flying 250,000, 500,000, or even 1,000,000 miles per year. Apparently, they believe that the size of their frequent mileage statements is a measure of their persistence, determination, and success rather than a log of time wasted sitting in an airplane.

Yes, laptop computers and pocket telephones can help you stay on top of things, but there's no way you can operate as efficiently and as effectively when you're traveling in an airplane and living in a hotel room than when you're working in your office. Today, a person has a lot of communication's alternatives to choose from before having to hop on an airplane to meet with someone face-to-face.

- ✔ First, why not try using the telephone? You can certainly have a conversation, or several of them, before you've got to fly off somewhere.

- ✔ Then you can send materials by fax, overnight delivery, or electronic mail, and after the materials have been received, you can have another series of phone calls to discuss them.

- ✔ You can even rent a video conferencing center so that you can talk to other people face-to-face

- ✔ And then, if you've done all of the above and you feel that it's still necessary to hop on a plane and see the person face-to-face, then do it.

And while you're examining your out-of-town total travel costs, you should analyze your visible, and *in*visible, costs. Your visible costs include the cost of the plane ticket, taxi fares to and from the airport, meals, and hotel rooms; your invisible costs include the cost of your time. You need to take into consideration the cost of your time because you're not only away from the office, but you're spending an awful lot of time sitting in traffic while you're going to and from the airport in both your home city and in the city you've flown to. And you're wasting a lot of time while you're in the airport waiting for the plane to depart.

ANECDOTE

Two hours waiting time for a 30-minute flight

One day I had to fly to Indianapolis on business. It took me 45 minutes to get to the airport, and then I waited another 20 minutes before I boarded the plane, and it was another 20 minutes before it left the gate. Then it was 15 minutes before we actu- ally took off. After I arrived in Indianapolis, it took me 35 minutes to get to my hotel. So I spent more than two hours sitting in a taxi or waiting for the plane take off for a flight that was only in the air for 30 minutes.

Don't waste your valuable time being an errand boy (or girl)

And while we're on the subject of *wasting* time, try not to waste your valuable time as an errand or delivery boy. Instead of wasting a couple of hours running something over to a client, have a messenger service or a taxi do it. You can save yourself time by not wasting it, and then you can continue working in your office. Addition by Subtraction.

I don't know about you, but I hate to fill out those air bills when I use an overnight delivery service. So here's a neat timesaving tip: Have your air bills preprinted! You can have not only your name, address, and phone number printed on the air bill, but you can also have the name, address, and phone number of the person to whom you're sending the letter printed on the air bill. Just call your overnight delivery service — Federal Express, Airborn Express, United Parcel Service, or whichever service you use — and ask them to send you preprinted air bills.

The 5th Wave By Rich Tennant

"OH SURE, IT'S NICE WORKING AT HOME. EXCEPT MY BOSS DRIVES BY EVERY MORNING AND BLASTS HIS HORN TO MAKE SURE I'M AWAKE."

Chapter 6

Take Control of Your Business Appointments

● ●

In This Chapter

▶ Preparing for meetings

▶ Managing meetings

▶ Making the most of your time in meetings

● ●

*E*very day we have meetings and appointments. Some of them are internal sales or staff meetings, or just a brief meeting with your boss, a colleague, or a coworker. And other times we'll have a meeting with someone who is from outside our organization. These meetings may take place within our offices, at their offices, or someplace in between, such as over breakfast, lunch, or dinner at a restaurant.

If you're meeting with your boss, a colleague, or a coworker, your meeting actually starts the moment you get up from your desk to go to the meeting. You've got to be friendly and cordial and walk into the meeting — on time — with a smile on your face. A smile makes a lasting impression.

Should your appointment be with someone outside your office, your meeting actually begins the moment you walk into the person's building. For all you know, the person who got into the elevator or walked into the building with you is the president or owner of the company; or he or she may be the person with whom you've got a meeting. Since you never have a second chance to make a first impression, and first impressions are usually lasting ones, you should try your best to be friendly and personable to everyone you meet, and that includes the receptionist, the person's secretary or administrative assistant, and anyone else you may see in the hallway. Display and use all of your social skills.

 When you walk through the front door of the office, have a smile on your face — it adds warmth to your voice — as you say "Hello" to the secretary or receptionist who will inform the person you're meeting that you have arrived. Warm up to those people and try to make them your friends.

> ## "Is this the party to whom I am speaking?"
>
> In ACT!, you have the capability to store the name of a person's secretary or administrative assistant, and you can even record the name of the receptionist who answers the phone when you call. When you walk in the door, you can ask the person behind the desk, "Are you so-and-so?" and then introduce yourself because you've spoken so many times on the phone. It makes a nice and lasting impression.

It Starts with a Smile and a Handshake

Do you like to work with, or do business with, a grouch? I sure don't! And I'm sure you don't either. We all prefer to do business with nice, friendly people, so even if the other person's a grouch, we don't have to become grouches ourselves. Instead, we must work hard at making and maintaining favorable impressions with everyone we come in contact with. It starts by having a smile on your face, a twinkle in your eye, and a warm and open handshake as you introduce yourself and say, "It's nice to meet you" or "It's nice to see you again."

If you're carrying a briefcase, carry it in your left hand so that when you greet the other person, your right hand will be free as the two of you can shake hands. Another reason for holding your briefcase in your left hand is that it keeps your right hand drier. No one likes shaking hands with a person whose hand is moist and clammy.

Dress and Act Appropriately

A question that I'm often asked is "How should I dress for work and for my business meetings?" The answer is rather simple: Your choice of clothing should be appropriate to the business environment. If you're working for an advertising agency, the dress may be rather casual — blue jeans and a tee shirt. But if you're working for IBM or some big investment banking house, you've got to wear a deep blue suit, white shirt with a "power tie," and wing tip shoes. The flashy red braces (suspenders) would be appropriate at the investment banking firm, but not at I.B.M.

And when you're having a meeting with people from outside your firm, you should feel comfortable dressing in the same manner as they do. If they're wearing business suits, you should also; and if they're dressed casually, then it's OK for you to do so. But no matter what you've chosen to wear, you should always look your best. Your business suits should be freshly pressed, your shirts should be starched, and your shoes freshly polished. Your fingernails should always be clean and trimmed and your hair neatly groomed. The amount of jewelry you choose to wear is really a personal decision, but in most instances, the less jewelry you wear, the better.

Have you ever been in an elevator and thought that the "aroma" of another passenger's cologne or perfume was a bit too strong? Well, a strong fragrance may be appropriate in a social setting, but in business, you don't want your scent to arrive ahead of your handshake. I personally believe that the less fragrance you wear, the better. And under fragrance I would include everything from perfume to cologne to scented deodorant.

And while we're on the subject of scents, you should pay attention to the foods that you eat. I know that onions and garlic may be your favorite foods, but in a business situation, you're trying to draw the other person closer to you, and when people smell of onions, no one wants to come near them.

And finally, business and politics don't mix. When you're meeting someone for business purposes, your personal beliefs and opinions should be placed in the background. Avoid wearing anything that identifies you with any religious belief, political or social persuasion, or outside organization.

During a Meeting, Where Should You Sit?

It may never have occurred to you before, but where you choose to sit in a business meeting can have a dramatic effect on the outcome of the meeting. Let's assume that you're meeting with a client in his office. If you're sitting at his desk, there will probably be two chairs placed in front of the desk, and it's *assumed* that you will sit in one of these, and the other person will sit in his chair, on the other side of the desk.

But if you accept this seating arrangement, there's a barrier — the desk — separating the two of you, and during a meeting you want to remove as many barriers as possible. If, on the other hand, you were to sit *next* to that person — instead of sitting on the opposite side of the desk — you would have a much greater opportunity to maintain control of the conversation and the meeting. And because you're sitting next to each other, you have the opportunity to dramatically improve the flow of conversation between the two of you. As an additional benefit, you won't even have to look at your notes and materials upside down.

Getting your chair around to the other side of the desk can be a little tricky, but once you've done it a few times, it's really easy. And besides, what's the person going to say after you've done it? Nothing. So here's what you do:

- ✔ First, you sit down in the chair that will be the easiest for you to pick up and move, and as you're exchanging pleasantries, you remove your papers from your briefcase.

- ✔ Then, as you're about to start talking business, you stand up, pick up your chair, and move it to the other side of the desk so that you're sitting next to the person.

- ✔ While you're moving your chair, you say in a soft tone of voice something like: "I'm sure you won't mind me sitting next to you. I think you'll find this material to be very interesting."

By picking up and moving your chair, while simultaneously stating your intentions to do so, there's really nothing the other person can do to stop you. The whole thing happens so quickly that by the time the person has had a chance to respond, you're already sitting next to him.

Here are some tips about how you should position yourself during a meeting:

- ✔ Whenever you're sitting with another person at a table — be it in one of your offices or at a restaurant — you should always sit next to the other person instead of sitting across from each other.

- ✔ It does make a difference it you sit on the left or right side. If you're right-handed, you should sit on the person's right side. This way, when you're writing, the person will be able to read your notations as you're writing them because your writing hand will not hide your pad. If you're left-handed, you should sit on the person's left side for the same reasons.

- ✔ When you're making a presentation to two people and you're sitting at a square table, you want the two of them to be sitting next to each other. This way, you can address the two of them at the same time. If you're sitting between them, you'll find that whenever you address one person, you're no longer able to look at the other. And when you're trying to share the same piece of printed information with two people who aren't sitting next to each other, one of them is always looking at it upside down.

- ✔ If you're sitting at a long table, like a conference table, you should still try to get the two people to sit next to each other. Then you should sit down on the same side of the table right next to them.

- ✔ The chair you choose to sit in can also be a contributing factor to the eventual outcome of your meeting. When possible, you should always sit in a straight-backed chair. This will keep you alert and focused.

- ✔ Try your best to avoid sitting in a soft, comfortable, lounge chair or couch because it becomes too easy for you to relax and lose your competitive mental edge.

- ✔ Try to avoid sitting in a chair that is lower in height than the chair of the other person. The person who is sitting in the higher chair is able to *look down* on you and will have more power and control over the flow of the meeting. This situation usually occurs when you're sitting on a couch and the other person is sitting in a straight-backed chair.

And finally, I would like to give you my thoughts on where business meetings should take place. It's my feeling that important business meetings should take place in the office, not in a restaurant. Business breakfasts, lunches, and dinners are fine for getting to know a person, but they are not good places to try to conduct important business because of the lack of privacy, constant interruptions, and continuous distractions.

Things to Bring to Your Meetings

I'm constantly amazed at how unprepared some people are when they come to a business meeting. I've had business lunches where the person I was meeting didn't even have a pencil or a piece of paper to write anything on. And I've given time management seminars where the people for whom I was making the presentation didn't have anything to take notes with. That being said, here's a list of things you should always have with you when you go to a meeting:

- ✔ A pen or pencil

- ✔ A letter-sized pad of paper

- ✔ Your appointment book and calendar. If you're using a computerized calendar, always take along a print-out of your scheduled activities for at least the next four weeks.

- ✔ Business cards. You never know when you might run into someone who could offer a potential customer or client, or someone who could help you in a future career move.

Always carry a small pen in your pocket or purse and business cards in your wallet. This way, when you need to write something down, you've got the necessary tools.

Always Call Ahead to Confirm Your Appointments

When I was first starting out in business, I scheduled appointments days or weeks in advance and then just showed up at the person's office at the appointed time and on the agreed-upon date. There was only one problem. Sometimes I found that the person I was to meet had gotten tied up with something and couldn't see me; other times I arrived at his office only to learn that he was out of town for the day; and worst of all, there were times that the person hadn't even put me into his calendar. To say that this was a waste of time and money is an understatement!

I learned a lesson — the hard way. Always confirm an appointment before you leave the office! You probably weren't aware of this, but almost 50 percent of the appointments that you schedule will need to be postponed. In today's fast-paced, high-pressure business world, there are just too many things that can happen at the last minute to keep a meeting from taking place. But if you call to confirm your appointments, before you leave the office, your day won't go up in flames just because the person wasn't able to see you. Here are some tips on confirming appointments:

- ✔ Always confirm an appointment at least a day ahead.
- ✔ If you have a long drive to get to your appointment, you should also call the morning of the appointment so that you know that nothing unexpected has come up.
- ✔ If you have an early-morning appointment, always take the person's home phone number, and give the person yours. Should something come up at the *very* last minute, you both have a way of reaching each other.
- ✔ If you have an early Monday morning appointment, always take the person's home phone number and call on Sunday to remind him or her of your meeting on Monday.
- ✔ If you're going out of town for a business meeting, call several days before you're scheduled to leave, and call once again on the day you're scheduled to leave.

A colleague of mine once got on an airplane for a meeting with a customer in New York. When he got to the customer's office, he learned that the person had been called out of town unexpectedly the day before. Because my colleague hadn't confirmed the appointment, he found that the entire trip was a total waste of time and money.

Whenever you schedule an appointment, always give the person the correct spelling of your name. Then ask the person to take down your phone number and write it in his or her book. Say something like: "Let me give you my phone number so that if something unexpected comes up, you can give me a call so we can reschedule it." This statement serves two purposes: First, it forces the other person to actually write your name down (yes, some people schedule appointments without writing them down). Second, it lets the person know that you're very serious about your own time when you ask the person to call you if there's a conflict.

Try Your Best to Be on Time

Now, if you're going to go out of your way to thoroughly prepare for your meetings and then confirm them a day or two ahead of time, you should try your best to arrive on time. Even if you have to sit in the reception area for a few minutes while the person you're meeting with concludes a phone call or wraps up a meeting, it makes a great impression when you're on time. It not only shows that you take your job seriously and lets the person know that you're there to talk business, but that you also respect his or her time.

To keep yourself on time, *try* to arrive at all of your appointments at least five to ten minutes early. You'll find that when you try to get there early, it increases the odds that you'll be there on time. You may also want to set the time on your watch five to seven minutes fast. This way, you'll always know that you've got a few minutes as a cushion. In business, I believe that it's far better to wait for a few minutes because you're early than to make the other person wait because you're late.

Make the Most of Your Waiting Room Time

If you've got to spend a few minutes sitting in someone's reception room, do something useful and constructive with this down time. You can use this time to review the information in your files one more time, or you can use this time to catch up on some of the reading — newspapers, magazines, newsletters, trade journals, or any of the memos and reports — that have accumulated in piles on the top of your desk.

When you're traveling, use the time while you're in the airport and on the plane to update your expense accounts, compose memos, write letters, work on your business plans, or just catch up on your reading. Most people complain that they don't have enough time to get everything done, but if you look for ways to save time in small pieces, you can find lots of opportunities to convert wasted, unproductive time into profitable time.

If You're Running Late, Call Ahead

Have you ever gotten tied up in a meeting that just wouldn't end, and as a result were running 30 or 60 minutes late for your next meeting? Well, sometimes meetings do run long, or you get tied up on the phone and you can't get off. When this happens, there's nothing wrong with calling the person you're meeting to say that you're running late.

While you're speaking to this person, you want to ask two questions: "If I can get over to your office in so many minutes, would you still have enough time to meet with me?" And if the person says "Yes," then tell him or her that you're walking out the door. And if the person can't keep the appointment, say something like: "Since you're all booked up for the remainder of the afternoon, do you have some time tomorrow morning, or would the following afternoon be better?"

Calling ahead serves two useful purposes: First, the other parties will certainly appreciate receiving the call because it lets them know that you respect and value their time. Second, by calling and finding out if the other parties are still available, you can avoid rushing to a meeting that isn't going to take place. By letting your fingers do the walking before you leave the office, you can convert the time that would be wasted sitting in a reception area into time that can used much more productively back in the office.

 When you're trying to schedule an appointment with someone, always give two choices. "Would you prefer meeting on Tuesday at 10:00 a.m. or on Wednesday, right after lunch?" This way, you're changing the conversation from "Do you want to set up an appointment?" to "When would you like to set up an appointment?"

Always Check Your Briefcase Before You Leave the Office

I know that this probably sounds stupid because it's just common sense, but you should always check the contents of your briefcase before you leave the office for a meeting or an appointment. You just don't want to get to a meeting and discover that you left a document, a file, some miscellaneous form, or some other piece of information sitting on your desk. This becomes very important when you have an appointment scheduled for early the next morning: You certainly don't have time to go into your office. Make sure that you check your briefcase before you leave at the end of the day.

Manage Your Business Meetings

Meetings play such an important part in everyday business life that it's a crying shame that so many of them are unproductive. From the studies I've seen, most of the people working in corporate America are spending at least 40 percent of their time sitting in these meetings. And I would hazard a guess that this figure is understated because it probably doesn't include the time spent in unscheduled, or impromptu, meetings.

And if you were to define a meeting as any time two or more people get together to talk about something pertaining to business, then we're probably spending at least 90 percent of our time in meetings. And the unfortunate thing is that the majority of these meetings are so poorly run and so poorly organized that they're nothing more than a complete waste of everyone's time.

When the purpose of a meeting isn't well thought out, the participants may not know what they're supposed to be discussing, what they're trying to accomplish, or even why they're there in the first place. In the end, decisions aren't made, important issues aren't resolved, and nothing gets done. A lot of valuable and precious time is wasted, and the only decision made is to hold another meeting. But it can't be scheduled because the person who called the meeting doesn't have his calendar with him. The following sections contain some tips on how you can turn unproductive meetings into action-oriented meetings.

Distribute an agenda

If someone's scheduling a meeting, you and everyone else should know why. If the meeting doesn't have a well-defined purpose, it shouldn't be held. You also need to know what's expected of you and what you're trying to accomplish. Are

I could have sworn I put it in my briefcase . . .

I once knew a man who liked to schedule early morning appointments. But he often forgot to look in his briefcase before he went home at the end of the day. Invariably, he would have to come into the office before he went to his meeting because he needed some miscellaneous form that he had forgotten to take with him. And he never realized why he always felt tired and looked like he had been run over by a train.

you getting together for the purpose of discussing a new business opportunity, solving a business problem, or just to share information and bring everyone up to date on the status of specific projects or clients?

The best way to inform meeting participants of what the meeting's about is by preparing an agenda. In most cases, a detailed agenda should be written and distributed well in advance of the meeting. This way, everyone will be thoroughly prepared to discuss the items on the agenda.

By insisting that a written agenda be distributed in advance, it forces the person who's calling the meeting think about why the meeting is necessary in the first place.

If you're the person calling the meeting, always prepare an agenda. And if you're the person who is being asked to attend a meeting, insist that an agenda be prepared so that you can properly prepare yourself for the meeting. Figure 6-1 shows a blank agenda form.

After the agenda has been distributed, it's even possible that some of the items on the agenda can be dealt with over the phone or by written correspondence, and if that's the case, these items should be removed from the agenda.

A great question to ask at the beginning of any meeting is "How do we know when this meeting is over?"

After the meeting starts, it's the responsibility of the meeting leader to see that everybody sticks to the items on the agenda.

Have specific starting and ending times

It's unfortunate, but some people just don't take meetings seriously. They come in late, they leave early, and they talk during the meeting.

It's rather easy to get people to change their previous pattern of behavior, however, if you let them know that you want your meetings to become more productive and meaningful. You start by insisting that everyone arrive on time.

The next time you're in charge of an office meeting, close and lock the door so that late arrivals will have to knock to get in. You can then use their late arrival as an opportunity to inform them that they're *expected* to be on time in the future.

Latecomers also need to know that you're planning to stick to your agenda, that there is only a limited amount of time available for discussion of each point, and that you plan to adjourn at the designated time.

Sample Agenda Form

Date of Meeting

Place

Starting Time

Ending Time

Person Calling Meeting

Purpose of the Meeting

Desired Outcome of the Meeting

Meeting Participants

1.

2.

3.

4.

Agenda Items/Time Allotted for Discussion on Each Item

1.

2.

3.

4.

5.

(Note: The most important items should be listed at the top of the agenda and should be discussed first. The person who prepares the agenda should also include the amount of time that will be allowed for discussion of each of these points.)

Figure 6-1:
A sample agenda form.

And when you're one of the people who was asked to attend a meeting, it's OK to insist that it start on time, and it's OK to point out that the discussion has strayed too far from the items on the agenda. If the person who called the meeting isn't going to take control of it, then you should speak up and remind him or her that time's running short and you've got other things to do, or another meeting to attend, as soon as this meeting is over.

Announce the meeting place

You probably won't believe this, but whenever I attend a meeting, there's always one person who comes in late with some *lame* excuse about going to the wrong office or conference room. To avoid any confusion, whenever you schedule a meeting, be specific as where the meeting will be held. And if you're holding a meeting at an off-site location, be sure to give the street address of the building along with the name and location of the meeting room. In some cases, you may want to include a map so that everyone knows how to get there.

Why's the meeting being held?

Just because someone wants to schedule a face-to-face meeting doesn't mean that the meeting *must* be held. After you get the agenda, it's OK to call the person and ask about the particulars of the meeting and what outcome is expected from the meeting. After you speak on the phone, you may discover that you can accumulate the necessary information without ever having the meeting.

Do you have to be there at all?

Just because you've been invited to attend a meeting doesn't mean that you've *got* to attend. You just wouldn't believe how many people attend meetings where their presence isn't necessary. But they waste a lot of their valuable time sitting there anyway. So if you don't think you'll have much to offer at a meeting, it's OK to call the person who scheduled the meeting and say so. Why waste your valuable time sitting in a meeting discussing things that are not of direct concern to you when you could be doing some important and meaningful work at your desk?

Do you have to attend the entire meeting?

Occasionally, the situation arises in which a person's presence is needed for only a small portion of a meeting. Should that be the case, when you're asked to attend a meeting, pick up the phone and ask the person who scheduled the meeting if you could attend only the portion that applies to you. This way, you don't have to waste hours of time listening to others discuss things that aren't of immediate concern to you.

Impromptu meetings can be a Big Waste of Time. When people call and say that they want to see you, you don't have to drop everything you're doing to have that meeting. It's OK to ask why they want to get together with you, what it is that they want to discuss, and what they want to accomplish. In many instances, a face-to-face meeting can be replaced by just a few telephone calls and some correspondence between the two of you.

What is the purpose of the meeting?

When you're asked to attend a meeting, you should always know the purpose of the meeting. Will you be expected to make a decision, or will everyone just be sharing information? Is the meeting being called in order to solve a problem, plan for the future, bring everyone up to date on the status of a project, discuss new business, or something else? When you as a meeting participant know what's expected of you, you're better able to prepare yourself for the meeting.

What materials should you bring?

I know this sounds silly because it's just common sense, but when a meeting's called, each of the participants should be informed by the agenda sheet as to what materials or other information they're expected to bring with them.

If you're the one who is calling the meeting, try to distribute all of your handouts or other information *before* the meeting takes place. This way, everyone will have the opportunity to read and think about the topics of discussion before the meeting starts.

I once sat on a committee where the committee head made it a practice of distributing the packet of information to the committee members at the beginning of each meeting. We were then expected to read the material and make decisions based upon that material without having any time to think about the things we had just read. I thought this was a very sloppy way to run an organization, and I didn't stay on this committee for very long.

What do you do next?

At the conclusion of the meeting, the person who called the meeting should take a few minutes to summarize the points that were discussed and determine what's to be done next. If additional work needs to be done, those tasks should be assigned, and the people who are doing the work should be told when the tasks need to be completed.

If you're the person to whom the work is being assigned, you should ask some questions — and take detailed notes on what you're being instructed to do — so there can be no misunderstandings about the format in which it's supposed to be done and the due date for completion. If another meeting needs to be scheduled, a date and time should be set before everyone walks out the door.

Keep minutes of the meeting

Someone's got to keep minutes of the meeting so that everyone will know what was discussed, what decisions were made, and what is to be done next, by whom, and when. These minutes should be distributed within a few days of the conclusion of the meeting.

Make the last person who arrives at the meeting take the minutes. Since no one wants to be responsible for taking the minutes, you should see people's arrival times improve.

Chapter 7

Maintain Control of Your Conversations

In This Chapter

▶ Getting other people to talk

▶ Controlling the conversation

▶ The right way to ask questions

▶ Tips on being a great conversationalist

*H*ow many conversations do you have during a typical workday? You probably don't have the slightest idea, and frankly, I don't have any idea how many conversations I have, either. But I know that we spend a great deal of time interacting with other people each and every day. We're talking to people on the telephone, getting together in *formal* meetings in a conference room, holding *informal* meetings in someone's office, and having many *impromptu* meetings as someone stops us while we're walking down the hall to get a cup of coffee.

And that's just the people we work with in our own organization. During the day, we're also interacting with people from the outside. They may be customers, clients, prospective customers, the people who supply us with goods and services, and the people who would *like* to be selling us goods and services in the future.

Before you begin asking yourself why I included a chapter on how to maintain control of your conversations in a book on time management, let me take a moment to explain. Each of us spends a lot of time interacting with other people, but we don't necessarily do a good job of *communicating* with each other. As a result, we don't get the information we need to do our jobs correctly.

So I've included this chapter because I think that if we're able to improve our ability to communicate and get the information we need, then we can spend less time in meetings or on the phone and more time working on our important work, tasks, and projects.

You Get Information by Asking Questions

The easiest way to go about getting information is to ask questions. And as you get better at asking questions, it becomes easier for you to obtain the information you need to do your job. Let me give you a few examples of how you can do your job more quickly if you're good at asking questions:

- ✔ When you're given an assignment, you need to know what you're expected to do, how you're supposed to do it, and when it's got to be done. You obtain this information by asking questions.

- ✔ When you're trying to sell someone a product, service, or idea — and we're all selling *something* — you've got to find out what it is that the other person wants, needs, or desires before you can show how your product, service, or idea can fill that want, need, or desire. You obtain this information by asking questions.

- ✔ When you want to get information about what's happening within your company or organization, you sit down with a colleague or coworker and ask some questions.

- ✔ When you want to find out what one of your competitors is up to, you ask some questions.

- ✔ When you meet someone of the opposite sex and you want to find out if he or she is free for a date on Saturday night, you've got to ask some questions. (Time management is one thing, but this *really* is important!)

The better you are at asking questions, the easier it will be for you to obtain the information you need to get your work done, to help your company prosper, to further your career, and maybe even to better your social life.

Encourage the Other Person to Talk

People love to talk about themselves, so let them. And by asking a series of questions — sometimes over an extended period of time — you'll end up learning a great deal about their business affairs, business activities, on-going business relationships, your competition, and almost anything else that's going on in their lives.

Questions enable you to tune into other people and learn what they're thinking; and questions can help you to identify their real needs and real motives. And it's by asking questions that you can identify existing problems that you can help solve, discover potential business, or even find new career opportunities for yourself. Here are three things to remember:

- There's often a big difference between what people say and what they think and feel deep down inside.

- When you talk about yourself, you're a bore. When you encourage the other person to talk, you're a brilliant conversationalist.

- During your business meetings, listen more than you speak. As a general rule, you should listen at least 60 percent of the time. If you find that you're talking too much, it's time to ask another question.

Keep a Tight Lip Yourself

Now I know that you probably love to talk, especially about yourself and your accomplishments (I can talk about *me* for hours). But you'll go much further in business and your career if you encourage the other people to keep talking and you just sit there asking questions and listening attentively. And besides, you can't learn very much when you're the one who's talking.

If you're asked a question during a conversation, give a brief answer and then follow up your answer with another question.

Talk about being tight lipped. Several years ago, I read a newspaper story about the late Bill Casey, the former director of the Central Intelligence Agency. He was so tight lipped that if your jacket had caught on fire, he would tell you so only if you asked him the question: "Is my jacket on fire?" And then his reply would be: "Yes."

He (or She) Who Asks the Questions Controls the Conversation

When you're able to ask a person a series of questions, you're able to maintain control over a conversation. It's easy to ask that first question, but it takes some work and effort to be able to ask a second, a third, and a fourth question. By doing so, however, you place yourself in the desirable position of being able to control the flow of the conversation.

Your objective in asking these questions is to keep the other person talking so that you can get some useful information. (Such as: Where do you live? What's your telephone number? Do you have plans this weekend? Never mind. . . .) The more information you have available to you, the easier it is for you to do your job.

Would you like to say a few words?

You've probably never realized this, but when you're able to keep another person talking during a conversation, you give yourself a competitive edge. You see, people can think at a rate of about 1,200 words per minute but only talk at a rate of about 250 words per minute. So when people are talking at 250 words per minute and trying to focus on what they're saying, you can be thinking — at 1,200 words per minute — about what you want to say in response. You're thinking more than five times faster than they are talking.

Whenever you're talking to people who appear to be losing interest, beginning to daydream, or falling asleep, just ask a question and you'll bring them back to life. Now they not only have to wake up and clear the cobwebs from their brains, but they also have to listen because they know that they're expected to give you some kind of response.

Try to discover the hot button

Many people in sales use a phrase that defines their reason for asking a lot of questions: They want to discover a person's *hot button.*

What's a hot button? When you know what someone likes or dislikes; when you know what excites or concerns a person; when you know what a person's problems are, then you've discovered his or her hot buttons.

And when you know what to say and when to say it, it becomes much easier for you to get people to say "Yes" to whatever you're proposing or suggesting. (And when you know what *not* to say and when *not* to say it, you can keep yourself out of an awful lot of hot water.)

Get to know the hot buttons of your boss, your colleagues and coworkers, your largest customers and clients, and the significant other in your life, and you'll dramatically improve your relationships with all of them.

The Art of Asking Questions

Asking questions is an art. It's easy to just ask one or two questions, but it takes a lot of hard work to be able to ask a person a series them. You'll find that it takes a little bit of practice to learn how to ask the right questions in the right way at the right time; but after you get the hang of it, you'll be amazed at how much information people are willing to volunteer, just because you asked.

To keep a conversation going, always ask open-ended questions

When you ask open-ended questions, it not only encourages people to continue speaking, thus keeping the conversation going, but gives them the opportunity to fully explain their thoughts, opinions, or comments. With an open-ended question, you're asking people to give you an informative and descriptive answer

To ask an open-ended question, all you've got to do is phrase your question in such a way that it includes one of the five "W" words or the "H" word. These words are.

- ✔ Who
- ✔ What
- ✔ When
- ✔ Why
- ✔ Where
- ✔ How

Now, how can a person give a "Yes" or "No" answer to a question that includes a Who, What, Where, Why, When, or How without appearing evasive?

When I was in high school, I would often have the following conversation with my mother:

> Mom: *Jeff, where are you going?*
>
> Me: *Out.*
>
> Mom: *When will you be back?*
>
> Me: *Later.*
>
> Mom: *Who are you going with?*
>
> Me: *Friends.*

(Just like Marlon Brando in *The Wild Bunch,* right?)

Avoid asking close-ended questions

The flip side to an open-ended question is a closed-ended question, which is a question that can be answered with a simple "Yes" or "No." When you give someone the opportunity to answer a question with just a "Yes" or "No," you've created a situation where the flow of conversation can easily die. You just can't have a meaningful conversation when all you're getting is yes or no answers.

Calvin Coolidge, the 30th president of the United States, had the nickname "Silent Cal" because he didn't say very much. One day a reporter said to the President, "I'll bet you ten bucks that I can get you to say more than two words." And Silent Cal replied, "Nope!"

Don't ask questions in a negative way

When a question is asked in a negative way, it can change the course, mood, tone, and flow of a conversation and take it in the wrong direction. You always want to talk about things from a positive perspective. For example, instead of saying, "What don't you like about . . . ," you could say, "What would you like to see improved?" Or rather than say, "What did I do wrong?" you could say, "What should I have done differently? How could I have done it better?"

When you don't understand, ask for clarification

If, during your conversation, you ask someone a question but you're not completely sure what the answer means, it's OK to ask for clarification. This is another way you to show your interest in what's being said. You can say something like the following:

Can you go into a bit more detail?

What does that mean to you?

How did you arrive at that conclusion?

By asking for more detail, you'll get some additional information.

Paraphrase, summarize, or simonize

During a discussion, your conversation partners always need some positive feedback — be it a smile, a nod of the head, or a twinkle in your eye — as encouragement to continue talking. And by paraphrasing or summarizing what was just said, you can encourage your partners to continue speaking. It also provides reassurance that you're trying your best to understand what it is that they are saying.

To paraphrase a person's previous statement, you can start your sentence with one of the following phrases:

> *If I understand you correctly, you're saying . . .*
>
> *It seems to me . . .*

By summarizing all the things that were just said — and feeding it back — you can pull everything together so that you can confirm that you fully understand what's been discussed.

Other techniques to keep a conversation going

In addition to asking direct questions, there are several other techniques that you can use to encourage people to continue talking and to show them that you're interested in what they are saying.

Echo the speaker's words

The *Echo* technique is an easy way for you to keep someone talking, and when you use it effectively, you don't have to do too much thinking or talking yourself. This technique is especially useful if you're stuck and can't think of anything more to say because it can buy a few moments of time so that you can think about what you want to say next.

To use the Echo technique, just take the last few words of the sentence that the person just said and repeat them as if you were asking a question. Here's an example.

> *"I just came back from a meeting with my boss."*
>
> *"Your boss?"*
>
> *"Yes. He just gave me another project that he says he needs tomorrow."*
>
> *"Tomorrow?"*

"Yeah. It's for Pepperdine Manufacturing. You know, the new account he landed last week."

"Last Week?"

"Yeah. He was on a plane coming back from Toledo, and he started talking with this guy who was in the next seat. . . ."

You get the idea. In theory, you can use the Echo technique to keep someone talking for hours at a time. In reality, you can't use it for more than a few moments because it won't take too long for the other party to catch on to what you're doing. So, for a little variety, you can throw in an occasional "Oh?," "Uh huh," or "Hmmmm." Don't stop reading just yet. In the following section, I describe this marvelous conversational technique in more detail.

Just say "Oh?," "Uh Huh," or "Hmmmm," and nod your head

As an alternative to echoing each and every statement during a conversation, you could throw in an occasional "Oh?, "Uh Huh!" or "Hmmmm," just for variety. No matter what the person says, you simply respond with "Oh?, "Uh huh!" or "Hmmmm," and the person will continue talking.

This technique is another easy way for you to signal to other people that you're still listening. You also let them know that you would like them to continue speaking. It's especially effective when you nod your head, as a sign of agreement, at the same time. Let's go back to the last conversation:

"I just came back from a meeting with my boss."

"Oh?"

"He just gave me another project that he says he needs tomorrow."

"Tomorrow?"

"Yeah. It's for Pepperdine Manufacturing, you know, the new account he landed last week."

"Oh?"

"Yeah. He was on a plane coming back from Toledo, and he started talking with this guy who was in the next seat . . ."

 If you would like to have some fun and improve your relationship with your spouse or significant other, try using the Echo technique and these other related techniques when you come home from work this evening. Lead off with a question like:

How was your day today?

See how long you can keep the conversation going. You'll quickly see his or her eyes begin to light up with the realization that you're *really* paying attention. At the conclusion of the conversation, you'll know *everything* that happened during the day, and he or she will think that you're a brilliant conversationalist.

Mirror the person's feelings and emotions

When your partner in conversation is expressing emotions or articulating feelings about something, you should reflect — mirror — those emotions or feelings. As a part of your response, you should make eye contact, show concern, and nod in agreement, or disbelief, as the situation may dictate. This way, you acknowledge to the other person that you heard what was just said and you offer an emotional response. You can usually pick up the emotion or feeling from the tone of voice, the choice of words, or a look in the eyes. Someone looking for emotional support may say something like:

> *Do you think that's fair?*
>
> *Do you think I did the right thing?*

But when someone's asking an emotional question, you don't necessarily need to offer an answer or response. Instead, it may be entirely appropriate to respond to the question by asking a question. You can say something like this in response:

> *What do you think?*

Listen more and talk less

Asking questions is just the first part of being a good conversationalist. If you're going to be good at asking questions, you've got to be good at listening to the answers. You must listen closely to what the other individual is saying so that you can give positive feedback and, when appropriate, ask another question. It is in this way that you're able to guide the flow of a conversation into the direction *you* want it to go.

He who talks *dominates* the conversation. He who listens *controls* the conversation. The same thing applies to "Shes."

Tips for Being a Brilliant Conversationalist

✔ Do show interest in what the other person is saying.

✔ Do make an effort to understand what the other individual is trying to say.

✔ Do make an effort to understand the other person's point of view, even if you don't agree with it.

✔ Do let the other person know that you disagree with his or her point of view at the appropriate time.

✔ Do remain quiet when silence is the best answer to a question.

✔ Don't enter the conversation with preconceived ideas.

✔ Don't argue, even if you disagree.

✔ Don't interrupt unless you have a very good reason.

✔ Don't pass judgement too quickly.

✔ Don't offer your opinion unless you're asked.

✔ Don't give advice or behavioral feedback (tell the person how his or her behavior affects you) unless you're asked.

✔ Don't allow yourself to react emotionally to a statement; keep your cool and don't get angry.

✔ Don't cut other people off. Let them finish their thoughts before you offer yours or ask another question.

Winning in a conversation means using active listening techniques to control and guide the flow of the conversation so that you and your partners have the opportunity to fully express yourselves.

Chapter 8

Help People Make Decisions . . . Faster

● ●

In This Chapter

▶ Getting someone to say "Yes"

▶ Getting an organization to say "Yes"

▶ Handling objections effectively

▶ Negotiating

● ●

*I*f you thought that the biggest time waster in American business today was time wasted in meetings, you're mistaken. The biggest time waster in American business today is the inability of people to make decisions. In corporate America, we all spend hours of time in meetings, but when it comes to making a decision and actually doing something, the only decision that's made is to schedule another meeting. And when decisions are not made in a timely manner, windows of opportunity open and close very quickly, usually before anything gets done.

One day Mitzi and I, (Mitzi's my wife), were trying to decide which movie we wanted to see, and because neither of us could make a decision, we missed the starting times of *all* the movies.

Now why do so many people find it difficult to make a decision? Because they're afraid that they're going to make a mistake; they're not confident that they're making the *right* decision; and as a result, they become paralyzed. And when someone avoids making a decision, nothing gets done. So if you want to get ahead in this world, you've got to be good at making decisions yourself and at helping other people make decisions.

There's a common tool that an individual or an organization uses to put off, delay, or postpone the making of a decision. It's called *The Objection!* But dealing with and overcoming objections is a daily part of our business and personal lives. Every day, we're selling our thoughts, ideas, and concepts, as well as our products and services, to others — be it trying to get the company's Management Information Services Department to order a new piece of computer software, trying to close a multimillion dollar deal, or getting a date for Saturday night. And when we're able to compress the time it takes for someone to make a decision, we're able to get our work done more quickly.

Your Objective Is to Get the Person to Say "Yes"

I don't know what you do for a living — hey, I'm just the author — but if you're like almost everyone else, you've got to be selling something. And you're selling something to someone every day. It may be a product or a service to a new corporate account, or a new idea to your boss, or maybe you're trying to convince a new employer that you're the best candidate for the job, or maybe you're trying to persuade your new neighbor down the hall to have dinner with you tomorrow night.

But no matter what it is that you're selling, you've got to be able to get the other person to say "Yes." People make decisions for their reasons, not yours or mine (I know that may be hard for you to accept), so when you're able to discover what those reasons are — their *hot buttons* — then the process of getting someone to say "Yes" isn't *quite* so daunting.

People make decisions for their reasons, not yours, and when they can feel, touch, and see something, it's much easier to get them to say "Yes."

The ABCs of selling

When you're trying to convince someone to say "Yes" to whatever you're selling, you should always remember selling's "ABCs."

Advantage: Always promote the *advantages* of the features of your product, service, or idea.

Benefit: Talk about how these features will be of value and provide *benefit* to the person you're

trying to convince. Describe how these features will help solve problems or improve the quality of life.

Commitment: Get the other person to make a *commitment,* to indicate that he or she wants to own the product, service, or idea you're selling.

Don't take "No" for an answer

The only way you can get people to say "Yes" is by asking them to say "Yes." If you don't ask, you don't get! Now the first time you ask a person to say "Yes," he or she will probably say "No" and at the same time give you a reason for saying no — it's called an objection. (And you'll probably be scared to death, but you shouldn't let that stop you from asking the person to say "Yes.") An objection isn't the end. You just need to talk a bit more and discuss why the answer was no.

To get someone to say "Yes," you've got to be persistent. I saw these interesting statistics one day in a magazine article. Of those who asked the other person to say "Yes," look what happened to them after they were told "No."

- After they got their first "No," 44 percent called it quits and went back to the office.

- After they got their second "No," an additional 22 percent quit and went back to the office.

- After they got their third "No," another 14 percent quit and went back to the office.

- After they got their fourth "No," another 12 percent quit and went back to the office.

These statistics tell me that 66 percent of the people called it quits after they heard their second "No"; 80 percent called it quits after hearing a third "No"; and after hearing the fourth "No," 92 percent packed up their bags and went home, without having made any money.

So if you want someone to say "Yes" to whatever product, service, or idea you're selling, you had better be prepared to stick around for a while. You should plan to ask the person to say "Yes" at least five, six, or seven times before you decide to call it quits. Just because a person says "No" once or twice doesn't mean that he or she won't say "Yes" if you continue to ask a third, fourth, or fifth time.

If you're not being rejected, you're not trying hard enough. (My editor wrote this query: "Jeff: I think that applies to my writing career. I've been rejected a number of times, but not for quite a long time — mostly because I haven't sent out any of my articles for quite a long time. I need to get back to doing that.")

A treatise on seafood

There was a barracuda swimming in a tank of water with another fish that just happened to be the barracuda's favorite meal. There was only one little problem for the barracuda: His meal was enclosed in a glass container. Every time the barracuda tried to eat this fish, he crashed into the glass and bumped his nose. He did this over and over and over and over again, and his nose became very, very, very sore. After a few days of this, the fish was taken out of the glass container and was free to swim wherever he wanted to. And the barracuda starved to death.

You build on agreement

The process of getting people to say "Yes" is the process of building on agreement. As you successfully deal with each objection, you eventually change people's opinions about your product, service, or idea. Your goal is to move people from feeling indifferent to feeling positive about whatever you have to offer.

You can't overcome indifference

When people say, "I want to think it over" or "I'm in no real hurry," that's usually an indication that they aren't really sold on the idea. Either your proposal or presentation hasn't convinced them that your product, service, or idea will help solve a problem, or they are not sufficiently uncomfortable with their present situation to want to do something about it. This indifference often stems from the four basic "Nos."

- ✔ **No Trust:** I really don't trust you.

- ✔ **No Need:** I'm not aware of a need for your product, service, or idea.

- ✔ **No Help:** I'm aware of a need, but you haven't convinced me that your product, service, or idea will satisfy it.

- ✔ **No Hurry:** OK, you can satisfy my need, but my problem doesn't really bother me enough yet for me to pay to make it go away.

In order to convince people to say "Yes," these four "Nos" first have to be identified and then dealt with one at a time.

When you perceive that a person's attitude is one of indifference, It's time to start probing. You probe for areas of discomfort or areas of dissatisfaction with her present situation. (For more information about asking questions, see Chapter 7.) You do this by asking open-ended questions, questions that can't be answered with a "yes" or "no." Your goal is to help people become aware of a problem, or to help them realize that they aren't entirely satisfied with something. After you've done so, you have the opportunity to point out that the product, service, or idea you're offering provides a solution to that problem.

People are always more comfortable when they identify a problem and then discover its solution all by themselves. You're just there to help them along.

Look for that magic moment

In every successful sale, there is a *magic moment* when the buyer is most likely to agree with you and say "Yes." And you've got to watch for and pick up those signals. It could be just a simple physical gesture, such as leaning forward slightly, that indicates "I'm ready to say yes," or there could be a twinkle in the eye or a slight smile. When you hear, feel, or see such a signal, you must stop your presentation and try to get a commitment immediately.

Your objective is to close the sale by getting your potential customer to say "Yes," not to complete the presentation.

Ask "How?"

One of the most effective closing methods is getting people to discuss *how*, not if, they are going to buy. Make a request for action. To close the sale, you've got to ask for the order. If you don't ask, you probably won't get it.

Who Makes the Decisions?

In every organization — be it a large multi-national corporation or a sole proprietor who works out of his or her home — there is a method or a process set up for making decisions. And if you're going to be successful in getting someone to say "Yes," you've got to know how the organization goes about making decisions.

If the decision is to be made by more than one person, you need to know who the other people are, how they fit into the organization, and what their overall level of involvement in the decision-making process is.

After you know who the decision makers are, you should meet with them individually or speak with them on the phone, if that's appropriate, in order to try to win them over and sell them on the benefits of your product, service, or idea.

Who has the authority to say "Yes"?

When you're trying to get someone — or an organization — to make a decision, you've first got to learn who has the authority to make that decision. Who has the authority to say "Yes"? After you learn who that person is — because he or she may not be your initial contact — then you've got to sell him or her on the merits of whatever you're proposing.

If you're unable to deal directly with the decision maker, there's a pretty good chance that you're going to waste a lot of time, energy, and money.

Who has the authority to say "No"?

Within every organization there may be a number of people who don't have enough authority to say "Yes," but they *do* have the power to say "No" and can effectively kill whatever you're proposing. You must discover who those people are and get them to support you.

A "No" is a "No" until it's a "Yes"

No matter how nice and friendly and courteous a person is, a "No" is a "No" until it becomes a "Yes." Occasionally, you'll come into contact with people who give you every indication that they're going to say "Yes," but you can never get them to make a commitment. They'll talk to you at length, both on the phone and in person. But you can't get a commitment. They lead you on; they raise your expectations, but still, they don't say "Yes." Instead, they just leave you hanging because they don't say "No."

Beware of these kinds of people. They're dangerous. They don't have the courage to tell you the truth: That they're not interested. Or even worse, they don't have the authority to say "Yes." And the really infuriating part is that they couldn't care less that you've invested a lot of time, effort, and money on them, and it was all done at their encouragement.

Are you dealing with a decision influencer?

Sometimes you'll find yourself dealing with a person who is in a position to influence the final decision but is not in a position to *make* the final decision. For example, if you're dealing with the president of the company, this person may need to get the final approval from the board of directors before he or she can say "Yes." Or someone may need to get the OK from a supervisor or manager before giving the go ahead. Or, on an individual level, a person may not be able to give you a final answer until he or she has had an opportunity to discuss it with his or her spouse.

In situations like these, you've got to be sure that you've "sold" the decision influencer. If you haven't, he or she won't be very enthusiastic about presenting it to the other people who will participate in the final decision.

To find out whether the person your dealing with has the authority to make a decision, or if he or she needs to consult with someone else, you should always ask this type of question somewhere along the way:

> *Before you make your final decision, is there anyone else whom you want or need to consult?*

Court your champions

A champion is a person inside the organization who stands to gain something — prestige, recognition, or some other benefit — by supporting your program and defending your cause. As you meet the people who are part of the decision-making process, try to identify those people who will work on your behalf and help promote your product, service, or idea within the organization. You should always keep them advised of your progress.

Beware of blockers

There are also people who, for one reason or another, will go out of their way to try to block or sabotage your activities and put a halt to whatever you're trying to accomplish. Maybe these people have an axe to grind, maybe they're against change, or maybe they aren't happy that a new idea is being promoted by someone else instead of them.

To neutralize these individuals, you need to find a way to work around them so that other people will become more involved in the decision-making process, and the blockers' involvement will be minimized. If these people are your only contacts within the organization, then you've got to find someone else to talk with because otherwise, you're dead in the water. This is where a champion can be of help, and it's always helpful to have a coach available to give you some tips.

Get yourself a coach

Every once in a while, you may find yourself in a situation in which you're not sure what you should do next. You may not be sure who the decision makers are or how the organization goes about making decisions, and you need some help in navigating through these unfamiliar and uncharted waters. In this situation, you should look for someone who has done it before, a person who can give you some ideas, tips, techniques, and strategies on how to deal with this situation. This person could *coach* you through each step in the decision-making process.

Your coach can help you prepare your proposal or presentation, give you suggestions as to what you should say and how you should say it, and assist you in creating an overall strategy so that you can get the other person, or the organization, to say "Yes."

Handle Objections Effectively

Now the meat and potatoes of getting someone to say "Yes" is your ability to handle objections effectively. This is the main course. You asked all those questions so that you could get them to give you *all* the reasons that they don't like the product, service, or idea that you're trying to sell them. You encouraged them to be honest and open with you about what it is that they want and don't want; like and don't like, need and don't need. And now that you've been given a list of all the reasons that they're going to say "No," you're in a position to deal with each objection, one by one, and convince them that it's in *their* best interest to say "Yes."

Objections are like a minefield: If you don't locate, uncover, and remove all of them, one at a time, they'll blow you away.

Here are some tips on dealing with objections:

> ✔ When you prepare for a presentation, put yourself in the other people's shoes and make a list of every possible objection that you think they could give you. Then write down an appropriate answer or response to each of these possible objections.

- ✔ Don't be afraid of objections. An objection often indicates a sincere interest by people, and it merely means that they aren't in agreement with you at this particular moment.

- ✔ Get the people to give you *all* their objections, and then you can begin discussing the most important ones first.

- ✔ Don't deal with each objection at the moment it's given to you. By responding to each of them, you'll certainly be giving more weight and importance to some of them than they deserve, and at the very least, you'll be wasting some of your valuable time doing it.

- ✔ In the absence of a response, most objections simply go away. The important ones will be brought up again.

There are two kinds of objections

Objections can be classified into two categories: factual and emotional. One is valid; the other may or may not be.

- ✔ **Factual objections are based on logic.** A valid objection is based on logical and factual reasoning. It's valid because this is the way the person perceives the facts to be. And even if the person's facts may be incorrect, based on unsubstantiated information, or even on a rumor or false innuendo, it's still a valid objection.

  Factual objections can be discussed in detail because you're analyzing the "facts" of a situation. Incorrect information can be corrected, and there can be a complete flow of conversation.

- ✔ **Emotional objections are extremely difficult to deal with.** An emotional objection is neither logical nor factual. It is based on an emotional response and would often be considered an excuse or a smokescreen. Emotional objections sound logical, but when you take the time to think about and analyze them, they don't make any sense.

When a person is giving you one objection after another after another, and none of them seems to make any sense to you, then you're probably dealing with a person who is making a decision based on an emotional reaction. No amount of factual information or logic will turn around an emotional objection. The person is saying "No" but won't explain the *real* reason for saying "No."

If your instincts tell you that you're getting emotional objections, it's your cue to attempt to change the flow of the conversation back to a discussion of the basic facts. If you're unable to do so, it's time to pack up and move on.

People often make the decision to say "Yes" based on an emotional reaction or response, and then they often justify that decision with factual information.

Techniques for overcoming objections

During your conversation with your potential customers, they are going to be making statements — offering objections — that indicate that they don't want or aren't ready to buy the product, service, or idea you're selling. To get them to say "Yes," you need to find ways of responding to these statements and keeping the conversation going. The following few sections discuss some techniques you can use to overcome objections.

Answer a question with a question

When you're asked a question, you don't necessarily have to give a direct answer. Use your answer as an opportunity to ask the person another question so that you can learn more about what he or she is thinking. Remember: Whoever asks the questions controls the conversation.

Let people speak

Encourage people to talk about the what they want or don't want, like and don't like, or need and don't need. Resist the temptation respond to each statement. And don't interrupt while they're talking.

Agree that the point is a good one

It's OK to say, "The point that was raised is a *good* point." Making this statement doesn't mean that you agree; it only means that you agree that the point raised was a good one. To indicate that you think the point is a good one, you can say something like:

> *I can see why that would be of concern to you.*
>
> *I can understand your feelings.*
>
> *That's an interesting observation that you just made.*
>
> *You've brought up a good point.*

And even though you may not agree with what the person has to say, you should try your best to express yourself in a positive way. Instead of saying "No," you can replace it with

> *Yes, but . . .*

This way, it *appears* that you're always in agreement with the other person when in fact you may not be.

Clarify those statements

If you would like the people with whom you're talking to give you a little more background information regarding a specific statement, you can ask them to clarify by saying something like:

> *How did you happen to arrive at that conclusion?*
>
> *What is it that makes you feel that way?*
>
> *It seems to me that you have a very strong reason for saying that. Would you mind telling me what the reason is?*

Identify all the important points

The more you're able to get other people to talk, the easier it will be for you to identify and isolate their most important points. To encourage people to talk, you may want to ask these kinds of questions:

> *Is there anything else you're concerned about?*
>
> *Are there any other points you feel need to be addressed?*

One of the reasons you ask questions is to try to discover what it is people *really* want, not what *you* think they want. After you've done that, it's much easier to get them to say "Yes."

Feed back statements

To confirm that what you heard is what was *meant*, you should feed back statements by saying something like:

> *If I understand you correctly, you said . . .*
>
> *If I understand you correctly, you're concerned about . . .*
>
> *If I understand you correctly, you believe . . .*

Soften the objection by eliminating confrontation

No matter what someone says — especially when he or she gets excited — try your best not to get into an argument. You may win the argument, but you'll never get that person to say "Yes." Instead, you can respond in this manner:

> *I can understand why you feel that way, however . . .*

The phrase, "I understand," when said in a quiet, sympathetic tone of voice, can be very helpful in defusing a potentially explosive or confrontational situation, without requiring you to state whether you agree or disagree with the statement.

Isolate the most important objection

Try to isolate the most important objection to whatever you are selling or proposing. In a way, the person is telling you that this objection is the *only* reason for not making a decision now. And if you can deal with this one objection, then the person is ready to say "Yes." To isolate the objection, you can say something like:

> *Other than [insert objection], is there any additional reason that you can think of for not giving your approval to go ahead with this right now?"*

> *If I understand you correctly, [insert name], if I could show you [convince you, display to you] that this [product, service, concept, or idea] will in fact save you [time, money], would you be prepared to give us the go ahead this very moment?*

Always take a deep breath before you begin speaking

Before you respond to an objection, you should always take a deep breath. This does two things for you: It gives you the opportunity to fill your lungs with air so that your voice will sound deeper and more powerful, and it will buy you a few moments of time to collect your thoughts.

To stress a point, hand over your pencil

Whenever you want to stress a point, give your customers a pencil and a piece of paper and ask them to write something down. This technique will guarantee that they will not only pay attention to you, but they will also listen to what you're saying as they write stuff down.

Picking on an insurance salesman for fun and profit

A friend, who was a life insurance salesman, once told me with great pride how he had effectively overcome each and every objection that one of his prospects had given him. He was so proud because he thought that he had done a great job of answering every question. So I asked him: "How much life insurance did the man purchase?" With that, Bob gave me a strange look and began to stammer as he looked away from me and down at the papers on his desk.

"Well," he said sheepishly, "he didn't buy any life insurance."

"But you just said that you did an absolutely marvelous job of overcoming his objections."

"Well I did, but . . . ."

Then I said, "But Bob, if he didn't buy any life insurance from you, then you didn't overcome his objections!" With that, Bob gave me that "It's about time for you to get out of my office" look, so I left.

When you've got to add a column of numbers or multiply several numbers, give your customers-to-be a pencil and a piece of paper and let them do the calculations. (If there are a lot of numbers to add, subtract, multiply, or divide, give them a calculator.)

When you allow people to participate in this manner, they can actually see and understand how you arrive at the final results. If they are the ones who do the calculations and write down the numbers, they are much more likely to believe that the results are correct. They're not *your* numbers, they're theirs.

When you want to emphasize the many benefits of the product, service, or idea that you're selling, ask people to write down the key points, one at a time, as you say what to write.

The balance sheet is a great selling tool

When you want your customers to create a list of reasons to buy whatever you're selling, have them create a *balance sheet*. You hand over your pen and a blank sheet of paper and ask them to draw a line across the top of the page and a line down the middle. Have them write For above the left column and Against above the right column, as shown in Figure 8-1.

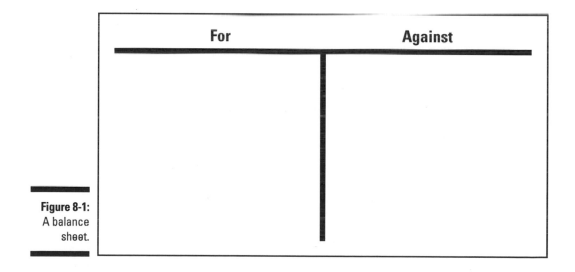

Figure 8-1:
A balance sheet.

Then ask your customers to start listing the advantages of your product, service, or idea, one item at a time. If they are having trouble coming up with these items, you dictate them as they write them down. While your customers are writing, take advantage of this opportunity to emphasize every detail. Don't stop until the list contains at least 20 items.

Now, here's where you get to the fun part. When you and your customers have gotten to the point where you've run out of additional reasons for a "Yes" response, you then say:

> *Now let's list all the disadvantages of not [using, buying, doing] my [product, service, idea].*

And now you become invisible. You don't say anything. You just sit there quietly and watch them *attempt* to fill in the Against column.

When they finish, you ask for a "Yes" response by counting the Fors one at a time. As you count off each item, you read each item aloud. When you're finished, you disappear again and don't say another word until they do something.

Just stop talking!

Has someone ever asked you a question, and when you didn't respond to it, the other person didn't say anything further either . . . and there was just silence? Wasn't the silence deafening? And the longer the silence lasted, the louder it got.

Well, you can use silence as a very subtle but dramatic selling tool. When it comes down to the final question of whether or not your customers will say "Yes," you ask your question and you stop talking. You don't say anything more; you sit; you wait! You don't say another word!

Silence creates tension, and the longer it lasts, the more tension it creates. The silence can last for 10 seconds, 15 seconds, or what seems to be an eternity, and it keeps getting longer. Still, you don't say one single word! You just sit there. You take a deep breath; you try to sit still in your chair; you clasp your hands together and squeeze your fingers tightly so that you won't fidget; and you try not to perspire too much. And you wait.

And your mind is racing. You're asking yourself, "What are they going to say? What are they going to do? What's going to happen next?" You don't know, but you keep waiting, silently. And you keep reminding yourself: *Whoever speaks first has lost.*

If you can wait until they speak, they will usually say "Yes." They'll buy whatever you're selling.

Create a sense of urgency

People are motivated to make a decision when they feel that their opportunity to do so may be lost. If you're dealing with a procrastinator, it's important to demonstrate not only the benefits of your product, service, or idea, but also the importance of making a decision NOW! And to do that, you have make that individual feel that there's a sense of urgency. Help your procrastinator seize the moment.

Ten ways to avoid killing a sale

After you've worked so hard to get people to the point of saying "Yes," you don't want to blow it at the very last moment by saying or doing the wrong thing. People become very nervous when it comes time to make a decision or sign a piece of paper, so you've got to make it easy for them to say "Yes." The following are some key phrases that can kill a conversation or a sale. In their place, you should use words and phrases that will make the process of coming to a decision less threatening.

✔ You don't ask someone *if* he or she is ready to say "Yes"; you just *assume* so.

✔ You don't ask a person to buy something. Instead, you say, "Let's give it the go-ahead," or "Let's get the ball rolling," or "Why don't we give it a try?" Meanwhile, you're pulling out your order pad, form, or application. Then you ask, "Now, what is the correct spelling of your first name?"

✔ You never sign a contract; you initial an agreement or ask for approval.

✔ Contracts become paperwork.

✔ You don't talk about costs or expenses; they become investments, gains, or benefits.

✔ When you're talking about costs, speak of them on a daily or monthly basis, and you should state the profits as an annual return. Little numbers for expenses; big numbers for profits or returns.

✔ Talk in terms people understand and relate to. People buy with dollars down and dollars per month, but the returns are annualized.

✔ You don't buy something; you own it.

✔ You don't sell products or services; you sell benefits and solutions to problems.

✔ There are no problems, only points to be addressed.

And after your meeting's over, keep detailed notes of what happened

Over the years, I've found it to be extremely helpful to keep detailed and meticulous notes of all of my meetings and conversations so that I wouldn't forget what was important to the other person. These notes were then placed in my file on that person for easy referrence, and became a permanent record of what was discussed, what decisions were made, of who was supposed to do what, and when it was supposed to be done.

Included in the notes would be my personal comments, thoughts, and opinions.

This is another reason that you'll really enjoy using a program like ACT! As Chapter 4 explains, with ACT! you can keep all your notes electronically — inside your computer — and you'll eliminate the need to write notes on small pieces of paper that get lost on the top of your desk and add to the overall clutter of your office.

After "Yes," the Fun Begins: You Start Negotiating

Just because a person has said "Yes" doesn't mean that you're out of the woods yet. In fact, the good stuff is just beginning. You now get to negotiate the terms of the transaction, preferably without giving away the company. You see, you want to *negotiate* the terms of your transaction; you don't want to make compromises or concessions. Your ultimate goal is to achieve a mutually satisfactory agreement where both of you think that you got the majority of the things you wanted. If you think that you were taken to the cleaners, then you gave away too much.

When you're negotiating, you never want to give something up without always getting something in return.

Negotiate from a position of strength

Every negotiation starts with the respective parties having a general impression of their own strength and the strength of the person sitting across the table. When you begin discussing the individual items that will make up the terms and conditions of your agreement, you want to start out strong, show confidence, and convey the impression that you're negotiating from a postition of strength.

When you have a strong opening, you can make the other party think that your bargaining position is a bit stronger than he or she thought it was, and you'll probably do better in your overall negotiations.

Get all the issues on the table

Effective negotiation can begin only after all the issues — major and minor — have been put on the table. That means you've first got to take the time to create a complete list of all the points of concern, *before* you start negotiating each of the various items. The greater the number of variables, the more opportunities you have for negotiating an agreement that everyone will be comfortable with.

In any negotiations, you and the other party will feel that some items are more important than are others. Your objective is to create a situation where you can make a small concession yet receive something that is of substantial benefit in return. When both you and the other party have been able to make small concessions — while getting large benefits in return — you've had effective and successful negotiations, and you both have won.

A fundamental basis of effective negotiating is that whenever you make a concession, you *always* get something in return — you never want to make unilateral concessions. And getting something in return is always much easier to do when you're able to provide the other person with a large number of alternatives, all of which are equally acceptable to you.

That's what makes negotiating such a fun game to play because both of you can walk away feeling that you've won. So, while you're negotiating the terms of your agreement, you should keep searching for new variables that you can discuss. The more items you have on the table, the better your chances of assembling a package that will be acceptable to both of you.

A word or two about concessions

I would like to add a word or two on the subject of agreeing to make concessions: Don't make them too readily. Even if you're chomping at the bit to say "Yes," take a moment or two — or a few days — to ponder your decision. Make it look like giving in to this concession hurts. If you give in too quickly, the other party will decide that they could have done better if they had tried a bit harder, and on the next item they probably will. When this happens, no matter how good a deal they got, they won't be happy, and the deal itself may start to unravel. The best way to keep a deal together is not to agree to demands or to make concessions. Always demand at least *something* in return, or refuse to go any further. This will generally be the most effective way to tie the whole package together.

Don't negotiate one item at a time

When you're negotiating the terms of a deal, there could be just a handful, or several hundred, issues that need to be discussed and agreed upon. But if you're negotiating each one of them in isolation — one at a time — the final results are often unsatisfactory. If you're tyring to negotiate one item at a time, you've created a situation where you can have only one of three outcomes, none of which will be satisfactory to either of you: If you win, the other party loses; if they win, you lose; and if the two of you were to cut it down the middle, then you both lose, and the only thing you will have gotten is the opportunity to move on to another point and continue the win-lose process.

Whose ox is being gored?

If you're the seller, negotiating one item at a time is a prescription for disaster. However, if you're the buyer, negotiating one item at a time can be a very effective negotiating tactic because it can coerce the other party into making unilateral concessions.

Let me give you an example of what happens to you, the seller, if you negotiate each item one at a time:

A prospective buyer says to you that he would like to buy 10,000 of your widgets but feels that your price is too high. So he tells you that if you were to cut your cost by 10 percent, he'd be happy to place the order, and you say OK.

Now that he's gotten you to cut your price, you start discussing shipping dates. You tell them that you can deliver the complete order in 60 days. But he wants it in 15, so you agree on 30. You've lost again.

And finally, it's time to talk about payment terms. Your normal terms are a 50 percent deposit with the order, and then the balance will be shipped COD. He explains that his company couldn't possibly do that. Their policy is to pay 50 percent on receipt of the order and the balance in 30 days. The two of you talk and he finally agrees to give you a 25 percent payment now, pay 50 percent on delivery, and the balance within 30 days.

Because the terms of this sale were negotiated one at a time, you lost on every item of discussion, even though you were so excited because he told you that he wanted to buy 10,000 of your widgets.

But look at how you could have negoitiated the terms of this sale if you had talked about all three points — price, delivery date, and payment terms — together. Here are a few different scenarios:

- ✔ When he asked you to lower your price, you could have asked him then how he planned to pay for the widgets by saying, "I can cut 10 percent off the price, but I'll need a deposit of 75 percent now with the balance on delivery, which will be in 60 days."

- ✔ If he had first said that he needed delivery in 15 days, you could have responded by saying, "Our normal delivery is within 60 days. However, we can get you a delivery in 15 days, but not at this price. I'll have to charge you 10 percent more, and our normal terms are 50 percent now and the balance on delivery."

I'm sure that you're beginning to get the picture. By discussing all three points at the same time, there are a lot of different variables that can come into play, and maybe the final terms are: Delivery within 21 days, at an 8 percent increase in price, with a 30 percent payment today, 50 percent on delivery, and the balance payable in 30 days. Since these are all terms that the parties can live with, and they feel good about the results of the negotiation, everyone walks away feeling like a winner.

Negotiating one item at a time is not a satisfactory method of negotiating the terms of any agreement because these individual items don't exist in isolation. They're all part of an overall *package,* the details of which have to be worked out.

Before you start negotiating, take the time to ask a lot of questions so that you can identify all the different issues and points of discussion that need to be laid on the top of the table. This approach helps you get a sense of the other party's real needs and objectives. And during your conversations, let the other party know that you're willing to discuss anything, but don't make any commitments until you've gotten a complete list of all the points that need to be addressed.

Part III
Improve Your Ability to Communicate Information

In this part . . .

In the next few chapters I'm going to give you a lot of tips, ideas, techniques, and strategies that you can use to make it easier for you to communicate information with *all* of the important people in your business life. First I'm going to show you how you can use the telephone more effectively. Then in Chapter 10, I'm going to help you get more mileage out of your voice mail system. In Chapter 11, I'm going to show you how you can write better letters, memos, and reports. And finally, in Chapter 12, I'm going to give you some tips on how you can spend less time dealing with your e-mail.

Chapter 9

Make the Telephone Your Friend

You're Always Communicating

If you were to look at your daily activities, there are two certainties, in addition to death and taxes:

- ✔ You're going to spend a lot of time in meetings.
- ✔ When you're not in meetings, you're going to be on the telephone.

Chapter 6 discusses things you can do to make your meetings shorter and more productive. And now that we're tackling the telephone, let's take a step back and look at it's basic purpose: To allow us to communicate information with other people.

Look at how far we've come with the telephone in just the last 40 years. We've gone from phones you had to dial (we still say "dial the phone," but when was the last time you *dialed* a phone?), to Touch Tone phones, to having the computer dial the phone for us. When I was a kid, we had two phones in the house. There was a phone for the downstairs and another one upstairs; today we've got wireless phones that we can use anywhere in the house or yard and mobile phones that we install in our cars or carry in our pockets, purses, or briefcases. And at this moment, I can't even imagine what's in store for us as we enter the 21st century.

But putting all this fancy, high-tech stuff aside for a moment, the phone is still a device that you and I use so that we can communicate with each other.

How Do You Come Across on the Phone?

I know you've been using the phone since you were about four years old, but have you ever thought about how you come across on the phone? And no matter how good you are on the phone, you can still work on improving your telephone techniques.

Your feelings and emotions come across loud and clear

Have you ever been really angry about something and then got on the phone to call someone else — who had nothing to do with the source of your anger — and then let this poor unsuspecting soul have it? I know that I have, and usually I felt so bad about it afterwards that I often called to apologize for my rude behavior.

Well, whatever your feeling is inside — happy, sad, joyful, depressed — it will be reflected in your voice as soon as you pick up the receiver and start talking to someone. If you were speaking with an individual face-to-face, he or she would see — and respond to — your nonverbal messages, such as your facial expressions, eye movements, and posture, as well as the gestures you make with your hands, arms, and legs.

And when you're on the telephone, even though the party at the other end of the phone can't see these nonverbal gestures, your attitudes, feelings, thoughts, and opinions are immediately transmitted by the tone of your voice, it's pitch, the speed with which you talk, and even your choice of words. So whenever you're speaking on the phone, you're going to be conveying a message. It may be one that indicates that you're happy to talk and want the conversation to continue, or it could be one that indicates that you're bored, disinterested, and have a desire to be doing something else at this very moment.

Keep a smile on your face

You may find this hard to believe, but you'll come across much better on the phone if you can keep a smile on your face and project that smile onto the other person while you're talking on the phone. People warm up to you when you meet them face-to-face and smile, and they'll do the same thing when you smile at them through the phone.

For many years, I've kept a picture of a smiling face in front of me as a reminder to smile when I'm on the phone. It helps me sound more friendly and open. My suggestion to you: Put a small mirror on your desk so that you can watch yourself smile when you're on the phone.

Be enthusiastic

Have you ever had conversations with people who sound as if they've just come back from a funeral or a wake? They're talking in a very dull and dreary monotone. The tone of voice is completely void of life and energy, and this is when they're calling to tell you *good* news! I don't know about you, but when I get these kinds of calls I want to crawl under the desk and hide.

So when you get on the phone, put some life, energy, and emotion in your voice. Don't be afraid to express yourself verbally and emotionally. Make your voice so interesting that the person at the other end of the phone wants to hear what it is that you've got to say. (In Chapter 13, I've a section, "Make your voice sound interesting," that talks about how you can expand the range of your voice when you're speaking in front of an audience.)

Have fun when you're on the phone. Be yourself. Let your sense of humor show through and don't forget to laugh. Laughter can be a great ice breaker.

Always take a deep breath before you begin to speak. When you have air in your lungs, your voice has more depth and power. (And if there's no air in your lungs, you're very likely dead.)

Hear how others hear you

I know that up until now, you've probably never given a moment's thought to your telephone technique, but it can be a real ear opener when you record some of your calls and hear yourself as other's hear you. You would be amazed at how many times you said things such as "you know," "and," and "um," during each sentence. Then there are the sentences that you start but never complete. And finally, there's your voice itself. What does it sound like? Is it energetic and enthusiastic, or does it come across like a limp wash rag?

But no matter what your voice sounds like today, with just a little bit of practice on your part, it's very easy to improve your ability to express yourself and communicate with other people over the phone. If you play back a tape of yourself speaking on the phone and hear what you're saying and how you're saying it, you'll become much more aware of the speech habits you've picked up. You can start working on breaking those habits so that you speak with more clarity. The first thing that you'll become aware of is how many times you say such things as "you know" or "um." In no time at all, you'll be able to stop yourself from saying these things.

For just a few dollars, you can go to an electronics store — like Radio Shack — and get a microphone that's designed to record telephone calls. The microphone attaches to the handset of your phone with a tiny suction cup and plugs into the microphone jack of your tape recorder.

Before you run to the electronics store, see if your telephone answering machine has the capability to record conversations. In many machines, this is a built-in feature. (Before you start recording your calls, however, you should find out if you have any legal responsibility to inform the other party that the call is being recorded.)

The first few times I recorded myself on the phone, I was appalled at how I *thought* my voice sounded, and to this day, I still don't like hearing my voice on tape. But as I thought about it, I realized that I had been speaking with people for years and most of them enjoyed talking with me, some for even hours at a time. So the concern that I had about the tone of my voice was *my* problem, and nobody else's.

What Is the Purpose of the Call?

Being aware of how you sound and come across on the phone is one thing, but why are you making a call in the first place? In today's high-pressure business world, we don't have the luxury of wasting time, yet one of the biggest time wasters of all is the phone call that has no apparent purpose. Whenever you're about to make a call, you should always ask yourself these questions:

- ✔ Why am I making this call?
- ✔ What information do I want?
- ✔ What information do I wish to convey?
- ✔ How much of the other person's time do I need?
- ✔ What do I do if the other person is not there and I get his or her secretary, assistant, or the receptionist? (I'll talk about this later in the chapter.)
- ✔ What do I do if I get the other person's voice mail? (I'll be discussing voice mail in the next chapter.)

Here are some tips that can help you to prepare for your phone calls:

- ✔ Make a list of the items that you want to discuss with the person.

- ✔ Arrange the sequence of the items so that the most important items will be discussed first.

- ✔ Have the files or other papers to which you'll need to refer at your fingertips.

- ✔ If you are planning an important or difficult call and you're not sure exactly what you want to say or how you want to say it, write everything out on a piece of paper. A word of caution here: When you get the other person on the phone, have your notes available for reference, but don't read them.

Spend a few moments thinking about and preparing yourself for each call before you make it. Treat each call as if it were a face-to-face business meeting.

If you think your call will take more than a few minutes, you may want to say something like this:

> *Jim, I'm glad that I was finally able to reach you. I've got a handful of things I would like to talk to you about that could take five or ten minutes [insert other lengths of times]. Do you have some time now, or should we schedule a conference call for later this afternoon or tomorrow morning?*

When you know that it's going to take you an hour to go through all the things that you've got to talk with a person about, schedule a conference call so that the two of you can block out the time on your calendars. You should also let the other person know, in advance of that call, what you're going to be talking about so that he or she can be thoroughly prepared.

If you're calling to schedule an appointment, always offer people two different times on different days. You could say something like, "Are you free on Monday afternoon, or would Tuesday morning be better?" This changes the flow of the conversation from *if* they will see you to *when* they will see you.

Beat the odds

Because everyone's so busy, it's almost impossible to reach a person on the phone the first time you call. As a result, everyone ends up playing telephone tag. You know how the game's played: I call you and leave a message, and then you call me and leave a message; and this goes on and on. Eventually we talk, or we get tied up with other things and forget about it.

But there are a few facts about the telephone that you should be aware of. The chance of actually reaching a person on the first try is less than 20 percent. What I mean by this is that there's only a one in five chance that when you call a specific person, he or she will be available to take your call. And there's an 80 percent probability that the person you hope to talk to will be tied up in a meeting — or on the phone. So, if you want to reach an individual on the phone, you've got to be persistent and should expect to call at least five times.

Don't leave messages

If there's someone you want to speak to, it's your job to track him or her down. And just because you left a message doesn't mean that you'll be called back — your call may be much more important to you than it is to the other person — and even if you are called back, the odds aren't very good that you'll be there to take that return call.

So, when you need to speak to someone, here are some techniques you can use to increase your odds of getting through.

- ✔ **Work with the secretary.** If the person you're trying to reach is in meetings, try to find out when the person will be available to take a call. If the person is on the phone, ask the secretary if he or she has any idea how long the call will last. Then ask whether it would be better for you to be put on hold for a few moments or call back in fifteen minutes. When the secretary says, "Let me take your number and I'll have So'n'so call you back." Just say, "Thank you, I'll call back later," because So'n'so probably won't be calling you back.

- ✔ **Get a direct number.** Try to get the person's direct number so that you can bypass the secretary, administrative assistant, or switchboard entirely.

- ✔ **Call early in the morning.** Many business people are at their desks as early as 7 a.m. each morning. So ask the secretary if the person you're trying to reach comes in early in the morning.

- ✔ **Call after work.** Many people are also working long after 5 p.m., so perhaps you can get through if you call after 5:30 p.m.

- ✔ **Call during lunch.** Many people work through lunch — or eat at their desks. So give it a shot and try your luck by calling at 12:30 p.m.

This is another area where ACT! has really improved my productivity. First off, I can't lose track of a call. If I don't reach an individual today, ACT! automatically rolls it over to tomorrow. Second, when I'm told that someone's out of town for two weeks, I just click the pop-up calendar and change the date of the call. In two weeks, that person's name appears again. And third, I love ACT!'s alarm. When I'm told that someone's tied up in a meeting for about another 20 minutes, I just set the alarm, and in 20 minutes, I'm reminded to make the call.

Take notes of the conversation

I know that I've said it before, and I'll probably say it again before this book is finished, but when you speak to a person on the phone, you should keep notes of your conversation and place them in the file you keep for that person. Though you may be blessed with a phenomenal memory, with the passage of time, it becomes difficult to remember exactly what a person said and when he or she said it.

When you get off the phone, you should write a brief note to summarize what was said, who's got to do what, and when it's supposed to be done. This note should be put in the appropriate file. And if there's work to do, it should be added to your Master List.

This is another area where ACT! excels. After the call, you can enter your notes in the person's notepad, and if there's work to do, you can enter that item on the Task List. The whole thing takes just a few moments. No muss. No fuss. And no pieces of paper to file.

How to call a stranger

Every once in a while, you may need to call someone who is a complete and total stranger. If you're in sales, you're doing this kind of thing almost every day, but if you're not, calling a stranger can be an absolutely terrifying experience. Now, I don't have the slightest idea why you may be calling a stranger; maybe you're doing some fund raising for your favorite charity, or perhaps it's time to explore new career opportunities and you're looking for a new job. Whatever the reason, here are some tips on how to call a stranger:

- ✔ **Get the person's name.** The first thing you need to do is get the name of the person to whom you would want to speak. To do this, you should place an *exploratory* call to the company's main number where you ask the person who answers the phone (probably a receptionist, operator, or secretary), "What is the name of the person who is the . . . [president of the company, head of human resources, and so on]?"

- ✔ **How is it spelled?** Then you ask for the correct spelling of the person's name.

> ✔ **Why do you want this info?** If the person who is giving you this information starts to ask you lots of questions like "Who are you?" and "What do you want?" just say "I want to send Mr. Such'n'such a letter." Then say, "Thank you so very much for your help" and hang up the phone.

> ✔ **Call later in the day or tomorrow.** Now that you've got the person's name, call later in the day or the following morning, and ask whether he or she is available.

> ✔ **Does the person have a direct phone?** As you're asking whether Mr. Such'n'such is in, you can ask in an offhanded way, "Oh, by the way, what is his direct phone number?"

Now that someone has put your call through, one of several things is going to happen.

> ✔ The person is at his or her desk and will actually take your call.

> ✔ You get the voice-mail system.

> ✔ The secretary will answer and screen the call.

Let's explore each situation.

Your call goes through

Let's say your call is put through and you find that the person actually answers his own phone. He says, "Hello," and you start to panic. Just take a deep breath and say, "Is Mr. Such'n'such available?" (You ask this question because you want to try to get Mr. Such'n'such to say "Yes.") He says, "Yes, this is Mr. Such'n'such." And you say, "Mr. Such'n'such, my name is So'n'so, of [company name or other affiliation], and I was wondering whether you had a moment?" (You ask this question because you want to know whether he's available to talk at this moment or whether it would be better to call back later.) If he says that he's got a moment, you start delivering your spiel.

If he's tied up, just ask, "May I call you back later this afternoon, or would tomorrow morning be better?" At this point, he may ask you why you're calling, so you should give him a short answer and then say, "Thank you for your time. I'll call back when you have more time to talk." (If you were calling Ms. Such'n'such instead of Mr. Such'n'such, please remember to replace the "he" with a "she" and the "him" with a "her.")

You get voice mail

Take another example. If you are trying to call someone and get his or her voice mail, you may or may not decide to leave a message. However, if you do leave a message, you shouldn't expect to receive a return call. (I'll be discussing voice mail in the next chapter.)

You get the secretary

A good secretary is trained to screen the boss's calls, so you should be prepared to answer a few questions, but you don't want to volunteer much information. When the secretary says, "Hello, this is Mr. So'n'so's office," you ask, "Is Mr. So'n'so available?" (With this question, you want to try to learn whether he's in the office, on the phone, in a meeting, or away from his desk.) The secretary then asks, "Who's calling?" To which you reply, "This is Mr. This'n'that. (If you're a woman, you should say, "This is Ms. This'n'that.") Is he available?" (You repeat the question because you want the secretary to give you information without volunteering any yourself.)

At this point, the secretary *may* put your call through or possibly put you on hold to tell the boss that you're on the phone. (If the secretary comes back and asks you the name of your company and why you're calling and then puts you on hold again, it's a pretty good indication that the boss is having calls screened.) Another possibility is that the secretary may start to ask you more questions. It's at this point that you want to try to make the secretary your friend.

Most secretaries feel that it's their job to *protect* the boss from unwanted telephone calls, and they're trained to say "No" to whoever is calling.

Make the secretary your friend

Now you have to make the secretary your friend. When the secretary starts asking you questions, the first thing you should say is, "To whom am I speaking? Are you So-and-so's secretary or assistant? (Write down the name so you won't forget it.) If you're speaking to a temporary secretary or someone who's just filling in, just say, "Thank you very much. I'll call back later." (You don't want to waste your time talking with someone who can't be of much help to you, so get off the phone as fast as you can.)

If you are speaking with the secretary, he or she will probably begin by asking you questions as to who you are and why you're calling. To these questions you should give short, concise answers, and once again ask, "Is So'n'so available?" At this point, the secretary probably will say that this person is in a meeting and ask if you would like to leave a message.

Now you've got two choices: To leave or not to leave a message, that is the question. What you choose to do depends on the situation and how comfortable you feel in talking with the secretary. You may want to go into detail as to why you're calling and see whether the secretary can be of help to you — perhaps refer you to someone else within the company — or you may just want to say, "Thank you very much for your help. I'll just call back later. Will So'n'so be available later this afternoon, or would tomorrow morning be a better time to call? And by the way, does So'n'so come in early in the morning?" (Again, you want to try to discover when the person may be available to receive a call.) Remember:

✔ Don't try to sell your product, service, or idea to the secretary. The boss is the decision maker, not the secretary. Your job is to sell the secretary on putting your call through to the person you want to talk to.

✔ If you aren't having any luck getting past the secretary, try calling another department to see whether you can get someone to give you the boss's direct number.

✔ Call the office of someone who is higher than the person you're trying to reach and use that person's name as your referral. Then you can say something like, "I was speaking with Ms. Bigfoot's office and she suggested that I speak with Mr. Littlefoot. Is he available?"

Dialing for dollars

If you're in a business where it's important for you to spend time on the phone, you should know that there are certain times during the day when you're most likely to find the person sitting at his or her desk and available to take your call. As a general rule, people are usually in their offices from 9 a.m. to 11 a.m. and from about 2 p.m. to 4 p.m. You should always block out those times on your calendar so that you can get on the telephone and make your calls.

Don't waste your valuable telephone time doing tasks that can be done at another time, can be done by someone else, or don't need to be done at all.

What do you do when your phone rings?

Up until now, I've been discussing how you can get through to people when you're calling them. But what do you do when *your* phone rings? You need some techniques that will help you with your incoming calls, and that's what you're going to get in the following section.

You don't have to answer every call

Just because the phone rings doesn't mean that you have to answer it. Whenever the phone rings, it's an interruption. And if you're in the midst of doing something important, the last thing you want to do is allow yourself to be interrupted.

It's OK to let your voice-mail system, answering machine, secretary, or receptionist take the call. If you answer the phone every time it rings, you'll never get any work done.

Use the screening feature of your voice-mail system to see who is calling. You can let the machine answer the phone, and if it's important, then you can pick up the receiver. And if it isn't important? Keep working!

Improve your productivity by using a telephone headset

Does your neck ever get stiff from cradling the telephone handset between your ear, chin, and shoulder? Do you find it difficult to take notes while you're on the phone — because you just can't find an easy way to hold the phone to your left ear, use your left elbow to keep the pad of paper from moving, write with your right hand, and remain comfortable, all at the same time?

If you answered "Yes" to any of these questions, you should be using a telephone headset instead of the traditional handset. In fact, if you spend any time at all on the phone, you should be using a telephone headset. I've been using one for years and have found that it's not only comfortable, but it has greatly improved my productivity and efficiency as well.

Today's headsets are so light and comfortable that after you put one on, you'll quickly forget that you're even wearing it. And when you're on the phone, you'll have the use of both your hands, so you can concentrate on the conversation instead of the pain in your neck or the tenderness in your ear.

Plantronics makes a full line of headsets for both the corporate user and the person who runs a business out of the home. You can reach Plantronics at 345 Encinal Street, Santa Cruz, CA 95060. For a catalog and a current price list, call 800-426-5858.

Who's calling?

When you do answer the phone, your need to know the answers to two questions: "Who's calling?" and "What do you want?" (You can be a bit more tactful and less blunt when you're speaking with the other person, but you need to know who the other caller is and the purpose of the call.)

If a caller doesn't identify him or herself or is very vague about the purpose of the call, it's OK to say, "Good bye!" and hang up the phone.

If you do want to talk to the caller, you should ask, "How much time is this going to take?" If the call will just take a few minutes, you may wish to have the conversation now; otherwise, you should schedule a time to talk later in the day. Most important, you want to avoid spending 30 minutes on a call when you should be completing your important work.

Get rid of cold callers

It seems that whenever I pick up the phone, there's someone at the other end trying to sell me medical insurance, penny stocks on the Vancouver Stock Exchange, a new long-distance phone service, or something else that I don't need or want. You can always tell who these people are because they all start their calls in the same way:

Caller: *Is Mr. Mayer there?*

Me: *Yes, this is he.*

Caller: *How are you today?*

And when callers say, "How are you today?" you *know* that they're trying to sell you something.

If you let these people get started with their sales pitch, it's difficult to get rid of them — you don't want to be rude — because they're always asking you to answer questions that are impossible to disagree with, such as "How would you like an investment that has a very high rate of return with no risk?" The best thing you can do is to cut them short and just say, "I'm not interested!" and hang up the phone.

Now, the two or three minutes that it takes to answer an unsolicited call may not sound like much, but multiply that by several dozen calls each day and you've eaten up a huge chunk of time that you should have spent working on your high-priority projects. (And you wonder why you never get anything done.)

The next time you get an unsolicited call, try this: Just press the hold button on your phone and see how long it takes for the salesperson to realize that you're not there any longer.

Don't say to salespeople, "I can't talk to you now; just send me something in the mail." First of all, you don't need any more junk mail. And second, after they send you their materials, they're going to start calling again to ask whether you've had a chance to look at it.

Cutting off a long-winded speaker

Every once in a while, I get calls from people who are happy to talk forever. (Don't they have work to do?) So here are a couple of tips on how you can regain control of the conversation:

- ✔ Listen to the person and wait patiently for the first opening that he or she gives you so that you can take control of the conversation. When the caller pauses to take a breath, just jump right into the conversation and say, "Now, what can I do for you?"

- ✔ Tell the caller at the start of the conversation that you were just walking out the door and only have a minute.

- ✔ Tell the caller that you have someone in your office, so the conversation will have to be short.
- ✔ Say that you've got a long-distance call on hold on the other line.
- ✔ When the conversation begins to drag, put the caller on hold for a moment, and when you come back on the line, tell the caller that you have a long-distance call that you've got to take.

Watch your socializing

I know that it's nice to chat with friends, but if you do it throughout the day, it's a very easy way to lose track of a lot of time. Just add five minutes of socializing to each of your calls, and by the end of the day, you could easily lose an hour or two. And let's not forget about those five-minute calls that end up lasting an hour. So try to keep the number of your social calls at a reasonable level, and be aware of how much time you're spending on each of them.

No one has enough time during the course of the workday, and one of the ways you can give yourself more time is to minimize the number and length of your social calls. As an alternative to talking over the phone, perhaps you should meet for lunch or dinner.

Dealing with angry callers

Every once in a while, you're going to have to talk to people who are very angry and upset. Unless you've done something to anger these people, you must remember that they are not angry with you, but rather with a situation or a problem. Don't take personally any of the things that they say about you, your company, or your products. Just let such callers vent their feelings and blow off some steam. Within a few minutes, they will wear themselves out, the fury and rage will subside, and they will regain their composure. When angry callers calm down, you can try to help solve their problems.

While a caller is ranting and raving, you can say, "I understand how you feel . . ." or "I can see that you're very angry. . . ." (The statements don't mean that you agree with any of the things being said.) Try your best not to get sucked into an argument with an angry caller because that will only get you upset, making an already intense situation more explosive.

You don't have to tolerate crude or obscene language. If a caller is being abusive, it's OK to say something like, "Mr./Ms. Foul Mouth, I'm willing to deal with your complaint, but I'm not willing to take this kind of verbal abuse. If you don't stop, I will terminate this call." If the caller doesn't stop immediately, hang up.

Coping with difficult telephone conversations

I don't know how often this happens to you, but now and then I find that I've gotten myself into a difficult phone conversation, and I'm having a hard time trying to get myself out of it. Sometimes things just aren't going my way, and other times my mind's coming up blank. So here are a few tips for dealing with these types of situations:

✔ **Put the caller on hold.** When you need a moment to regroup yourself or to get the other person to calm down, just put the caller on hold for a few moments. When you get back on the line, you'll be better prepared to continue your verbal jousting.

✔ **Hang up on yourself.** If things aren't going well during a phone conversation, just hang up — in mid-sentence — on yourself. The other person will think that there was just a glitch in the line. Here's how you do it: While you're saying something important, just hang up on yourself, right in the middle of your sentence. By the time the conversation resumes, you will have given yourself a few minutes to think about the topic of your conversation. (Depending upon the dynamics of the situation, you'll have to decide whether you want to call back immediately, wait a few minutes and then call back, or wait for the other person to call you.)

Thank the caller for complaining

A person who takes the time to complain is a person who wants to continue doing business with you. By complaining, people are telling you what it is they want or need from you. When people call to complain, don't become defensive or argumentative. Just thank them for telling you what it is that they're unhappy with, and then say something like, "Thank you for taking the time to call. I'm glad you bought that to my attention. We'll do our best to solve this problem for you."

Don't pick up someone else's phone

Have you ever walked by someone's desk when the phone was ringing and decided that you would be a nice person and answer the phone? But after you picked up the phone, you found yourself with a big headache instead. The caller had a problem and he or she wanted you to help solve it. (Well, you *did* pick up the phone, didn't you?) Or the caller wanted to leave a detailed message for someone, but you couldn't find a pencil or a piece of paper, so you tried to commit the message to memory, and then you forgot to tell the intended recipient about the call.

So the next time you hear someone else's phone ringing, just let it ring and go back to work. After so many rings, the call will be transferred to the person's voice mail or to the receptionist. And if no one picks up the phone, the caller will call again.

Chapter 10

Increase Your Productivity with Voice Mail

Sometimes I long for the "good old days" when everyone had a secretary who was always available to take messages. But times have changed. The secretaries are gone, we're typing all of our own letters, and we've got machines that answer our phones for us when we aren't there. Now, if these machines are used properly, they can really improve a person's productivity. But when they aren't, they can be a real nightmare.

Why Use Voice Mail?

The telephone has one terrible shortcoming: Both the caller and the callee must be present at each end of the telephone for a conversation to take place. But statistics tell us that almost 80 percent of all business calls are not completed on the first attempt. Of these calls, at least half of them are one-way transfers of information, and almost two-thirds of all phone calls are less important than the work they interrupt. So here are some reasons that you should be using voice mail:

✔ Voice mail enables you to share information without actually speaking to the other person.

✔ Voice mail lets you communicate in non-real time. You don't have to wait until noon, rise at 6 a.m., or stay awake until midnight to call someone on the other coast, in the Far East, or in Europe.

Would you rather leave a message with a person or a machine?

A recent survey conducted by the Voice Messaging Educational Committee of Morris Plains, NJ found that 58 percent of the callers surveyed would rather leave a message on voice mail than with a secretary or receptionist. Of these:

✔ Nearly half feared that a secretary or receptionist would lose some of the details while taking down the message.

✔ Eighteen percent felt that more detail could be conveyed through voice mail.

✔ Sixteen percent preferred delivering the information in their own speaking style.

✔ Voice-mail messages are usually much shorter than the actual telephone call.

✔ Voice mail is available 24 hours a day, seven days a week. (Some systems are even designed so that when a voice-mail message is received after normal business hours or on the weekend, the system will then call the recipient at home to inform him or her that a voice-mail message has been received.)

✔ Voice mail can reduce the length of time you're stuck on hold.

Don't Leave Your Callers in Voice Mail Jail

Have you ever called someone, and when the voice-mail message came on, it said something like: "The party you have reached at extension 1234 is not in. Please leave your message at the beep." And you weren't given any other choices? You didn't know how to get an operator! You didn't know how to get the person's assistant! And you were reluctant to leave a message because you weren't sure that the person at *extension 1234* was the person you wanted to be speaking to in the first place! So you hang up the telephone, feeling angry and frustrated, and as you look at the timer on the phone, it tells you that this call took 58 seconds, and nothing happened. You've been placed in Voice Mail Jail.

Or maybe you have called someone, and when the message came on, it said something like, "Hi, this is Phyllis and I'm not in at the moment. If you would like to speak to my assistant, press 0; otherwise, leave a message at the beep." So you press 0, and a few moments later, you're transferred to Phyllis's assistant,

Tim, whose message says, "Hi, this is Tim, and I'm not available right now, so if you would like to leave me a message, I'll call you when I return. If you would like to speak to a receptionist, press 0." So you press 0, and you're transferred to the receptionist, and no one picks up the phone. So you hang up, feeling angry and frustrated, and as you look at the timer on the phone, it tells you that this call took 2 minutes and 25 seconds, and nothing happened. Once again, you've been placed in Voice Mail Jail.

In the first instance, the person who recorded the message just didn't include any options so you could get out, or exit, the voice-mail system. And there's no excuse for this. In the second example, detailed exit instructions were given; unfortunately, no live person was available to take the call.

The biggest complaint that callers have about voice-mail systems is the inability to reach a live person on demand.

Here are some tips about what you should include in your voice-mail messages:

✔ Always leave instructions so that the caller can be transferred to someone else. ("Press #48, and you'll be transferred to my assistant, Jim; press 0, and you'll be transferred to the operator.")

✔ Leave instructions so that callers can leave messages without having to listen to your message each time they call. ("If you would like to skip this message in the future, press 1.")

Recording Your Message

Some people like to record a basic message once and never make any changes to it. Others like to record a new message every day so that they can leave a detailed schedule of their activities for the caller. This type of message is very helpful to both the caller and the callee because it helps improve the odds of their being able to reach each other since the caller knows when the callee is expected to be in the office and behind the desk. Let me give you a few examples of very good voice-mail messages:

✔ _Hello, this is Fred Smith. It's Friday, January 20th, and I'll be out of the office all day today and all day on Monday. Please leave me your name, number, and a brief message. I will be checking in for messages throughout the day. If you need to speak to someone immediately, press 0._

✔ _Hello, this is Carol Collins of the Building Managers Association. It's Tuesday, August 22. I'm sorry I missed your call. I am out of the office today. If you're calling in regard to completion of the US Industrial survey and you need some_ *extra time, please leave me a message as to when you think you can send it to me. If you have any questions that you need answered today, please call Sherry Ackerman in Dallas. Her number is 123-456-7890. If this call is in regard to other matters, please leave me a message and I'll get back to you as soon as I can. If you need help immediately, please press 0.*

✔ *Hello, this is Kelly Green. It's Monday, October 17, and I'm in the office today; however, I'm going to be tied up in meetings for most of it. I will check in later, though, so please leave a message and I'll get back to you as soon as I possibly can. If you need immediate assistance, press 0.*

Here are some things you should remember when you record your voice mail message:

✔ Your message should be informative, courteous, and brief, and it should always encourage the caller to leave a message.

✔ Smile before you start speaking and the warmth of your smile will come through in your voice. This way, you'll leave a friendlier greeting.

✔ To put some *life, energy,* and *enthusiasm* into your voice-mail message, get up from your chair, stretch for a moment, get the blood in your body circulating, and then record your message. You don't want your message to sound as if you recorded it just before you had to go to a funeral.

✔ When you record your voice mail message, always speak slowly, distinctly, and clearly.

✔ If you're going to ask people to leave you messages, you've got to check your messages throughout the day, and you must be diligent about returning your calls.

✔ After you have recorded your voice-mail message, call yourself up to listen to how it sounds. Does it have enough energy and enthusiasm? Is it short and concise? Does it say what you want it to say? If not, record it again.

Tips for Leaving Voice-Mail Messages

Recording a voice-mail message is one thing, but leaving messages is an entirely different, and more important, subject. In today's business world, almost everyone has voice mail, so whenever you make a call, you should be prepared to leave a message. This means that you should think about what you want to say and how you want to say it — *before* you make the call. Here are some tips on how to leave better voice-mail messages:

- Don't start leaving your message until you hear the machine beep. (I know that almost everybody should know this, but you would be surprised at the number of people who start talking before the outgoing message is finished.)

- Before you start speaking, take a deep breath so that your lungs are full of air. This will give your voice more depth and power.

- When you speak, speak slowly, clearly, and concisely so that the person can understand what you're saying. Don't swallow your words.

- Make your voice sound interesting. Speak with enthusiasm. Put some energy into your voice.

- When you leave your name, in addition to saying it, you should spell it out. ("This is Jeffrey Mayer, M-A-Y-E-R.")

- Always give your phone number twice, once at the beginning of the call and again at the end of the call. While many of the people you call may already have your number, they may be calling in for their messages and may not have your number with them.

- When you leave your message, state the most important points first, with the lesser points following.

- If you're including your mailing address, speak slowly and spell out the name of your street and city after you say the address. ("50 East Bellevue Place, B-E-L-L-E-V-U-E, Chicago, Illinois.")

- Leave a specific time, or a window of time, when you'll be available for the person to call you back. For example: "I'll be in my office and available tomorrow morning." Or, "I'm always in my office every afternoon after 2:00."

Be energetic and enthusiastic. Let your personality brighten the other person's day.

What if my voice-mail messages aren't returned?

If you leave voice-mail messages several times with a person and they aren't returned, try to talk with the person's assistant, someone else in the department, or the receptionist to find out if the person you're calling is in town and available. If you're unable to reach this person, try to get the name of someone else you can speak with.

After you've called someone a few times and have left voice-mail messages that haven't been returned, try to reach the person's assistant or someone else in the department. Find out when the person you're trying to contact may be available to take your call. Don't sit around waiting for a return call that won't be forthcoming.

But I get too many messages

One of the biggest complaints I get about voice mail is that people get too many messages, and it takes too long to listen to them. Here are some tips that can help you deal with this problem:

- ✔ Increase the playback speed of your calls. When you listen to your messages, speed them up so that you can get through them quicker. (This feature may not be available on all voice-mail systems or home answering machines.)

- ✔ Limit the length of time for each message. If you've got long-winded people, limit the length of time that a person can leave a message to 60, 90, or 120 seconds at most. (When you record your message, tell callers that they have only 60 seconds to leave their messages.)

- ✔ Limit the number of calls your voice-mail box can hold. I know this may sound like it's defeating the purpose of the voice-mail system, but if you're getting too many calls, try limiting the number of calls that your voice-mail box can hold. When your box is full, the caller will be told something like: "This voice-mail box is full." Now the caller will have to call someone else, call back later, or send a letter or e-mail message.

- ✔ If you get a message for something that doesn't pertain to you, transfer the message to the person who is responsible.

Taking care of business

After you get messages, you've got to do something with them. They won't do you much good if you just store them in your "voice-mail archives." So here are a few suggestions:

- ✔ If there's work to do, you should note it on your Master List or put it into ACT!.

- ✔ If the information is important, you should take notes on a big piece of paper — one note per page — and put it in the appropriate file. (Don't forget to date your papers.)

- ✔ When you're finished listening to your messages, erase them.

Chapter 11

Write More Effective Correspondence

In This Chapter

▶ Who is your audience?

▶ Good writing isn't easy

▶ Write better letters

*I*t wasn't all that long ago that computers were a novelty, and we still used adding machines and pocket calculators. But times have changed. Today, almost everyone in corporate America has a computer sitting on the top of the desk, and we're being asked to do some things with them that we haven't done in a long time: Write letters, memos, and reports; create presentations; and send and reply to e-mail messages. I thought it would be appropriate to include a chapter on how to improve your writing skills because so much of our communication is done by the written word.

Who Is Your Audience?

Good writing makes it easy for you to communicate your ideas to other people, and it helps them make better business decisions. In today's busy world, no one has time to read, so the people who are responsible for making business decisions want to get the information they need from their letters, memos, reports, and e-mail messages and then make a decision without wasting a lot time. So, to make everybody's life easier, you've got to be good at putting your thoughts and ideas on paper, using words that the reader understands, and then arranging this information in a concise and thorough way that's easy to comprehend.

In addition, you have to give consideration to the people who will be reading your letter, memo, or report. For example, a report for your company's president, chairman, or board of directors would be written in a different manner than a weekly status report to your supervisor or manager. Likewise, a letter to a customer or client wouldn't be written as if it were an e-mail message.

Your goal is to not only communicate information to other people, but to obtain a favorable response from them.

Good Writing Isn't Easy

Good writing requires hard work. It is a laborious and slow process because we can think much more quickly than we can write. And that's why it's so much easier to write today, using high-speed computers and high-powered word processors, than it was a century ago, using a pen and inkwell, or even ten years ago, with an IBM Selectric typewriter. Today, the computer gives you the opportunity to spend your time thinking about what it is you want to write, instead of worrying about formatting text or trying to cut and paste words, sentences, or paragraphs from one part of a document to another with a razor blade.

Give yourself plenty of time

After you get started in the writing process, more ideas will begin to flow, and this will help you to focus on what you're *really* trying to say. That's why it's so important that you give yourself plenty of lead time when you're writing. After you write something, put it aside for a little while and then come back to it. When you resume your writing, you'll see new ways in which you can improve upon what you put down on paper.

When you're writing a letter, memo, or report, make sure that the content of the document says what you want it to say in the way you want to say it. Your goal is to write well, not necessarily quickly.

Whenever I write something, even if it's just a short letter, fax, or memo, I always print it out, read it, and put it aside for a little while. When I come back to it, I *always* find that it doesn't say exactly what I wanted it to say. So I do little bit of editing, make some changes, and then send it out.

When you're writing something and you seem to be stuck, just put it aside for a little while and then come back to it. By taking a break and giving yourself a little bit of time to think about your problem, you can usually solve it without much additional effort.

Print out a copy of your document. Hard copies of a document often look and read a bit differently than they do when viewed on the computer screen. So when you're editing a document, print a copy of it, and you'll probably see things that you didn't notice while you were looking at it on-screen.

Use familiar words and phrases

Have you ever gotten a letter from someone and, after reading it, didn't have the slightest idea what it said? So you read it a second or a third time, and it still didn't make sense to you? It's frustrating, isn't it!

When you're composing your letters, memos, or reports, you want to make it easy for the reader to understand what you're saying, so write short sentences, brief paragraphs, and use words that are familiar to your reader.

In today's fast-paced and hectic world, most of us don't have the time to pull out a dictionary to look up the meaning of a word we're not familiar with.

When you select your words, challenge yourself. Keep a dictionary and thesaurus at your fingertips so you can search for better, more descriptive words to express your thoughts and ideas. But don't use words you've never seen before or that are unlikely to be unfamiliar to your readers.

Write in a conversational style

Writing isn't much more than putting the spoken word down on paper. And you can make writing a lot easier if you just imagine that you're having a face-to-face conversation — like two friends sitting around a coffee table having a nice friendly chat — with the person you're writing for. Here are some writing tips:

- ✔ Before you start writing, always ask yourself : "What is the most important piece of information that I want the reader to know?"

- ✔ Get to the important points quickly. State the purpose of your letter, memo, or report in the first sentence of the first paragraph. The reader doesn't have the time to wade through three paragraphs or three pages of text to learn why you're writing a letter in the first place.

- ✔ Short sentences are easier to read. Present your thoughts and ideas to your reader in short bursts, and keep the length of your sentences to no more than 15 to 20 words. However, you do need to add a little variety in your writing. So write some very short sentences and some longer ones every once in a while.

- ✔ Tie your thoughts together. Make your writing clear, concise, and to the point.

✔ To add variety to your letters, memos, and reports, include charts, graphs illustrations, or pictures. The visuals can often eliminate the need to write many words of text.

✔ If you're having a bit of difficulty putting your ideas on paper, read the sentence aloud, and when you get to the part that's giving you trouble, just imagine that you were looking at someone and ask yourself, "What would I *say* next?"

✔ If you're going to be using abbreviations, such as the features of your company's newest product, explain what the abbreviations mean to your reader.

✔ If you're going to use initials for the names of organizations, you should first write out the name in full and then show the abbreviation in parentheses. From that point forward, you can use the organization's initials. (To make the insertion of long names into a document much easier, use your word processor's search and replace feature. You type in an abbreviation for the long name in your text, and when you're finished, you search for the abbreviations and replace them with the long name.)

✔ The more white space, the better: The more white space you have on a printed page, the easier it is to read. When writing, your goal is to give the reader the most information in the fewest number of words. And that takes some work. Abraham Lincoln once said, "I would have written a shorter letter, but I didn't have the time."

✔ Run your spelling checker and your grammar checker before you print the final version of your document. With today's powerful word processing programs, there's just no excuse for misspelled words and typographical mistakes. They make you look sloppy, and they make it more difficult for the reader to get through the document. (But don't put all of your trust in these newfangled devices. Your spelling may be perfectly fine, but you might just use the wrong word (for example, two, too, to). And a grammar checker isn't going to help you at all if you don't actually know the rules of grammar. There is no substitute for rereading everything before you present it.)

✔ Have another pair of eyes read your documents. Sometimes we become blind to spelling, punctuation, or other grammatical errors, errors that are easily discovered when we have another person proofread our documents.

✔ Listen to the sound of your written words. What sounds good usually reads that way. To check the smoothness of your writing, read it out loud.

✔ Set artificial deadlines for yourself. If you have a report that's due on the 15th of the month, set your deadline for the 10th. This will motivate you to get started early, and it will give you plenty of time to think about and edit your work after you've finished. Your goal is to have a great final draft, not a great first draft.

Edit your letters, presentations, and reports

Revising, rewriting, and editing your work are all a part of good writing. Good writing consists of a constant effort to find and eliminate the unnecessary word, no matter how small. As you're editing your work, you should ask yourself these questions:

✔ Is each sentence complete?

✔ Is each paragraph complete?

✔ Is each section complete?

✔ Is my punctuation correct?

✔ Does my text read smoothly?

✔ Are my arguments, ideas, and relationships thoroughly developed?

✔ Have I spelled the names of persons and organizations correctly? (My editor thought this was an extraordinarily important point.)

Grab the reader's attention

No one has time to read long letters, memos, reports, or other documents. We're all just too busy. So, if you want someone to read the things you write, you've got to make it easy for them. And one of the ways you can do this is by putting the most important information at the beginning of your document.

To grab your readers' attention, you've got to start with the first word in the first sentence of the first paragraph. If you can't *grab* their attention, they'll put your document down and may never pick it up again.

Put your most important information in the first sentence of the first paragraph and all of your supporting facts and other information in the sentences and paragraphs that follow. When you write in this manner, you can shorten your readers' reading time because they don't have to dig into each paragraph to try to find out what you're trying so say.

When you write the first draft of your document, your most important points probably will be at the end of the document, and all of your supporting information will be at the beginning. So, when you start editing your work, just move your major points and conclusions from the end of the document to the beginning.

When you need to send a long document, write a one-page cover letter that summarizes the information in the document, in addition to sending the document.

Purchase your stamps by mail. Do you hate standing in lines, especially at the post office? I sure do! Well, you don't have to any longer. Now you can purchase your stamps by mail (Form 3227) and pay for it with a check. You can also order your stamps by phone (1-800-782-6724), 24 hours a day, 7 days a week, and charge it to a credit card.

Write Better Letters

Everyday we're writing letters. It's an everyday part of our business lives. And in the following section, I'm going to provide you with some great tips that will help you improve the chances that your letter will be opened and read.

Get your letters opened

When you send a letter, you want the person who receives it not only to open your envelope but then to take the time to read it and respond to it. Here are some tips on getting people to open your letters:

- Type your return address directly on the envelope. Don't use an address label. If possible, write the name and address of the recipient in longhand. A handwritten address always gets someone's attention. (When an envelope bearing an almost illegible scrawl appears on my desk, I always open it first.)

- Hand stamp you letters. Big colorful, commemorative stamps make your mail look more interesting.

- Mail all your letters first class.

- Write "Personal — Please" with a red pen on the bottom-left corner of the envelope. (I've been doing this for years, and it works! It's much more effective than typing "Important" or "Personal" across the bottom of the letter.)

Get your letters read

After you've been successful in getting someone to open your envelope, you want that person to read your letter. Here are some tips:

- The first sentence of you letter should jump out and capture your reader's interest and attention so that he or she will want to read the rest of it.

- Add a postscript. The postscript is usually the first or second thing that a person reads, so include a postscript that grabs the reader's attention and generates enough interest to get your entire letter read.

✔ Always try to start a letter with the word "You"; it makes the reader want to continue reading.

✔ Mention the person's name and the name of his or her company throughout the letter. This makes your letters more personal and friendly, and it is a powerful way of getting the reader's attention.

✔ Stress the benefits to the person reading the letter. Say what's in it for the reader. "You get this . . . ," "You get that . . . ."

✔ Eliminate the word "I" from your letters. "I" is the least important word in the English language.

Make your letters easy to read

After you've gotten someone to open your envelope, read the opening sentence, and read the postscript, you then want that person to go back and read the entire letter. Here are some tips:

✔ Indent your paragraphs. They're easier to read this way. And skip a line between paragraphs.

✔ Use a serif typeface (this book is printed in a serif typeface — except for the sidebars and running heads — and so is your daily newspaper). The typeface you use should be at least 12 points in size. This improves readability.

✔ Use a ragged right margin. A justified right margin makes your letters look as if they were mass-produced.

✔ Keep your letters short and concise and not more than one page in length. (If you're sending a handwritten note, keep it under three sentences in length. Think about what you want to say, say it, and sign it.)

✔ At the end of the letter, indicate that you will be doing something: "I'll be calling you within a few days to get your thoughts on this."

✔ Hand sign your letters.

Remember the three magic phrases: "Thank You," "Congratulations," and "Thinking of You."

Chapter 12

The Ins and Outs of E-Mail (or Is It the Ups and Downs?)

● ●

In This Chapter

▶ Writing good messages

▶ Learning e-mail etiquette

▶ Allocating time for e-mail reading

▶ Using e-mail wisely

● ●

E-mail is an electronic medium that millions of people use to share information. It's become extremely popular in corporate America because it's more efficient than using the telephone, less formal than writing a letter, and much faster than snail mail, (the United States Postal Service). When e-mail is used properly, it's a huge time-saver because it allows you to share information with someone down the hall, or halfway across the world, in just a moment's time. But if you're spending one, two, or even three hours per day responding to your e-mail messages, it can become an enormous time waster because it takes away from the time that you should be spending on your other work.

Keep It Short and Sweet

The whole concept behind using e-mail is that it's fast, short, and sweet. You don't worry about spelling, punctuation, or grammatical errors. You don't edit or proofread your writing. You just write your message and send it. It's sort of like an electronic memo pad.

Make it easy to read

Even though most e-mail messages are less than three paragraphs in length, you should put your most important information in the first sentence of the first paragraph and your background or supporting information in the following paragraphs.

Use the subject line

The subject line is the most important part of your e-mail message. It's the first thing the recipient sees, so it should be short, concise, descriptive, and informative. If action is required on the part of the reader, put it in the subject line — for example, "Please attend Tues. meeting" or "Need Reply by Wed. morning."

Make your subject line so descriptive that it grabs your readers' attention, and they'll probably read your message first. You often have 25 to 35 characters for a subject line, so make the most of them.

Keep the message simple

When you write your e-mail message, write short, easy-to-read sentences and paragraphs. Put the most important information in the first few sentences of the first paragraph. Here are some tips:

- Try to keep your e-mail messages on one screen. If a message takes more than one screen, you should shorten it.

- If you're including a list of items, use a bulleted or numbered list. It's easier to read (like this list).

- If you must send a long message, attach the file as an enclosure. Write a brief description of the message in the subject line. The e-mail message itself should be a more detailed description of the enclosed file.

- When you attach a document to an e-mail message, write a brief but thorough description about the document you're sending. Don't forget to include the purpose of the document, detailed instructions regarding what the recipient is supposed to do with the document, and the date you need a response. This item of business should then be added to your Master List or into ACT!.

If you receive an e-mail message that's stamped with a receipt notification and you don't want to open it, just forward a *copy* of the message to yourself and read the copy.

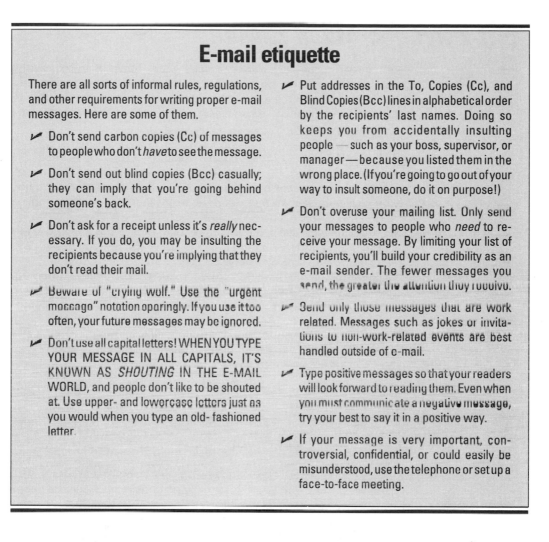

E-mail etiquette

There are all sorts of informal rules, regulations, and other requirements for writing proper e-mail messages. Here are some of them.

✓ Don't send carbon copies (Cc) of messages to people who don't *have* to see the message.

✓ Don't send out blind copies (Bcc) casually; they can imply that you're going behind someone's back.

✓ Don't ask for a receipt unless it's *really* necessary. If you do, you may be insulting the recipients because you're implying that they don't read their mail.

✓ Beware of "crying wolf." Use the "urgent message" notation sparingly. If you use it too often, your future messages may be ignored.

✓ Don't use all capital letters! WHEN YOU TYPE YOUR MESSAGE IN ALL CAPITALS, IT'S KNOWN AS *SHOUTING* IN THE E-MAIL WORLD, and people don't like to be shouted at. Use upper- and lowercase letters just as you would when you type an old-fashioned letter.

✓ Put addresses in the To, Copies (Cc), and Blind Copies (Bcc) lines in alphabetical order by the recipients' last names. Doing so keeps you from accidentally insulting people — such as your boss, supervisor, or manager — because you listed them in the wrong place. (If you're going to go out of your way to insult someone, do it on purpose!)

✓ Don't overuse your mailing list. Only send your messages to people who *need* to receive your message. By limiting your list of recipients, you'll build your credibility as an e-mail sender. The fewer messages you send, the greater the attention they receive.

✓ Send only those messages that are work related. Messages such as jokes or invitations to non-work-related events are best handled outside of e-mail.

✓ Type positive messages so that your readers will look forward to reading them. Even when you must communicate a negative message, try your best to say it in a positive way.

✓ If your message is very important, controversial, confidential, or could easily be misunderstood, use the telephone or set up a face-to-face meeting.

Write e-mail messages that are easy to respond to

Make it easy for people to respond to your e-mail messages. When you write your message, be sure to include enough information so that recipients can give you a quick answer or response. Phrase your messages so that readers can reply with a "Yes" or "No," and if you're going to ask for a reply, mention it in your subject line.

But I Get Too Much E-Mail

If you're getting too much e-mail or it's taking too many hours of your day to respond to it, maybe somebody isn't using the e-mail system in the manner in which it was intended. So let me ask you a question: How much time would you spend reading and responding to these messages if they had been sent to you the old-fashioned way, on paper?

Would you be in such a hurry to respond to them and get them off of your desk? Would you drop everything and deal with them immediately? Of course not! In the old days, these paper memos could sit in your in-box for days, if not weeks, before you got around to them, and the world didn't come to an end.

But because the same message is now being sent to you electronically, you feel this primal urge to read and respond to it immediately. But are you in such a hurry to read your e-mail messages because they're so very important, or because you know that if you don't get to them regularly, they will just back up on you and eventually overwhelm you? Here are some tips on how to cope with the e-mail onslaught:

- ✔ Set aside specific times during the day that you'll go through your e-mail to see what's arrived and what's important. Don't interrupt yourself every time an e-mail message arrives.

- ✔ If it's not necessary for you to respond to each and every e-mail message that you receive, don't!

- ✔ When you must respond to an e-mail message, make your response short and sweet. Give "Yes" and "No" answers when possible, and if you have to write a few sentences or paragraphs, make them concise and to the point.

- ✔ If you're getting copied (Cc) or blind copied (Bcc) e-mail messages that don't specifically apply to your job or daily responsibilities, ask the people who have been sending these messages to take you off their lists.

- ✔ Don't allow the arrival of e-mail to interrupt your important work. If your computer beeps or sounds a trumpet to announce the arrival of each new e-mail message, then turn this feature off. And if your computer's hard drive starts making all sorts of whirring noises whenever you get an e-mail message, you may want to turn off your e-mail as well.

Check your e-mail box regularly. If you don't check your e-mail box regularly, you lose the major advantage of using e-mail over snail mail.

Be Careful with the Freedom of E-Mail

Just because e-mail's supposed to be an unstructured environment, you shouldn't allow yourself to get carried away. There's just too big a difference between writing e-mail messages to your boss, colleagues, and coworkers, and writing anonymous messages on the Internet. When writing e-mail messages to the people within your own company or organization, you should use the same diction and common sense that you would use if you were writing a letter, having a conversation on the phone, or having a face-to-face meeting.

Don't flame out

If you're feeling hurt, angry, or insulted about something, don't write out your thoughts as an e-mail message and send it off, especially if you're upset with your boss, manager, or supervisor. In e-mail lingo, there is a term for this use of e-mail; it's called *flaming*.

When people let their emotions flare up and then send blistering e-mail messages, they're flaming. (It's sort of like throwing a temper tantrum.) And when the person who received the message fires off a fiery response, you've got yourself a *flame war*. (We used to have these kinds of fights — food fights — in the high school cafeteria, but this is the 90s and we're more civilized now.)

Try your best not to become a participant in a flame war, especially at the office. You've certainly got more important things to do. In most instances, the sender just sent a message that you misinterpreted, or vice versa. Or maybe the sender wrote something stupid, or vice versa. If you have a problem with someone, pick up the phone or schedule a face-to-face meeting so that you can talk things out.

Smileys improve e-mail communication :-)

Because e-mail messages can easily be misunderstood or misinterpreted, e-mail junkies often use smileys to convey feelings, moods, or emotions.

To see a smiley, you must put your left ear to your left shoulder and look at the computer screen sideways. Today, there are hundreds of smileys. Here's a sampling of some smileys and their meanings:

Smiley	Meaning
:-)	Happy
:-(	Sad
:-II	Angry
%-)	Happy confused

Smiley	Meaning
8-0	Shocked
;-)	Winking
:'-(	Crying
:-*	Kiss
X-(	Brain dead

Protect Yourself Against E-Mail Break-Ins

If you leave your computer unattended, make sure that no one else can use your e-mail program while you're away. You certainly don't want someone else writing a letter to *your* boss describing what *you* think of him or her. And never give your e-mail user name and password to anyone else.

There's no substitute for personal interaction. Every once in a while, rather than ask a question of a coworker via e-mail, get up from your chair and stroll down to that person's office. You'll stretch your legs and get the break you probably needed but wouldn't otherwise have taken.

Save Important Information

When you send or receive an e-mail message that contains important information, print out a copy of it and put it in the appropriate file so that you can find it when you need it.

The 5th Wave   By Rich Tennant

" WELL, I'M REALLY LOOKING FORWARD TO SEEING THIS WIRELESS E-MAIL SYSTEM
OF YOURS, MUDNICK."

Part IV
Looking Out for #1

The 5th Wave — By Rich Tennant

"THE SHORT ANSWER TO YOUR REQUEST FOR A RAISE IS 'NO.' THE LONG ANSWER IS 'NO, AND GET OUT OF MY OFFICE.'"

In this part . . .

With continued downsizing, the people working in corporate America, people like you and me, have to look out for ourselves. The days of lifetime employment are gone. There's no longer a benevolent employer that's going to take care of us throughout our career. If we don't look out for our own best interests, who will?

In Chapter 13, I show you how to improve your ability to communicate your ideas to a group of people. I know that most of us, myself included, are scared to death to stand in front of an audience and make a presentation, but when you can overcome that fear, you can do a very good job of convincing people to your way of thinking, and this skill will help you to promote your ideas, your company's products and services, and yourself.

In Chapter 14, I help you promote yourself. You start by collecting testimonial letters from satisfied customers, clients, and coworkers. To become the recognized *expert* in your field, get yourself quoted in the local newspapers, start writing articles for newspapers, magazines, and trade journals, and then write the definitive book. Public speaking is another way that you can promote yourself. Finally, I give you some tips on how to get more mileage out of your business cards.

In Chapter 15, I show you how you can get the right results by doing the right things. Goal setting is an enjoyable and challenging experience. You can set reasonable goals for yourself, accomplish them, and then push yourself toward accomplishing another set of goals.

In Chapter 16, it's time to wrap things up. As my good friend, Jim Paglia, said of me, "Jeffrey Mayer has identified the secret of success: Use your time to your advantage." The keys to success come from having a winning attitude and maintaining good work habits. You need to challenge yourself, take responsibility for the things you do, surround yourself with successful people, make the most of your time, and spend more time with your family and friends.

Chapter 13
Make Winning Presentations

· ·

· ·

Most of us never think about it, but the art of standing in front of a group of people and *really* dazzling them with a presentation is extremely important. Now, I know that you probably don't consider yourself to be a public speaker, but whenever you've got to stand up in front of a group of people, it's public speaking. When you're giving a report to your boss, colleagues, or coworkers, you've become a public speaker (even if you're sitting down). When you're sitting in a meeting and you're asked your opinions about something, you become a public speaker. And when you're participating in a brainstorming session, whenever you start talking, you transform yourself from being an observer to being an active participant — and a public speaker.

A Presentation Is a Show

When you start speaking, you become the center of attention; everybody's eyes are on you as they lean forward to hear what it is that you're going to say. I know it's scary. And you're probably feeling terrified because the spotlight's on you. But this is your opportunity to go out and sell your thoughts, your ideas, and yourself. So you should look at this opportunity to speak and to present this information as a performance, as a show.

And whether you like it or not, when you're making a presentation to one person or to several hundred people, for that brief time when you're standing in front of your audience, you become an actor. You're standing in the center of the stage, and you're the *star*. The same principles that make for a successful stage or screen performance will also make your presentation a success. You'll be exciting and entertaining, provide useful information, and persuade your audience to say "Yes."

Get rid of those butterflies

It's perfectly natural for you to feel butterflies in your stomach when you've got to stand up and speak before a group of people, or when you're participating in a discussion with your colleagues and coworkers while you're sitting in the conference room. Many professional athletes, actors, singers, and musicians feel a sense of terror just before they're about to perform, so why shouldn't you? But after they get started, that feeling of terror subsides. If you didn't feel nervous, tense, or apprehensive, you wouldn't be human.

With a little bit of practice, you can get rid of those butterflies in your stomach and use that nervous energy to improve the quality of your presentation. Here are some tips:

- ✔ While you are waiting for your turn to speak, you should use these few moments to "warm up." Think about your opening statements or remarks, and go over your material or notes one more time.

- ✔ If you will be addressing a group of people and are waiting to be introduced, read the first page or two of your presentation to yourself.

- ✔ Remind yourself to display lots of energy and enthusiasm and to smile. Remember that these people are your friends.

- ✔ Use your breathing to calm yourself down. Controlled breathing is a great way to get yourself to relax. Start by inhaling deeply through your nose, and then, with pursed lips, slowly blow the air out of your mouth as if you were trying to blow out a dozen candles on a birthday cake in one breath. As you exhale, you'll feel your diaphragm — the muscle that brings air into and pushes air out of your lungs — contract and become tighter. The more nervous you feel, the harder you should blow and the tighter you should squeeze your diaphragm. This technique will help you to dissipate a lot of nervous energy.

- ✔ Leave a nickel or a quarter in one of your pockets; if you're feeling stress or tension, you can squeeze the coin.

How do you want to be introduced?

When you will be speaking in front of a group of people, someone will usually take a moment to introduce you to your audience. A well-written introduction can build instant rapport between you and your audience and can win them over, even before you begin speaking. Here are some ideas that will help to guarantee that the person who introduces you will say the right things:

✔ Write out the introduction — in full — so that the person who introduces you won't start rambling when introducing you.

✔ The introduction should be double-spaced, using at least an 18-point font (this makes it easy to read), and take no more than 90 seconds to read.

✔ Any words or phrases you want the person to emphasize should be noted by *italics* or "quotation" marks.

✔ Ask the person who will be introducing you to read your introduction aloud at least two times *before* introducing you.

✔ Make sure you both know how to pronounce each other's names.

✔ Test the microphone before you approach the lectern to make sure it works properly.

Warm up your audience

When you're speaking in front of a group of people, you should try to loosen up your audience, and yourself, before you begin. This gives them a few moments to get settled, and it gives you a chance to burn up some of your nervous energy. The following sections describe a few techniques that I've found help to bring an audience to life

The "Good Morning" welcome

As you're walking to the front of the group, just after you've been introduced — with a big smile on your face — always say "Good Morning," or whatever greeting would be appropriate. And if the response you get from the audience is subdued, which it will be, you should say "Good Morning" a second time and encourage the audience to say "Good Morning" back to you with a bit more energy and enthusiasm. Do this three or four times, and you'll raise the audience's energy to a pretty high level. Now you're ready to begin your presentation.

The "Let's Get the Body Moving" stretch

Most of us spend too much time sitting and not enough time moving around, so if you would like to put some energy and life into your audience, ask them to stand up, stretch, and shake their arms and legs so that they'll get the blood in their bodies circulating again. (This technique can be particularly useful if the members of your audience have been sitting in their chairs for several hours, or if you're speaking to them just after they've had a meal.)

Getting your audience to stand up and stretch can be a little bit tricky because you can't just ask them to stand up and stretch. If you do, they'll give you some very strange looks and won't budge from their seats. So you've got to get them moving in stages.

You first ask the audience members to raise their right hands above their heads. Then you tell them to shake those hands. Next, you ask them to raise their left hands above their heads and shake them also. Then you ask them to raise their hands higher and higher so that they get out of their chairs and stand up. After they're standing, you ask them to shake their feet, one at a time, and before they sit down, ask them to shake the hands of the people that are sitting next to them. Then say, "Now that you've got your blood flowing again, let's all sit down. It's time to get started."

Open with a bang

You must plan for the opening of your presentation in the same methodical way that you plan the presentation itself. You need to grab your audience's attention and establish rapport with them. And you start with your opening line.

If you've got some special talents, use them. Can you sing? Dance? Draw? Can you tell stories? Can you tell funny stories? The use of humor can be an important part of making an effective presentation. Funny stories that are based on a personal experience or a real-life example can help you to illustrate a key point and make it easier for your audience to remember those key points. Remember, when you're in front of a group of people, just be yourself. Don't try to be something you're not.

Pay close attention to the length of your opening remarks. If your few moments of small talk are too short, then your audience won't be ready for you; and if it's too long, they'll begin to feel that you're wasting their time.

Talk with your body

No matter how well prepared you are when you give your presentation, it is your nonverbal delivery — your physical presence in front of your audience — that ultimately establishes your credibility. The first thing you should pay attention to is how you look in front of your audience. Here are some tips:

✔ Stand up straight, squeeze your shoulder blades together to open your chest, square your shoulders, and pick up your head.

✔ For more balance and stability — and a feeling of power — plant your feet firmly on the floor. To do this, spread your feet about an inch wider than your normal stance, bend your knees slightly, and gently rock forward and backward, for just a moment, so that you can feel your heels, feet, and toes come in contact with the floor. This will keep your weight evenly distributed on both feet.

✔ When you move, take long, purposeful strides in the direction you want to go, and then plant your feet on the floor again.

Fifty-five percent of your message is communicated through body language, 38 percent through your vocal cords, and only 7 percent through your words.

You've got two hands — use them

Because more than half of your message is conveyed by your body language, be animated and use your hands and facial expressions to help express yourself. Let your audience use their eyes and their ears to experience what you're saying. Here are some tips:

✔ Keep your hands in view. Don't put them in your pockets or behind your back.

✔ Let your gestures flow naturally. Speak with your hands and your arms. Practice being more animated with your gestures in front of a mirror so that you can see how other people see you.

✔ When you're making points, spread your hand out and count on your fingers so that your audience will know that you're counting for them.

✔ To keep from making jingling sounds when you're walking around, remove keys, change, and any other objects from your pockets.

Keep smiling. The warmth of your smile will help to win your audience over.

Keep your body moving

To keep your audience's attention, don't stand in one place or stay behind the lectern or podium for too long. Keep moving. Let your movement coincide with your words. When you become excited and begin to speak more rapidly, move quickly and it'll stir up the audience. When you calm down and begin to speak at a slower rate of speed, lower the tone of your voice and slow down your body movements. It'll keep your audience sitting on the edges of their seats.

✔ When you're giving a list of items, say the item, take one step, and stop, and then say the next item and repeat this movement as you're stating your list.

✔ When you're making specific points, turn and face a different part of the room — left and right, front and back.

✔ When you want to speak intimately, move forward and lower your voice.

✔ When you want to speak with more authority, take a step backward and speak more loudly.

✔ Talk to all the people in your audience: the people in the front of the room, the people in the back of the room, the people in the middle, and the people who are sitting on the far left and far right.

✔ When someone asks a question, walk toward that person.

When answering a question, listen to the question and then repeat it to the audience before you begin to answer it.

Look at your audience

When you're talking to someone, look at him or her. Eye contact is a very important part of defining, developing, and establishing relationships between people. And by looking into another person's eyes, you can often determine how well the two of you are connecting.

When you're speaking in front of a group of people, you want to establish a relationship with each person in the audience. You want them to feel connected to you, befriended by you, and you want them to give you some of their energy, which in turn will give you more confidence. Try to win everyone over. Let them feel the warmth of your presence and the warmth of your smile.

✔ When you're standing in front of a small group of people, scan the room and try to make eye contact with as many individuals as you can, *especially* those who aren't smiling and nodding their heads in agreement. Select a row and then scan from left to right (not front to back), and when you've looked at everyone in that row, scan the row behind it, from right to left, until you've worked your way through the entire audience. Then you should look at the people sitting in the front of the room and start over. Make all members of your audience feel that you're speaking directly to them.

✔ If you're speaking to a large audience, it may not be possible for you to look at each person, so you should make and hold eye contact with various sections of the room following the same pattern of movement. Start at the front of the audience and look from left to right, and then look at the next section of people from right to left, until you've worked your way through the entire audience, and then start over again.

✔ For a little variety, you can play some games with yourself as you're making eye contact with your audience. For example, you can look for everyone with big hair, everyone with short hair, or everyone with no hair. Then look for everyone wearing green, or red, or black, and then look at each person who is sitting in the middle of each section. (And if you see people with yellow hair, green hair, orange hair, or purple hair, don't stare at them because you may forget where you are in your presentation.)

✔ If you're losing some members of your audience — they're dozing off, appear to be daydreaming, or are talking with their neighbors — you've got to work at bringing them back. Walk towards them, give them more eye contact, and pay more attention to them.

To bring attention to your eyes, use a very light powder around them. To bring attention to your mouth, use Vaseline or a light lip gloss.

When you're looking into a person's eyes, don't try to look at both eyes at the same time. This causes you to shift your focus from one eye to the other, and the other person will see your eyes darting back and forth. Instead, you should focus on only one of the person's eyes at a time. This will keep your eyes in a fixed position.

Now where was I?

Most people find that it can be quite a challenge to hold their speaker's notes, look at the audience, and keep their place all at the same time. So here are a few thoughts:

✔ When you create your outline, only include the key words or phrases. Don't write out your sentences.

✔ Make your speaker's notes easy to read. Print them on a sheet of paper or on index cards, using a very large, easy-to-read font, such as Times Roman, 18 point. (You can use presentation software to create your speaker's notes. I discuss presentation soft-

ware in the section "Use Pictures, Graphics, and Charts to Enhance Your Presentation." For myself, I just create my speaker's notes in WordPerfect.)

✔ Hold your notes with your left hand and, as you speak, slide your thumb downward so that it's always on the next line of your presentation.

✔ When you take your eyes away from your notes to look at your audience, just look for your thumb and you'll know exactly where you are in your presentation.

Make your voice sound interesting

Most people make decisions based not on what a person says, but on *how* that person says it. And when you're speaking in front of a group of people, if your delivery is exciting, the presentation becomes exciting and your audience continues to listen. So when you can make the sound of your voice more interesting — by varying the volume, pitch, modulation, and intonation — it's much easier to keep your audience's attention. The next few sections offer some tips on using your voice effectively.

Pay attention to the speed at which you talk

Don't talk too slowly or you'll bore your audience to death; but don't speak too quickly either, or they may not catch everything you're saying. Just try to speak at the same rate of speed that you use when you're talking to a friend on the phone, about 150 to 200 words per minute.

Change your pace frequently

Vary your pace to fit the content or mood of what you're saying. When you're talking about something that's exciting, sound excited and speak a little more quickly. And when you're talking about something that's serious, sound serious and slow things down.

Raise and lower your voice

To keep your audience interested in what you're saying, you should change the volume at which you're speaking. When you get excited, it's okay to speak loudly and more quickly; and when you want to make a very important point, speak softly, or even whisper, and everyone will lean forward as they strain to hear what it is you're saying. When you whisper, everyone listens!

Pronounce all your words clearly and distinctly

Try to pronounce the beginning of your words cleanly and clearly, and keep enough air in your lungs so that you'll able to end your sentences with power as you put em*PHA*sis on the last syl*LAB*le of the last word. Always try to speak with power and conviction.

Always take a deep breath before you begin to speak. When a person begins speaking in front of a group of people, he or she often gets a rush of adrenalin and then starts talking faster and faster and faster. And like a hundred-car freight train, once you start talking too quickly, it's very difficult to slow yourself down. So always take a breath before you begin a new sentence and a deep breath before you begin a new paragraph. This technique will give you an extra moment to collect your thoughts, in addition to keeping you from talking too quickly. And remember: when your lungs are full of air, your voice sounds deeper and has more power.

For added emphasis, add silence

When you're giving a presentation, it's very easy to overwhelm your audience with information. You're giving them so many different things to think about that it's almost impossible for them to process it all. One of the ways you can help your audience grasp all the things you're saying is to use *silence* as a presentation technique.

✔ When you want to emphasize a specific point, pause for one beat before and after the word you want to make stand out. (A beat would be about a second in length, like your heartbeat when you're lying down and resting, not your heartbeat while you're standing in front of your audience.)

✔ When you want to emphasize the transition from one thought to another, pause for about two beats.

✔ To give your audience a few moments to reflect on the unusual, complex, important, provocative, or evocative statement you just made, pause for about four beats.

✔ When you want to emphasize something dramatically, make your statement and then stop talking. After a few moments the tension will start to build, and when it finally reaches a breaking point, you should commence speaking again.

And to keep your presentation from *appearing* canned — because you've given it so many times — you should occasionally pause, look toward the ceiling, and rub your chin with your hand, as if you're trying to remember something or you're trying to find just the *right* word, for three or four beats. This is particularly effective when someone's asking a question that you've answered a thousand times before.

Work on your voice

Here are a few easy and simple exercises that will help you add depth and power to your voice:

✔ **Humming down.** To lower the normal pitch of your voice, hum down the scale to the lowest note you can reach and hold it for as long as you can. Do this three or four times a day as you're getting dressed in the morning. Within just a few weeks, you'll find that you're speaking with a deeper voice.

✔ **Make your voice more interesting.** To make your voice sound more interesting, practice counting aloud. Start by counting from 1 to 10 and do this over and over again (and then from 1 to 20, and from 1 to 30). As you say the numbers, begin to make each one sound different from the previous number. Say some louder, others softer, some with a higher voice, and others with a lower voice. Try to make each one sound interesting. Do this for a few weeks, and you'll be able to keep your audience members sitting on the edges of their seats while you're reading the telephone directory.

✔ **Increase your lung capacity.** When your lungs are empty, they hold about two pints of air; when they're fully inflated, they hold about ten pints — a one-gallon differential — and when you're just sitting around watching television, your lungs contain about five pints of air. The greater the amount of air you have in your lungs, the richer the tone of your voice, the deeper the pitch of your voice, and the more powerful the volume.

To increase your lung capacity, just take a deep breath and, in a whisper, start counting very slowly. With your first breath, you may be able to count to 6, 7, or 8. Take a second breath and you should be able to count to 10, 12, or 13. With a third breath, you may get up to 15 or 16. And with your fourth or fifth breath, you'll probably be getting close to 20. Do this for just two minutes a day, and within two weeks, you should be able to count to 30, 35, 40, or even higher on a single breath.

With these simple and easy exercises, you'll increase your lungs' capacity, add power to your voice, and make it sound deeper and stronger.

Enthusiasm creates energy

Like laughter, enthusiasm is contagious. So let your enthusiasm about your job, career, product, service, or business show in your voice, your gestures, and in your energy level when you're standing in front of an audience. When it's apparent that you enjoy and are excited about the subject of your presentation, you'll keep your audience interested in the things you're saying.

Use Pictures, Graphics, and Charts to Enhance Your Presentation

When you're planning your presentation, you should always ask yourself, "What kinds of visuals will best enhance my presentation?" Do you want to work with slides, overheads, or flip charts in addition to your handouts? Visuals enhance the image of the presentation itself, and visuals get more of the audience's senses involved because they can see a picture of what you're describing. Visuals also enable you to walk a person through all the step-by-step details of your presentation. Here are some tips to make visual aids work for you:

✔ Just before you begin your presentation, run through your slides or overheads — for the twentieth time — to make sure that they're in the right order and facing forward.

✔ Talk to your audience. Don't talk to the screen, overhead projector, or flip chart. Just glance at the screen to see that it's showing the proper slide and then look at your audience as you continue speaking.

Use your computer to create your slides, overheads, charts, and speaker's notes

Today, you can use presentation software that makes it easy to create professional-looking slides, overhead transparencies, and charts without leaving your office. You can design and create charts, graphs, drawings, and illustrations that can be used to make professional slide shows, overhead transparencies, handouts for meetings, or any other type of information that you would present on paper. In just a matter of minutes, you can create presentations that have impact and get results. The following are very good presentation software programs: **WordPerfect Presentations:** WordPerfect Novel Applications Group, 1555 N. Technology Way, Orem, UT 84057; 800-451-5151. **Harvard Graphics:** Software Publishing Corp., 3165 Kifer Road, Santa Clara, CA 95056; 800-336-8360. **Freelance Graphics:** Lotus Development Corp., 55 Cambridge Pkwy., Cambridge, MA 02142; 800-343-5414. (If you would like to learn more about the Harvard Graphics program, pick up a copy of *Harvard Graphics For Dummies* at your local bookstore.)

Bring your computer into your meetings

Instead of taking those computer files and turning them into overhead transparencies or 35mm slides, just attach your computer to a desktop projector and bring it into your meeting. A desktop projector is a small, lightweight liquid crystal display projection panel that sits on top of an overhead projector and is connected to the computer with a cable. The projection panel captures any image that would appear on the computer's monitor — spreadsheets, charts, graphs, project schedules, document outlines, animated graphics, illustrations, and even video images — and displays them on-screen through the overhead projector. Proxima Corporation makes a complete line of LCD projection panels. Proxima Corporation, 6610 Nancy Ridge Drive, San Diego, CA 92121. Call 800-447-7694 for product information. (With the "slide show" feature of your presentation software — WordPerfect Presentations, Harvard Graphics, and Freelance Graphics — you can make your presentation directly from your computer.)

What Handouts Do You Want to Leave Behind?

Whenever you speak in front of a group of people, you should always prepare a handout that audience members can take with them. It doesn't have to be very detailed and complicated, and in most cases, a simple outline, bulleted points, or even a fill-in-the-blank form will do. You just want to use the handout as a reminder of your main points and as a promotional piece. Here are some tips:

- ✔ If you have a multipage handout, your name, corporate logo, and the title of your presentation should be prominently displayed on the first page. On the following pages, your name, address, and phone number should be placed in a header or footer. It's okay to continue plugging your company, but be subtle.

- ✔ Each sheet of paper should be numbered. If they become separated, the person can put the information back together again in the correct sequence.

- ✔ If you're handing out single pieces of paper, place your name, company name, business address, and phone number at the top or bottom of each sheet in your handout. This makes it easy for people to get in touch with you later.

- ✔ If you're the author of a book, make sure that you mention the title on one of the sheets in your handout. (Even if the book is unrelated to the topic at hand, you should still mention it because it increases your credibility.)

Make the Meeting Room Speaker-Friendly

For most of us, the setup of a meeting room isn't something we need to be concerned with very often. But since *Time Management For Dummies* is a reference book that you're going to keep on the shelf for years to come, this section could become very important to you if you should be asked to speak in front of a group of people. (It can also be helpful if you're the person who is responsible for setting up the room for a speaker.)

Whenever you're conducting a business meeting in a conference room or making a presentation to several hundred people in an auditorium, you should do your best to make sure that the conditions of the meeting room meet with your approval. Don't assume that the room will be set up in a way that will be advantageous to your presentation.

The layout of the seating, lighting, and acoustics of the room can have a significant impact on your ability to connect with your audience. If it's done properly, a great presentation will be fabulous, a good presentation will be great, and even a not-so-good presentation will come out okay. But if it's done wrong, even a great presentation can be a flop.

Work with the people who will be setting up your meeting room

Tell the meeting planner or the person who is in charge of setting up the room — several weeks in advance of your presentation — how you want the room set up. Draw diagrams to show the desired layout for the chairs and tables. Provide an itemized list of what you will need in the way of audio or video equipment. After you've had your initial conversation or meeting, confirm everything that was discussed, including any drawings or diagrams you've made for the layout of the room, in writing.

Here's a checklist of things you probably never thought about before that you should discuss whenever you're going to give a presentation:

- ✔ How big is the room? You always want to be close to your audience, so the smaller the room, the better. When you're close to your audience, it's much easier to generate energy, enthusiasm, and excitement.

- ✔ How many chairs should be set up? You never know how many people will actually show up for a presentation, but as a general rule, you should set up 30 percent fewer chairs than the number of people you expect. This will help to guarantee that the front of the room will fill up first and that your audience will be close to you.

- ✔ Have extra chairs available. Have some extra chairs stacked somewhere in the back of the room so that if it becomes necessary to set up additional chairs, they'll be available. Should you need to set up additional chairs, you'll find that this last-minute craziness adds to the energy and excitement in the room and gives everyone the impression that this *is* important because the turnout was so overwhelmingly large that you had to set up more chairs at the last minute.

- ✔ If you find that you're giving your presentation in a room that's got more chairs than people, instruct the people who are in charge of the presentation to ask the people in the audience to sit in the front of the room as they walk into the room, before they've settled comfortably into their chairs.

- ✔ How bright is the room? Make sure that the room is well lit so that you can see the audience clearly and so that they can see you.

- ✔ Does the room have a dimmer? If you will be showing slides or using other audio-visual equipment, make sure that the room has a dimmer so that the people in the audience don't have to take notes in the dark.

✔ Find someone to dim the lights. You don't want to interrupt your presentation, so find someone who will dim the lights when it's time to show your slides or overheads.

✔ If you'll be writing things on a flip chart, ask someone from the audience to come up and write down the information that you dictate. This way, you can continue to focus your attention on your audience. If you'll be doing the writing yourself, write quickly and clearly. And remember to bring your own markers.

✔ Make sure that all your visuals are big enough for everyone to see clearly.

✔ If you want to hang posters or other things on the wall, bring a roll of your own duct tape. To hang a poster, take four 12-inch strips and make each of them into a loop with the sticky side out. Then put a loop on each of the four corners of each poster and stick it to the wall.

✔ Keep the room cool. The temperature of the room is important. If you're expecting a lot of people, keep the meeting room just a little on the cool side, about 68 to 70 degrees, but not so cold that the audience members must put on their coats, scarves, and mittens. If the room becomes too warm, the people in your audience may lose their ability to concentrate and may even start to doze off. (Temperature becomes even more important if you'll be making your presentation just after your audience has eaten a meal.)

✔ What do you see when you look out the window? If the meeting room has a wonderful view, like the hotel's swimming pool, you've got to do something about it. If you can't shut the drapes, find out whether it's possible to change rooms or change the layout of the chairs and tables.

✔ Check out the equipment. Make sure that your equipment works, and make sure you have spare bulbs for your overhead or slide projector. If you'll be using someone else's slide projector, bring along your own 25-foot extension cord for the remote control switch. (And if you *really* want to be prepared for the unexpected, bring along a 100-foot electrical extension cord.)

Setting the Tables (and Chairs)

The closer you are to your audience, the more energy they can absorb from you, and the more you can absorb from them. Traditionally, the seating for a presentation is laid out in rows, like a classroom. Oftentimes, there's even an aisle placed in the center of the rows of chairs. But think about this arrangement for a moment: It's detrimental to the speaker.

When the seats are in rows, the members of the audience are unable to make eye contact with other members of the audience and see how the other people are responding to the presentation. And with an aisle going down the center of the room, directly in front of the speaker, the speaker's audience has effectively been cut in half. When looking straight ahead, the only thing the speaker sees is the back of the room.

Arrange the chairs in a semicircle

As an alternative for arranging the chairs in straight rows, have them arranged in a semicircle, with the speaker almost in the center. This arrangement will allow the audience not only to see the speaker, but to see the other people in the audience as well. It also brings the people who are sitting at the ends of the aisles closer to the speaker. This setup creates a much more intimate and more personal setting.

Arrange tables at an angle

If both tables and chairs are to be set up, they shouldn't be laid out in nice straight rows. The tables should be arranged so that they're at an angle to the speaker. This way, the audience can see both the speaker and the other members of the audience while they're taking notes. To avoid having an aisle going up the center of the room, the tables should be placed so that they're touching at the corners.

Variations on a theme

Now, there are many different ways of laying out a room, and I'm not going to try to address all of them. I just want to get you thinking about different ways in which you can improve the interaction between the audience and the speaker.

I can't stand still!

Do you prefer standing behind a podium or walking around? If you're comfortable standing behind a podium, then the microphone that's attached to the podium should be sufficient. But if you like to walk around, you should be wearing a lavaliere microphone around your neck — one that has a long cord attached to it — or a wireless microphone. If you're wearing a wireless microphone, always have a wired microphone available in the event you start picking up conversations between taxi cabs or landing instructions from a nearby airport.

And don't forget: If you're going to wear a wireless microphone, ask the sound technician to install a fresh battery.

Some Other Miscellaneous Things to Think About

If I haven't given you enough things to think about already, here are a few more:

- ✔ If you'll be using a microphone, double-check the sound quality and room acoustics before you begin your presentation.
- ✔ If there are phones in the room, have them disconnected.
- ✔ If Muzak is playing, have it turned off.
- ✔ If there's a public address system, make sure that no announcements will be made while you're giving your presentation.
- ✔ If you will speaking after a meal has been served, make sure that the people who are catering the meal instruct the waiters and waitresses not to take away dinner dishes after you begin speaking.
- ✔ Check to be sure that there will be no noise emanating from adjacent rooms, the hallway, or other surroundings.
- ✔ Keep water, food, other refreshments, and display materials in the back of the room.

If a meal, soft drinks, or coffee and rolls will be served, you should anticipate that something will go wrong. You may get the wrong food, at the wrong time, in the wrong room. So the day before the meeting is to take place and again on the day of your meeting, verify everything with the person who is in charge of catering your event. If your meeting is scheduled to start at 8:00 a.m., make sure that the caterer understands that you want the coffee and rolls to be there no later than 7:30 a.m.

I know that I've given you a lot of things to think about, maybe more than you ever wanted to know, but many of the things that can interfere with a successful speech or presentation are easily avoidable. And here's one final thought: Always arrive for your presentation at least an hour before you're scheduled to begin speaking. Doing so will give you an opportunity to see how the room has been laid out and to test all the equipment so that you're sure everything works properly.

How Well Did You Do?

After each presentation, critique yourself so that you can do an even better job the next time. Ask yourself questions like these: How high was my energy level? My enthusiasm? How well did I present my information? Did I relate to the audience? What could I have done even better?

Chapter 14
Promote Yourself

● ●

In This Chapter
➤ Collecting letters of reference
➤ Getting yourself quoted in the newspaper
➤ Writing newspaper and magazine articles and *the* book
➤ Promoting yourself through public speaking
➤ Using your business cards
➤ The art of networking

● ●

If you want to get ahead in business, and in life, you've got to sell and promote yourself. You've got to toot your own horn. You've got to tell your colleagues, coworkers, and even your boss when you do something important or noteworthy. And you've got to let your clients, customers, friends, and family know when something good happens to you.

Working hard and doing the right things are the basic building blocks of a successful career. And after you've laid that foundation, you ought to let others know that wonderful things are happening to you.

Collect Testimonial Letters

Every time you do something well, ask the person you did it for to send you a brief note that you can put in your file. When you do something well for a customer or client, ask for a letter. When you do great job on a project or do something very well for one of your company's customers or clients, ask one of your colleagues, coworkers, or even your boss to write you a letter saying what a great job you did. (And don't forget to ask if it would be okay for you to use the letter as a future reference.)

You just never know when these letters could help you in closing a big sale with a future customer or help you land your dream job. To say it plain and simple, letters of recommendation and testimonials from satisfied clients — written on their letterhead — are a great way to promote yourself.

When I started my time-management consulting practice, I asked my satisified customers to write me letters that I could show to people who were considering hiring me to get them organized. Some of those letters were so good that I'm still using them even though they're six or seven years old.

Testimonial letters or letters of recommendation can come from many sources in addition to satisified customers, clients, colleagues, and coworkers. You can also collect letters from your peers within your industry or from members of the professional organizations you belong to. The greater the status of the person writing the letter — the title on the letterhead — the more it helps to build your credibility. Though the person you're showing the letter to may not be familiar with the individual who wrote the letter, the person may know of the company and will certainly be impressed by the letter writer's title or position within the company.

Many years ago, a man asked John D. Rockefeller if he could borrow some money. Rockefeller thought about it for a little while and then decided not to give him a loan. He did, however, offer to do something even better. He said that he would invite the man down to the floor of the New York Stock Exchange and would put his arm on his friend's shoulder as the two of them walked across the trading floor. After the two of them took their stroll, the man was able to borrow the money he needed from someone else. This person felt that anyone who was such a good friend of John D. Rockefeller had to be a good credit risk.

Do you know any celebrities, community leaders, or other famous and important people? If you do, can you get them to write you a letter, send you an autographed photograph, or have your picture taken with them? If so, it'll give the impression to your prospective customers, clients, and anybody else that you yourself are special and important. Here are some tips about getting and using testimonial letters:

- ✔ Just ask people to write a testimonial letter, a letter of recommendation, or a thank you letter in appreciation for the good job you did for them, and they probably will. Oftentimes, the people will feel honored that you asked.

- ✔ After a person has agreed to write a testimonial letter, make a note to yourself to follow up in a week or two. If it hasn't arrived by then, the person has probably forgotten about it and needs a gentle reminder.

✔ If the letter writer is extremely busy, offer to write a sample letter yourself that the person could have typed on his or her own letterhead. This makes writing the letter much easier for the person you've asked, and no one can write as good a testimonial letter about you as you can about you. (If you feel a bit uncomfortable about tooting your horn, that's perfectly natural. Most of us are, but that shouldn't stop you from asking someone to write you a nice letter.)

✔ If you've got some great letters but they're a bit old, just mask out the date the next time you have them reproduced.

✔ When you make up a brochure or flyer, use some of the quotes from your letters.

✔ Have you thought about recording a testimonial on tape? Perhaps your satisfied client would allow you to make a tape recording of the testimonial. You can then put together a collection of these interviews on a single cassette that you can give to prospective clients or customers in the future.

The next time you send out a brochure or other promotional literature, personalize it. Use a colored marker to highlight key phrases, write handwritten notes in the margin, or use sticky notes to direct the reader to specific pages.

Testimonial letters should become an on-going part of your marketing and promotional efforts. With time, you'll have a collection of letters that show that you've done a number of different things well and have been able to help your customers and clients solve many different kinds of problems.

Have You Been Quoted in a Newspaper or Magazine Article?

When you're quoted in the newspaper or are the subject of a magazine article, it adds a great deal to your credibility. If you're quoted or interviewed often enough, you soon become the recognized *expert* on the subject.

Self-promotion really works!

In 1988, I decided that I wanted to write a time-management book, but after thinking about it, I realized that I would need some publicity about myself and my time-management consulting business before a major publisher would take me seriously. It took me several months of trying, but I finally persuaded Bill Gruber, a business columnist for the *Chicago Tribune,* to write a brief, three-inch piece about me. Several weeks later, I got a phone call from Jim Warren, also of the *Tribune,* who wanted to do a more in-depth interview.

All of a sudden, I found that I liked seeing my name in print — it also helped my business — and decided that I would try to get a national newspaper, like the *Wall Street Journal,* the *New York Times,* or *USA Today* to do a story about me. So I started making calls to editors, and I finally spoke to a senior editor at *USA Today,* who asked me, "Are you the guy in Chicago who cleans off desks for $1,000 a person?" When I said, "Yes," she said, "I'll have a reporter call you later this afternoon."

And on January 18, 1989, I was featured, pictures and all, in *USA Today* as "Mr. Neat, the Clutterbuster." Over the next few weeks, I was interviewed by *Newsweek* and some other national magazines, and within three months I had my book contract with Simon & Schuster for my first best-seller *If You Haven't Got the Time to Do It Right, When Will You Find the Time to Do It Over?*

I've now been interviewed by almost every major magazine and newspaper in the country, and I have done more than a thousand radio and television interviews. This publicity, coupled with my having written several best-selling books, has helped me become one of the country's leading authorities on time management.

Here are some tips on how to get the most mileage out of your newspaper and magazine articles:

- ✔ To make a professional-looking reprint of a newspaper or magazine article, cut out the name of the newspaper or magazine from the front page and center it at the top of a piece of white paper. Then cut out the article, center it underneath the publication's name, and photocopy the reprint. (If, after a while, you feel that the article's become dated, just mask out the date the next time you reproduce it.)

- ✔ For greater impact, have your article professionally typeset and then have your publicity reprints printed on a glossy paper. (If you would like to go one step further, have the newspaper or magazine's masthead reproduced in a second color.)

- ✔ To turn a radio or television interview into a publicity piece, bring along a camera and ask someone to take a photograph of you and the host during the interview. And don't forget to ask the host to send you a thank you letter for having been a guest on the program. (Always ask for an audio tape of your radio interviews and a video tape of your television appearances. These could come in handy if you later decide to create a promotional tape. You can also use their quotes on your printed materials.)

Writing, Anyone?

You can develop a great deal of credibility and establish yourself as one of the leading authorities in your chosen field when you write articles for newspapers, magazines, or trade journals. (The money's not very good — you may even do it for free — but the exposure is phenomenal!) Then you can take your printed articles and use them as additional promotional and marketing pieces.

Writing newspaper, magazine, or trade journal articles is one thing, but you can set yourself apart from everybody else when you write "the book." Once you write a book, you're on your way to establishing yourself as the leading authority within your area of expertise. As a published author, you'll receive a great deal of respect from your peers, and there will be a huge increase in your level of credibility. If you were to write several books, you may be able to position yourself as the *ultimate* authority.

Promote Yourself through Public Speaking

Public speaking is an excellent way to promote and market yourself. It gets you in front of potential customers and clients. It gives you credibility and exposure, and after you've done it a few times, you may discover that people are willing to *pay* you to make presentation.

Here are some tips on public speaking:

- ✔ Practice, practice, practice! If you haven't done a lot of speaking in front of groups of people, look for opportunities where you can go out and practice. The more you speak in front of an audience, the easier it gets.

- ✔ Make your first few speeches in front of groups of people where no one in the audience is a client or prospective client. This will give you the opportunity to practice in front of a *live* audience and work most of the bugs out of your presentation. And if you make some mistakes, it doesn't matter because no one in the audience is doing business with you.

- ✔ Watch how you speak. As you prepare for your presentations, rehearse in front of a mirror and try to imagine that you're standing in front of your audience. This way, you can see your facial expressions and watch your body movements.

- ✔ Listen to how you speak. Record your practice sessions so that you can hear what you're saying and how you're saying it.

✔ Listen to how your audience hears you. Bring a cassette recorder or a camcorder to your presentation and record your session. Listening to yourself on audio or watching yourself on video is a wonderful way to improve your presentation skills because you can hear, or see, what you said and how you said it.

✔ Take an acting class. If you would like a bit more practice performing in front of an audience, you might consider trying out for a small part in a community play or enroll in an acting or drama class at your local community college.

✔ Watch how other professional speakers perform. You can learn a lot by watching a pro give a speech. When possible, attend a seminar or borrow, rent, or buy some video tapes. Watch how the pros move on stage, use their voices, and make eye contact with the audience.

✔ Hire a coach. If you're really serious about your speaking, you may want to hire a voice and acting coach to help you improve your presentation style. A good coach can see what you're doing and help you with your diction, body movements, volume, pitch, and timing. You'll find these techniques to be very useful whenever you're making a presentation, whether it's in a client's office or to the company's board of directors. To find a voice coach, you can try calling the drama department of your local high school, college, or university, or maybe one of your local theater companies.

To be, or not to be . . . a speaker

One day, when I was writing my first book, *If You Haven't Got the Time to Do It Right, When Will You Find the Time to Do It Over?,* my editor at Simon and Schuster called to tell me that they were going to send me on a national author's tour. We talked for a few minutes, and afterwards it dawned on me that I didn't have the slightest idea how to conduct myself during a radio, television, or newspaper interview. So I went out and hired a voice and acting coach.

I studied with Leslie Holland, a local actress, once a week for almost a year, and it was one of the best things I ever did. I learned how to speak properly, how to enunciate my words clearly, and, most important of all, how to present myself in front of a television camera. The wonderful thing about this training is that it's helped me in many other areas of my business and personal life.

If you're interested in becoming a professional speaker — yes, people will actually pay you to speak — you may want to contact the National Speakers Association, 1500 South Priest Drive, Tempe, AZ 85281, 602-968-2552.

If you would like to improve your ability to speak in front of a group of people but don't plan to make a career out of it, give Toastmasters International or Dale Carnegie a call. They can be reached at Toastmasters International, P.O. Box 9052, Mission Viejo, CA 92690, 714-858-8255, or Dale Carnegie & Associates, 1475 Franklin Avenue, Garden City, NY 11530, 516-248-5100.

Don't Forget to Pass Out Your Business Cards

To get ahead in business you've got to promote yourself, and one of the best ways you can do it is by passing out business cards. Now a business card offers you several opportunities to promote yourself. When you give someone a card, it gives you the opportunity to talk about yourself, tell the person what you do for a living, and to talk about the goods, products, or services that your company sells.

Don't be shy about giving out your business cards: Give them out liberally. Every time you sit beside someone at a dinner party or a business luncheon, give the person who is sitting next to you a card and say what you do for a living. Pass out cards whenever you're standing in line. You could be waiting to cash a check at the bank or standing in line at a neighborhood cash station. Or maybe you're waiting to pay for your groceries at the supermarket, buying a ticket for the movies, waiting for the gates to open at the ball game, or standing at the ticket counter at the airport. You never know who the people standing next to you are unless you use the opportunity to start talking with them, introduce yourself, hand them a business card, and promote yourself and your business. Here are some additional tips on using business cards:

- When you give potential clients a business card, don't just give them one card: Give out two or three so that they can keep one for themselves and give the others to friends or associates. Business cards are cheap, so give them away every chance you get.

- Whenever you buy something from someone, don't pass up the opportunity to give that person a card and say what you do for a living. This kind of opportunity would include your dry cleaner, your banker, the person who cuts your hair, the person who sells you your clothing, as well as the butcher, the baker, and the candlestick maker.

- To make your business card more impressive, include the mobile phone number for the phone you carry in your briefcase, your car phone number, and your e-mail or Internet address.

Take Other People's Business Cards

As important as it is to give away business cards, it's even more important that you take other people's cards. From my own experience, I've found that many times people wanted to have me help them get organized, but they never got around to calling because my business card was lost and buried in a pile somewhere on the desk. But because I had their cards, I was able to follow up with them.

If there's money to be made from something, it's your responsibility to stay on top of things. You can't sit around waiting for other people to call you because they won't! So when you meet people, give them one of your business cards, and always take one of theirs so that you can follow up with them.

Always carry a pen or pencil and a handful of business cards with you so that you can jot down the name and number of the people you meet, in case they don't happen to have business cards with them. When you get back to the office, add their names to your list of people to call. (If you put the piece of paper with the name and number on it in a pile, it could be weeks before you see it again.)

This is another way that ACT! can help improve your daily productivity. Instead of having another small piece of paper or business card lying on your desk, you just add the person's name to your ACT! database and throw the piece of paper away. Then you can open ACT!'s notepad and write down who this person is, what he or she does for a living, where you met, and why you're going to be calling in two weeks. Then you add that person to your list of people to call. With this system, it's impossible to lose track of someone.

What do you do with your business cards?

How many business cards do you have lying in the lap drawer of your desk? Fifty? A hundred? Two hundred? More? If you're like most people, you've gone to a great deal of effort to meet people and collect their business cards because you thought these people could be of help to you in the future. But what good are these cards if you can't remember who these people are, what they do, where you met them, or why you've bothered to keep their cards in the first place?

This is another way that ACT! can help you become more productive. ACT! is a great place to store the information on your business cards because it gives you an easy way to find the person's name and number when you need it.

If you're really into collecting business cards and don't feel like typing the names, addresses, and phone numbers of hundreds, if not thousands, of business cards into ACT!, you've another alternative. You can scan your business cards with CardScan from Corex Technologies directly into your computer and then transfer the information into ACT!. **CardScan,** Corex Technologies, 233 Harvard Street, Brookline, MA 02146, 800-924-6739.

One day, I was having lunch with a client at a local restaurant when a man came over to our table and asked if I was Jeff Mayer. I said that I was, and he asked whether I was still in the business of helping people get organized. I said, "Yes," and then he asked me to call him. He didn't have a business card in his wallet, so I wrote his name and number on the back of one of mine.

As soon as I got back to my office, I added his name to my ACT! database, and included his name on my list of people to call. It took me almost three weeks before I was able to get him on the telephone so that we could schedule an appointment. But because of ACT!, this business opportunity didn't slip through my fingers.

The Art of Networking

As you go through life, you're going to meet people — lots of people. You're going to meet people at business meetings, at conventions and seminars, and in other business settings. And you're going to meet people in non-business settings as well. You may have a conversation with a person on an airplane, while you're exercising at your local health club, or while you're waiting for a table at a your favorite restaurant on a Saturday night.

And every once in a while, you'll meet someone who could be a potential business contact or someone who could help you with your future career moves. These are the people you should keep in touch with and get to know better. With time, you'll find that you' have lots of things in common and the two of you will become friends.

You should work hard to nurture and cultivate these relationships. Take the time to discover what's important and meaningful to these other people, and you'll eventually know more about them than they know about themselves. That's the secret of developing a close relationship and friendship. Business is built around relationships.

ACT! is designed to enhance your relationships

ACT! will help you further your relationships with the important people in your life. As you get to know other people better, you become friends. And one of the ways you can get to know people better is by asking questions. With the passage of time, you should know everything about them.

You'll be able to answer questions such as the following: What do they do for a living? How did they get into this line of work? What are their long-range goals, dreams, and desires? Where do they live? Are they single, married, or divorced? If they're married, what is the spouse's name? What does he or she do for a living? Where or how did they meet? Do they have children? How old? When are their birthdays? Wedding anniversary? What do they like to do on the weekends? What are their hobbies? What are their kids' hobbies? Where did they go to school? How do they spend their vacations?

Every time you meet with a person or talk on the phone and learn a little bit more about the things that are going on in that person's life, you just make a notation in ACT!'s notepad (see Figure 14-1). The notepad makes life easy because it gives you a convenient place to store lots of miscellaneous information.

One day, I had a business meeting with a potential consulting client, and during the conversation I asked him how his wife was feeling. He said that she was doing much better, and thanked me for asking about her. Then he asked me how I knew his wife had been ill. I told him that his secretary had mentioned that she was in the hospital during a previous phone conversation. What I didn't mention was that I had recorded that information in ACT! and reviewed it just before the meeting. That's how I knew to ask him how she was doing.

Figure 14-1:
ACT!'s
notepad.

ACT!

File   Edit   Font   Size   Style   Format   Spelling   Window   Help

JEFF

Company	Corporate Image Products
Contact	Tom Huffman
Phone	312-555-9665 Ext
Fax Phone	312-123-9876 cc 1
Main Num	

1 of 1

Lookup:
Last Name

Dear	Tom
Address	445 West Washington Street
City	Chicago

Notes for Tom Huffman

2/1/95:   Tom called, he's got three people that he works with that want to get organized. Call Sydney Sharpe, Helen O'Connor, and Ken Short.

11/9/94:   Rec'd bio & faxed it to Kathy Smith

11/8/94:   Tom may want me to help him with some "power tips" for ACT. He'll send me a resume that I can send to Carol Smith about a job opening

11/5/94:   Rec'd $ for consulting services

10/17/94: Left message about Tom's question in the ACT forum on CIS.

Spend your time with the people who are most important to you

There's an old sales and marketing adage called the *80/20 rule,* which states "You get 80 percent of your business from 20 percent of your clients." Said another way: In most businesses, a small number of clients typically generates the majority of the business's sales and profits.

I've heard people talk about this 80/20 rule for many years, and I'm sure that you have too, but there has always been something about it that bothered me. If, in fact, 80 percent of a company's business is coming from just 20 percent of its customers, then wouldn't it make a lot of sense to get to know these people better and minimize the time spent with everyone else? And as you get to know them better, they may be in a position to introduce you to some other people who may be potential clients or customers.

Get to know your friends better

We've all got good friends, people that are important to us, but because life and work are so hectic, we just don't get to spend enough time with them. In today's fast-paced, high-pressure world, you need to spend more time with the people who make you feel better, the people who build you up, the people who stimulate your creative energies. Therefore, I'm going to suggest that you sit down right now and make a list of the 10 business people whose companionship you like and enjoy the most. Figure 14-2 shows an example.

Now that you've made this list, call each of these people and set up a date to have either lunch or dinner together. In the future, you should plan to break bread with at least one of these people every week. As you meet more people, expand your list of "Business People I Like the Most" and have lunch with them regularly.

Once again, this is another way ACT! can keep you organized. When you schedule an activity such as "Call Jim Smith for lunch" — you may remember him from Chapter 3 — you can designate it as a recurring activity. With the click of a button, you can schedule a reminder to call Jim, say, once every other month for the next two years. This way, you won't lose touch with the important people in your life.

I was working with a client one day, and he began telling me about how he had forgotten to call his closest friend, who just happened to be his biggest customer, to wish him a happy 50th birthday. I suggested that we use ACT! to keep this from ever happening again. With ACT!'s recurring activity feature, we were able to enter the person's birthday for the next several years, and then we selected a lead time of 14 days so that the reminder would appear well in advance of the big day.

The Ten Business People I Like the Most

1.

2.

3.

4.

5.

6.

7.

8.

9.

10.

Figure 14-2:
Make a list of the ten business people you like the most.

Chapter 15

Do the Right Things and You'll Get the Right Results

Day after day, I hear people tell me about all the wonderful things they will be doing in the future. They talk, and they talk, and they talk, but when I ask then *how* they plan to do these wonderful things, they give me one of those "I can't believe that you're asking me this question" looks. I'm sure the same thing has happened to you at least once in the last month.

Now, there's a big difference between talking and doing, and there's an even bigger difference between daily activities and overall results. When you focus your energies on your *activities,* you can accomplish the majority of the things you set out to do because it's easy to manage *activities.* On the other hand, you can't manage *results.* Results are the end product; they're the pot of gold at the end of the rainbow. Results come after a lot of hard work and effort. And for many of us, favorable results don't come easy; we've got to work at it.

So instead of focusing on results, it's much more important to sit down and identify which activities need to be done and then go out and do them. And before you know it, you've achieved more than you ever dreamed.

Sweat the Details

Most people hate details. They don't like getting down to the nitty-gritty. They don't like getting down on their hands and knees and getting dirt under their fingernails. They don't want to be *bothered*. Details just get in the way.

But by focusing on the details, you can achieve not only the results you want, but you can usually do it in less time and with less effort. In today's unforgiving business environment, if you don't take the time to work out the details — before you get started on a project — you'll end up working much harder than you have to. The project's going to take longer to complete, and it will cost more than was originally budgeted.

Be smarter than the next guy, or gal

To succeed in today's fast-paced world, simply working hard doesn't cut it. You've got to be smarter and more creative than the next guy, and it's almost impossible to be creative when you're spending all of your time working or putting out fires and very little of your time thinking and planning. When you're able to separate your "thinking and planning" from your "doing," the "doing" becomes much easier.

In American business, "thinking" isn't considered "working." Only when a person's "doing" something is he or she considered to be working. It doesn't matter that the task that being done is busy work, not productive work. At least the person's working!

Do the things that are important

To be successful in today's extremely competitive business environment, you must spend as much time as you can doing the things that are important, the things that will make your company money, and as little time as possible doing the things that keep you busy but hardly productive.

On the wall of my office, I've tacked a small sign that reads, "How much money am I making from my present task?" This subtle reminder helps to keep me focused because it's just too easy to get sidetracked. When I find that I'm doing something that isn't making me any money, I stop doing it and start working on something that will put some money in my pocket.

That's why the Master List and ACT! are such enormous productivity-improving tools. By looking at your Master List or the ACT! Task List throughout the day, it's easy to identify which tasks are important. Then you set aside some time and do them.

A journey of a thousand miles begins with a single step . . . forward

If you want to be able to spend more time thinking, you've got to start looking at your daily activities, not your hoped-for results. You may remember the old Chinese proverb: "A journey of a thousand miles begins with a single step." Over the years, I've often thought about this saying because there was something about it that I was uncomfortable with, and finally I realized what it was. The proverb should be: "A journey of a thousand miles begins with a single step *forward."*

Live in the here and now

It's very easy to look way into the future and dream about all of the things you're going to do and achieve, but to do them successfully, you've got to be focused on the here and now. When you arrive at work in the morning, you should know what you're going to do before you sit down at your desk. If you come into the office and have to ask yourself, "What am I going to do today?" you're already in trouble. Manage your daily activities, and the results will take care of themselves.

Let's play Twenty Questions

A few years ago, I was having a conversation with several people who were career salesmen. (In case you're wondering, all of the people who were participating in this conversation were men. If there had been a woman in the group, I would have used the word *salespeople* in place of the word *salesmen*. And if all of them had been women, I would have used the word *saleswomen* in place of *salesmen*.) I found their conversation to be very interesting because they were always focusing on the end result. Here it was the beginning of January, and they were telling me how many widgets they planned to sell during the coming year.

But when I began to ask them some pointed and direct questions about *how* they planned to go about selling all these widgets, they became very uncomfortable. They began to squirm when I asked questions like: "How many appointments do you have scheduled with prospective widget buyers this month? This week? Today?" "How many people do you plan to call on the phone for the purpose of scheduling an appointment this week? Today? This morning? This afternoon?" "What do you plan to be doing at 9:00 a.m. tomorrow morning?"

And finally I would ask, "Why are you wasting your valuable time talking to me when you should be making a presentation to a prospective widget buyer?" To say the least, they didn't care for the questions I was asking and the conversation ended shortly thereafter.

Set Activity Goals

I don't know about you, but I'm not a long-term goal setter. I'm just a short-term goal setter. If you break things down into their smallest parts, everything becomes easier. Just spend your time and energy doing the right things every day. Set *activity* goals for yourself, not *results* goals, and the results will take care of themselves.

Set goals that are reasonable

Set goals for yourself that are reasonable and well within reach. If you're trying to achieve something that's way beyond your immediate grasp, you're likely to give up long before you' have a chance at achieving your goal. Yes, you should certainly have big dreams, goals, and desires, but if you want to make those dreams come true, you'll have to successfully complete a lot of little dreams along the way. So start by setting modest goals for yourself, ones that are within your grasp, ones that are easy to achieve. Then when your reach that first goal, set another, slightly more difficult goal for yourself.

Look at the goals you set for yourself in the same way that a high jumper approaches the challenge of a jump over the bar. He doesn't get up one morning and decide to jump 7 feet when the best he has ever done is 5 feet 9 inches. This high jumper may dream of clearing 7 feet, but for the time being, the immediate challenge is successfully clearing 5 feet 10 inches. After clearing this height, he can raise the bar another inch, or a fraction thereof, and try again. With each success, the high jumper challenges himself a little bit more and raises the bar higher and higher.

We should be approaching our goals in the same manner. We should be setting goals for ourselves, accomplishing them, and then setting another goal, one that's slightly more difficult. We shouldn't expect to make quantum leaps in our achievements overnight. That's not being realistic. But we should be able to move forward a little bit at a time, day in and day out. And after a while, if we take the time to look at where we are today and compare that with where we were when we started, we'll see that we accomplished more than we ever dreamed.

The winning time in the 1948 Olympic marathon would just be good enough to qualify for this year's Boston Marathon. Over the past 50 years, runners have gotten stronger, faster, and better, but it didn't happen at once; it happened a little bit at a time, over a long period of time.

Give yourself enough time

An important part of goal setting — the one that many people often overlook — is the part that pertains to time. Most people don't give themselves enough time to accomplish their goals. They always think that they can accomplish their goals in a shorter period of time than is reasonable, and then they feel that they failed because they didn't make their self-imposed deadline. In the end, they aren't being fair to themselves, and it's unfortunate. Had they given themselves more time, they could have accomplished their goals with flying colors. But because they're in such a hurry, they shorten their time frames and place an unnecessary burden on themselves. Somehow, they believe that a goal that would normally take a week to accomplish should be completed in a day, and a goal that would take a month to accomplish should be completed in a week.

Here's an example of goal setting that we all can relate to: losing weight. I don't know about you, but I could stand to lose a few pounds, and I know that I would like to lose it immediately. So what would happen if I starved myself for a week? Yes, I would lose my ten pounds, and would probably gain it back within a month, maybe even sooner.

But look how the dynamics of goal setting change when I break my big goal into a lot of little ones. Instead of trying to lose ten pounds as quickly as I can, what would happen if I changed my goal to lose a pound a week? If I lost a pound a week for ten weeks, I will have lost my ten pounds. To make this goal even easier, what if I tried to lose a quarter of a pound every two days? Is that reasonable? You bet! And after I lost the weight, do you think I would regain it? I don't!

Set many short-term goals

The shorter the time frame of your goal, the more real it becomes. It's okay to set long-term or annual goals, but if you want to achieve them, you have to create a plan that breaks them down into smaller and smaller goals. Annual goals should become quarterly goals; quarterly goals should become monthly goals; monthly goals should become weekly goals.

Now don't stop at weekly goals. Break them down even further. Have some fun and play some games with yourself. What is your goal for today? What is your goal for this morning? What is your goal for this afternoon? What is your goal for the next thirty minutes? (After you've broken your larger goals down into very small goals, they should appear to be within your grasp. If they aren't, then maybe you've got to rethink the your entire plan and start over again.) And when you've accomplished your short-term goal, take a moment to pat yourself on the back and congratulate yourself for a job well done, and then keep going.

Write your goals on paper

The most important part of the planning process is to write your goals down on paper so that you can see them. Identifying your goals and then putting them down on paper will take some time, thought, and consideration on your part, but as I've said before, the more time you can spend thinking and planning your course of action, the easier it will be.

When you write down your goals, always remember to date that piece of paper.

Writing your goals on paper serves several purposes. First, it shows that you are committed to accomplishing these goals, and by putting them down on paper, it gives you a point of reference. Now you can compare your progress at any given point in time with your original plan of action.

After you've stated your overall goals, you should keep a copy of them on display, where you and other people — your family, friends, and colleagues — can see them. Tape a copy of your long- and short-term goals on your bathroom mirror so that you can see them every morning and evening. And post a copy of your goals on the wall in your office.

Review your goals regularly

At the end of each week, spend a few minutes reviewing and analyzing your progress during the past week. This information can be very helpful as you plan your activities for the coming week. I would suggest that you do this every Friday afternoon as your work week is slowing down. By doing this on Friday, it will enable you to prepare yourself mentally for the challenges that lie ahead, so when you arrive on Monday morning, you'll know exactly what you need to do, and you'll sit down and do it.

Share your dreams with your friends

Share your goals and dreams with your friends, colleagues, and coworkers, and discuss your plans to achieve them. Many of your friends will have thoughts or ideas that can help you accomplish your goals, and they would certainly like to be kept abreast of your progress.

Maintain a daily record of your activities, and keep a daily list of the things you accomplished. These sheets of paper should be placed in a file folder labeled "Things I Accomplished." When you want to see how far you've actually come, just pull out the file and look at your list of accomplishments.

Chapter 16

A Winning Attitude and Good Work Habits Are the Keys to Success

● ●

In This Chapter

▶ The importance of good work habits

▶ Challenging yourself

▶ Expanding your horizons

▶ Being the best *you* that you can be

▶ Making the most of your time

● ●

I know that a lot of people are looking very hard for the secret of success, but they won't find it in a book, lecture, or seminar. You find success inside yourself. It's your attitude, your perspective on life, your willingness to learn, and your willingness to try new things that will determine your ability to achieve the things you desire. Only *you* can motivate yourself. Other people can show you how to do something, but you've got to do it *yourself.*

You Need Good Work Habits

Many of our work habits were acquired early in our careers, but just because you've done something one way for a long time doesn't mean that you've got to continue doing it the same way in the future.

The proof is in the pudding

Early in my business career, a close friend sat me down and asked me a pointed question. She said, "Jeff, which do you prefer: pleasing habits or pleasing results?" As I pondered her question, I became uncomfortable and started squirming like a worm on the end of a hook. After what seemed like an eternity, I sheepishly said that I preferred pleasing results. From that point on, I started to take a harder look at the things I did, why I did them, and how I did them.

Look at everything you do, and ask yourself, "Why do I do these things this way?" "What would happen if I did them a bit differently?" "Is it possible to streamline my activities and still achieve the same results in less time and with less effort?"

To be successful in today's highly competitive world, it's important that we ask these types of questions more often. And when you become more efficient and effective at work, there's another added benefit: You get to leave the office at a reasonable hour and go home!

Challenge yourself

Look for new mountains to climb and new rivers to cross. Just because you've never done something before doesn't mean that you shouldn't try to do it. Or even if you tried to do something and weren't successful, it doesn't mean that you shouldn't try a second or third time. Don't be afraid of failure.

People who are successful have failed before. (I know that I learn much more from my failures than from my successes.) Learn from your mistakes so that you won't repeat them a second time. Cherish your failures; it makes your successes sweeter and much more rewarding and fulfilling.

When I was younger, I had a wonderful tennis instructor who had a very interesting outlook on the game and on life. He said to me, "Jeff, if you're getting beat, change your game. And if you're still losing, change your game again. In the end, you may still get beat, but lose as many different ways as you can!"

If you haven't experienced failure, you haven't been trying hard enough. When you succeed, relish the fruits of your hard work. When you fail, see failure not as an end in and of itself, but as an opportunity for learning. It gives you the opportunity to look back and to analyze what happened. What did you do right? What did you do wrong? What worked? What didn't? And why? Then go back out and try again.

The only time you must not fail is the last time you try.

Expand your horizons

Do things you never did before.

- ✔ Look for new responsibilities and challenge yourself.
- ✔ Look for new opportunities and don't be afraid to take chances.
- ✔ Look into the future and expand your horizons.
- ✔ Learn about other things that go beyond your present area of expertise.
- ✔ Challenge your mind and imagination.
- ✔ Make decisions. People who hesitate go nowhere.

Take responsibility for the things you do

After you begin to set goals for yourself, you start to accept personal responsibility, and you become accountable for the things you do. When you take responsibility for your actions, you quickly discover who you are, learn what you're made of, and determine what it is that you stand for.

- ✔ When you make a promise, keep it!
- ✔ When you say you're going to do something, do it!
- ✔ When you promise something by a certain date or at a certain time, deliver it!

Surround yourself with people who are successful

If you want to be successful, you've got to think and act like you're successful. Success in business, and in life, is an all-consuming attitude. Successful people set high standards for themselves and have made a commitment to personal excellence in everything that they do.

There are plenty of successful people out there. Go out and search for them. Surround yourself with them. Catch their enthusiasm and let them catch your's. Give yourself the opportunity to share each other's successes.

Work hard and strive to do your best. Try to excel at everything you do.

Be the best you that you can be

Your greatest asset is the fact that you're unique. You are blessed with wonderful skills, talents, and abilities, and no one else has those same skills, talents, and abilities. Therefore, it's important that you work hard to be the best *you* that you can be.

Get a hit when it means something

I've watched a lot of baseball games in my life, as I'm sure you have too, where a ballplayer gets a hit that didn't mean anything. At the moment he hit the ball, the outcome of the game had already been decided.

But what happens when there's pressure: It's the bottom of the ninth, the winning run's on third base, and the game is on the line? How often does the batter come through with that game-winning hit? Not very often. Instead, he'll usually strike out, oftentimes without even taking a swing at the ball. (I'm a Cubs fan, so I've been watching this happen for decades.)

So who do you think is the more valuable player: the one who gets three hits in a game but strikes out when the winning run's on third, or the player who strikes out three times but hits the game-winning single in the bottom of the ninth?

As we go through life, there are always some defining moments and wonderful opportunities that come our way. When one of these moments comes your way, take a big swing, hit the ball, and make the most of it.

Make the most of your time

Now that you've read or skimmed *Time Management For Dummies,* it's time to put some of these wonderful time-management tips, ideas, techniques, and strategies to work. Because this is a reference book, keep it handy so that you can refer to it frequently. There's so much useful information in it that you should look through it every few weeks to see whether you can pick up some additional tips that will help you be a little more productive and efficient in your work.

Your overall objective in learning how to use your time more effectively is to get your work done on time and to do it well. When you've done that, it's time to go home.

With the time you've saved at work, you have more time for yourself. You can spend more time doing the things that you love and enjoy. You can spend more time with your family, friends, and the other people who are important to you. You can see a movie or a play, or watch a ballgame. You can read a book, magazine, or newspaper. You can take a vacation. You've earned it!

Part V
The Part of Tens

The 5th Wave   By Rich Tennant

"IT'S NOT THAT IT DOESN'T WORK AS A COMPUTER, IT JUST WORKS BETTER AS A PAPERWEIGHT."

In this part . . .

Every *Dummies* book has a Part of Tens, and I would guess that my book has more lists of ten than any other book in the IDG Books universe — all at no extra charge. If you happen to be just thumbing through the book, take a look at the next few chapters; they're jam-packed with my best tips, tricks, hints, and suggestions. If you've read the whole book to this point, think of this final part as dessert. So sit back and enjoy.

Chapter 17

Ten Desk Exercises to Stimulate Your Body

- -

In This Chapter

▶ Stretches for your hands and arms

▶ Stretches for the rest of your body

▶ Some info on a better keyboard, mouse, and chair

- -

Are you an office couch potato? Do you come into work, sit down at your desk, and stay there for the rest of the day? Do you take a break for lunch, or do you eat it at your desk? Well, if you do, it's time that you put some movement back into your life.

The human body was designed to move, and we spend too much time sitting at our desks and not enough time moving around. So here are some stretching exercises that will warm up, relax, and stretch the muscles in your hands, fingers, and the rest of your body. And because most of us would like to find ways to make our lives easier, I've included some information about how to automate your keystrokes with macros. If your hands hurt from spending too much time at the computer keyboard, I've got some good news for you: I'm going to tell you about the Kinesis Ergonomic Keyboard and the Kensington Expert Mouse. And if your back hurts, maybe you need a new chair. Steelcase's Criterion chair is a great one.

Be Nice to Your Hands

You probably don't give your hands and fingers much thought, but look at the extensive workout they're getting at your computer's keyboard. For example, if a person spends five hours per day typing at the rate of 60 words (360 keystrokes) per minute, that's 100,000 keystrokes per day, 500,000 keystrokes per week, and 25,000,000 keystrokes per year. Cut it down to 40 words per minute for only three hours per day, and you've still got more than 43,000 keystrokes per day and 215,000 keystrokes per week. In addition, your body isn't moving because you're sitting in the same chair for hours at a time.

To compound the problem, much of this work is done by the little fingers. We use our pinkies to press and hold down the Shift, Ctrl, Alt, Return/Enter, Backspace, and Tab keys. When you type for hours at a time, day after day, the muscles and tendons in the fingers, hands, and arms become susceptible to injury.

So here are a few simple exercises that will help your hands, arms, and fingers stay healthy. Take a few moments to do them several times per day.

- ✔ **Massage your hands.** Gently massage the palms of your hands and fingers for 30 to 60 seconds each.

- ✔ **Stretch your lower forearm.** To stretch the underside of your forearm, turn your palm facing up, and, with your other hand, gently press your fingers away from your body until you feel your muscles begin to stretch. Hold for 5 seconds and then relax. Repeat 3 to 5 times.

- ✔ **Stretch your upper forearm.** To stretch the topside of your forearm, make a fist, and with your other hand, press it toward your body until you feel your muscles begin to stretch. Hold for 5 seconds and then relax. Repeat 3 to 5 times.

- ✔ **Rotate your wrists.** Hold your arms away from your sides and slowly rotate both wrists ten times in each direction as if you were drawing circles with your fingertips.

- ✔ **Stretch your fingers.** Spread the fingers of both hands far apart and hold for 2 seconds, and then make your hands into fists and hold the fists for 2 seconds. Repeat 3 to 5 times.

Give your hands a break from typing at least once every 30 minutes. Shake them for a few moments to get the blood circulating and then switch to another activity that uses the hands differently before you resume typing.

Energize Your Body

The human body was designed to move, so you shouldn't stay seated in that nice comfortable office chair, in the same position at your desk, for hours on end. When you stay seated for too long, your muscles get stiff, you become fatigued, and your productivity goes south. Here are a few exercise that will get your blood flowing again and stretch your tired muscles; within a few minutes, you'll feel refreshed and invigorated.

Do these at least once in the morning and again in the afternoon. And while you're at it, don't forget to take a break. Get up from your desk and stretch your legs at least once every hour.

- **Stretch your whole body.** Stand up, raise your hands above your head, and try to touch the ceiling. For variation, try to touch the ceiling with one hand at a time. Hold the stretch for 5 to 10 seconds. Repeat several times.

- **Stretch your back.** Hold your arms straight out from your sides, and with your palms forward, take a deep breath and push your hands gently backward. Hold the stretch 3 to 5 seconds and exhale. Repeat the stretch 3 to 5 times. This exercise will help you to stand up straight and get rid of your rounded shoulders.

- **Roll your shoulders.** To loosen up your shoulders, stand up and pretend you're swimming the backstroke. First bring one arm backward, and then the other. Repeat 3 to 5 times.

- **Shrug your shoulders.** Slowly lift your shoulders toward your ears, and then roll them backward and down again, making a complete circle. Repeat 3 to 5 times.

- **Squeeze your shoulder blades.** Stand up straight, clasp your hands behind your head, and squeeze your shoulder blades together. Take a deep breath, and, as you exhale, allow your muscles to relax.

- **Stretch your neck.** Straighten and arch your back, sit up straight, and hold your head high. Relax your neck by lifting your head and try to gently touch your right ear to your right shoulder, stretching the muscles on the left side of your neck. Let your head roll down to the center, rest a moment and pick up your head again. Now try to touch your left ear to your left shoulder and let your head roll down to the center; then pick it up. Repeat this 2 or 3 times.

Automate Your Keystrokes with Macros

Because many of the things you do at the keyboard are repetitive, you can use the computer to automate those keystrokes. Keyboard macros — they're like the redial feature on your phone — will make you much more productive because the computer can play back a series of recorded keystrokes much faster than you can type them. And they'll also reduce the wear and tear on your hands and fingers, thereby reducing the possibility of sustaining a hand, finger, or arm injury. See the user's manual of your favorite software applications to learn more about how macros work.

Do Your Hands Hurt? Then Try a Different Keyboard

I spend a lot of time at my computer keyboard, and after a while, my hands, fingers, and forearms begin to ache. Somehow, I don't think that the human body was designed to spend hours on end typing away. So after a few visits to my favorite massage therapist, I decided to try one of those fancy ergonomic keyboards. A few days later, my Kinesis Ergonomic Keyboard arrived in the mail, and after using it for a few days, my hands stopped hurting. I've now written two books with it, and I just love it.

Kinesis's designers have given a lot of thought and consideration as to how the human hand and body relate to the keyboard, and they've done some neat things in their design of the keyboard. (The keyboard looks more like the control panel from the Starship Enterprise than a computer keyboard). Here are some of the things that they did:

✔ The keyboard is divided into two concave wells that are placed six inches apart. This separates the hands, allowing the elbows and arms to rest at shoulder width.

✔ The keys are positioned in a slight arc, instead of in a straight line, which takes into consideration that your fingers are of different lengths — thus conforming the keyboard to the shape of the hand.

✔ They repositioned some of the keys that were formerly pressed with the little finger — the Backspace, Delete, Ctrl, Alt, Home, End, PgUp, PgDn, Return/Enter, and Spacebar keys — and grouped them together in two sets of thumb pads.

✔ They added a foot pedal you can use in place of the Shift key, and they include a little bit of memory in the keyboard so that you can record keyboard macros and save yourself the time and effort of retyping the same words or program commands over and over and over.

If you've been experiencing finger, hand, or arm discomfort, the Kinesis Ergonomic Keyboard (shown in Figure 17-1) is certainly worth trying. **Kinesis Ergonomic Keyboard.** Kinesis Corporation, 915 118th Avenue Southeast, Bellevue, WA 98005, 800-454-6374.

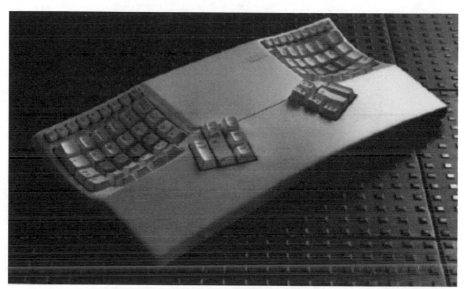

Figure 17-1:
The Kinesis
Ergonomic
Keyboard.

Tired of Mousing? Get a Trackball

If you would like an alternative to using a mouse, you should try Kensington's Expert Mouse trackball. Its ergonomic design offers you maximum mousing comfort while at the same time giving you precision control over your cursor's movement. And because a trackball remains stationary — you only move the ball, not the entire device — it doesn't take up much desktop space.

The Expert Mouse's large trackball — almost the size of a billiard ball — is easily controlled by your fingertips and offers very smooth cursor movement. The buttons, which are placed symmetrically on each side of the ball, have a light, easy-to-press feel and accommodate both left- and right-handed users. The real beauty of the Expert Mouse is in the software. It has several user-programmable functions that give you the ability to adjust and modify how the cursor responds to the movement of the trackball.

✔ **Custom Acceleration.** The Custom Acceleration feature enables you to adjust the cursor acceleration, which is the speed at which your cursor moves in relation to how far and how quickly you move the trackball.

✔ **Brilliant Cursor.** With a single click of a trackball button, your cursor will jump to different, predefined points, or *hot spots,* on your screen.

✔ **Slow Cursor.** The Slow Cursor feature gives you ultra-precise, pixel-by-pixel control over your cursor's movements. This feature is especially useful for placing graphics, drawings, or page layouts in exact locations on your screen.

One evening, my trackball stopped working. I called tech support, told them what happened, and they said that they would send out a replacement (it has a 5 year warranty). The next morning it arrived by Federal Express.

I've been using the Expert Mouse for years. It's easy to use; it's easy on my hands, arms, and fingers; and it helps me be more productive. **Expert Mouse.** Kensington Microware Limited, 2855 Campus Drive, San Mateo, CA 94403, 800-535-4242.

Does Your Back Hurt? Then Get a New Chair

If you're spending a lot of time sitting at your desk, you should be sitting in a chair that gives proper support of your back, neck, shoulders, and arms. These are some of the features you should look for in a chair:

- ✔ The seat height should be adjustable upward and downward.
- ✔ The back rest should be adjustable up and down and fit the curve of your lower back.
- ✔ The seat cushion should have a slight forward slope so that it doesn't dig into the back of your legs.
- ✔ The height of the arm rests should be adjustable so that they support your arms while you're typing.
- ✔ The chair should swivel left and right, tilt forward and backward, and roll on casters.

The Criterion chair, by Steelcase, is by far the most comfortable office chair I have ever used. I've been sitting in it for almost two years now — eight to ten hours per day — and I would be in *big* trouble without it. It's comfortable and well designed, and it provides proper support for my back and my arms. It would be impossible for me to spend so many hours sitting in front of my computer in a chair that wasn't as comfortable as the Criterion.

Steelcase has included every possible adjustment imaginable in its chair. The chair goes up and down, swivels left and right, and is supported on five casters. For maximum comfort, the back support can be adjusted up and down, and the seat pan can be tilted forward and backward. The feature that I like the most are the individually adjustable arm rests. They allow your hands to *float* over the keyboard, instead of resting on it. **Criterion Chairs.** Steelcase Inc., Grand Rapids, MI 49501. Criterion chairs come with either a high or a mid back. The arm rests are optional. For a catalog and a current price list, call 800-333-9939.

Chapter 18

Ten Computer Programs That Will Save You Time

▶ Lots o' software and other stuff to buy for your computer

*B*ecause this is a book about time management, and I'm a time-management expert, I think it is appropriate to tell you about some of the computer programs that I use to save me time and help me be more productive. (I know that I'm not supposed to be writing in the first person, but these are the programs that help me, and I'm sure that they'll help you.)

WordPerfect

I've been using WordPerfect products for years, and I think they're great! I wrote my first three books with WordPerfect 5.1 for DOS, and this book was written with WordPerfect 6.1 for Windows. The productivity-improving features in WordPerfect 6.1 enable me to spend all of my time and energy writing. I don't have to be concerned with the layout or format of the text because WordPerfect does it for me. WordPerfect 6.1 for Windows has increased my writing efficiency by at least 50 percent over WordPerfect 5.1 for DOS. **WordPerfect 6.1 for Windows.** WordPerfect Novell Applications Group, 1555 N. Technology Way, Orem, UT 84957, 800-451-5151.

ACT!

ACT! runs my life. It's the first computer program I turn on in the morning and the last one I turn off in the evening. By using it, I have been able to automate all of my follow-up tasks — my calls, meetings, and to-dos — and it has improved my daily productivity three- or fourfold. (Somehow I think you already know that I like ACT! I'm even writing *ACT! For Dummies,* which will be out in the summer of 1995.) **ACT!** Symantec Corporation, 10201 Torre Avenue, Cupertino, CA 95014, 800-441-7234.

Quicken

Quicken has enabled me to automate all of my financial record keeping. It keeps track of my bank balances, it prints my checks, it categorizes all of my financial transactions (my tax preparation costs have gone down by more than 50 percent), and it helps me stay on top of all my saving and investment programs. For many people, Quicken has been a reason to go out and buy a computer, and I heartily agree. **Quicken.** Intuit, P.O. Box 3014, Menlo Park, CA 94026, 800-624-6095.

WordPerfect Presentations

WordPerfect Presentations is an easy-to-use graphics and drawing program. I use it to create and design charts, graphs, drawings, and illustrations that are used in my slide shows, overhead transparencies, and handouts. I even used WordPerfect Presentations to create the screen shots of the computer programs that were used throughout this book. **WordPerfect Presentations.** WordPerfect Novell Applications Group, 1555 N. Technology Way, Orem, UT 84957, 800-451-5151.

UnInstaller

Removing old or unused programs from Windows can be a bit tricky because these programs put references to themselves all over the place. They may create .INI files for themselves (don't ask me what an .INI file is because I don't know) and add a few lines about the program in some file named SYSTEM.INI or WIN.INI (files that are needed to run Windows, but no one has been able to adequately explain to me what they are, why they're there, or what they do).

Microhelp's UnInstaller removes the program's files, searches your computer's entire hard drive looking for all these miscellaneous .INI things, and then gives you the opportunity to delete them, one at a time. UnInstaller is a great utility program. **UnInstaller.** MicroHelp, Inc., 439 Shallowford Industrial Parkway, Marietta, GA 30066, 800-922-3383.

Norton Backup and the Colorado Jumbo Tape Drive

Five years ago, it was easy to back up your hard drive onto floppy disks. But how do you back up a 250MB, 500MB, or 1000MB (1 *gigabyte!*) drive? The only way you can do it is with a cassette tape drive and backup software.

I've found the Norton Backup software and the Colorado Backup Tape Drive to be a great combination. I've automated the whole process, and it's made my life quite easy. Every afternoon at 6:00 p.m., the backup program automatically turns itself on and backs up all the files that have changed since my last full backup. About once a week, I do a full backup of my entire hard drive.

If you're not backing up your computer on a regular basis, you're taking an unnecessary risk because sooner or later, something bad is going to happen and you're going to lose some, or all, of your data. It's happened to me more than once, and Norton Backup has been both a lifesaver and a huge time-saver.

Norton Backup. Symantec Corporation, 10201 Torre Avenue, Cupertino, CA 95014, 800-441-7234. **Jumbo Tape Backup System.** Colorado Memory Systems, Inc., 800 S. Taft Avenue, Loveland, CO 80537, 800-451-4523. Colorado Memory Systems makes many different sizes and types of tape drives.

Norton Utilities

And speaking of lifesavers, I think everyone should have a copy of Norton Utilities. Norton Utilities is a collection of utility programs that are designed to keep your computer's disk drive in tip-top shape. If there's a problem, Norton Utilities has a utility that can fix it, and if you were to lose some information as a result of that problem, there's a Restore Utility that's designed to recover damaged Lotus 1-2-3, Symphony, Excel, Quattro Pro, dBASE, and WordPerfect files. **Norton Utilities.** Symantec Corporation, 10201 Torre Avenue, Cupertino, CA 95014, 800-441-7234.

Seiko Smart Label Printer Pro

How do you print a single label? Good question, isn't it? Somehow, I don't think that laser printers were designed to print a single label. And typing a label on one of those old fashioned things — an electric typewriter — was always a time-consuming task.

But printing a label with the Seiko Smart Label Printer Pro is easy. The SLP Printer Pro attaches to the serial port of your computer and prints labels from a roll, one at a time, instead of from a sheet. Seiko has even developed software that searches for the address in your letter and then automatically prints the label, with bar codes, for you. What could be easier? I use mine every day and find that it's a great productivity-improvement tool. Now it's time to get rid of that old typewriter. **Smart Label Printer Pro.** Seiko Instruments USA Inc., 1130 Ringwood Court, San Jose, CA 95131, 800-888-0817.

Bootcon

This may be a little technical, but please forgive me because it's important. You may not be aware of this, but when you turn on your computer, you load a lot of different *device drivers* — little programs that run devices such as your sound card, CD-ROM drive, flatbed scanner, hand-held scanner, and lots of other miscellaneous things — into your computer's memory. Now, this is OK if you're using the sound card, CD-ROM, and all those other things all the time. But if you're not, you're wasting valuable system resources, which can cause your whole system to run slower. That's where Bootcon comes in.

Bootcon is a utility program that enables you to select different system configurations so that you can decide which device drivers and other things you want to load into memory when you turn on your computer. **Bootcon.** Modular Software Systems, 25825 104th Avenue SE, Suite 208, Kent, WA 98031, 800-438-3930.

SuperPrint

I don't know how you feel about this, but I think it's a waste of time to be sitting at a computer and not be able to use it. This happens to me every time I print a document with the Windows print manager. After the print manager starts sending information to the printer, it takes control of the computer and won't give it back. In the mean time, I've got nothing to do except sit there, twiddle my thumbs, and feel frustrated. With Zenographics's SuperPrint, I don't have to sit and wait any more. I can continue working while SuperPrint prints.

After I press the print button, SuperPrint collects all the information that my printer needs in just a few moments. It then returns control of my computer to me so that I can continue working while it sends the printing information to the printer — *really* in the background. **SuperPrint.** Zenographics, 4 Executive Circle, Irvine, CA 92714, 800-566-7468.

Winfax Pro

One of the biggest timesaving and productivity-improving inventions in the last decade has been the fax machine. And although fax machines have made it possible to send and receive information in an instant, most of us still follow a cumbersome procedure: We print hard copies of that letter or document that we just created in the computer. Then we walk to the fax machine, insert the document into the paper feeder, and send the fax. This assumes that the machine isn't already in use. If it is, we wait.

And what happens when someone sends *you* a fax? Unless the machine is nearby, you have no way of knowing whether a fax has been received, so it may sit there for hours before you get it.

With Winfax Pro, you can send and receive all your faxes directly from your computer without ever touching a piece of paper. There's no more walking back and forth to the fax machine; no more standing in line waiting for the machine to become available; and no more greasy, curly paper to deal with. And best of all, when you receive a fax, you're notified instantly and can review it on-screen or print it. If you send a lot of faxes, Winfax Pro can save you a lot of time. **Winfax Pro.** Delrina Technology Inc., 6830 Via Del Oro, San Jose, CA 95119, 800-268-6082.

HyperACCESS

If you need communications software, Hilgraeve's HyperACCESS is very easy to use. It makes the process of transferring information from your computer to someone else's a breeze, and it supports hundreds of modems. And its virus-detection program prevents viruses from entering your computer as you're downloading files. **HyperACCESS.** Hilgraeve, Inc., 111 Conant Avenue, Monroe, MI 48161, 800-826-2760.

Protect your computer from viruses

Do you do any of the following:

✔ Do you ever download programs from private bulletin board services (BBSs)?

✔ Do you ever copy files from other systems by using floppy disks?

✔ Are you hooked up to a local-area network (LAN)?

If you answered "Yes" to any of these questions, your computer could easily become infected with a computer virus.

What is a computer virus? It's an infectious computer program that makes your computer do weird things. Some viruses are nothing more than mere annoyances that display cute, or not-so-cute, messages. Others can be very destructive. They lie in wait until a particular date, and then they go on a rampage and destroy files. Sometimes they will erase the entire contents of a person's hard drive.

To keep your system free of viruses, there are a handful of things you should do:

✔ Back up your files regularly. (If your computer is infected with a virus, you must remember to disinfect the restored files.)

✔ Never boot your computer with a floppy disk that you haven't scanned and disinfected first. (When you scan your computer with an anti-virus program, you search your computer's memory and program files for viruses. If a virus is found, the anti-virus program will removed the virus from your computer.)

✔ Always disinfect every file you download from a BBS, copy from a floppy disk, or copy from a network drive — before running it on your computer.

✔ Install an anti-virus program, like Norton Antivirus, and use the memory-resident virus-spotting portion of the program at all times.

Norton Antivirus scans your files and your directories whenever your computer is turned on. It can also scan each floppy disk for viruses before files are copied onto your computer. Should a virus be detected, Norton AntiVirus can quickly repair infected files. **Norton AntiVirus.** Symantec Corporation, 10201 Torre Avenue, Cupertino, CA 95014, 800-441-7234.

Chapter 19

Ten Tips for Out-of-Town Travel

. . . .

In This Chapter

▶ Several ways to make traveling easier

. . . .

*T*raveling today is a real pain in the butt. I don't care what the airlines say, all we ever do is sit and wait, and wait, and wait. We wait to board the plane. We wait for it to leave the gate. We wait for it to take off. We wait for it to land, And if we don't carry everything we own with us, we wait for our luggage. The following travel tips should help to reduce the stress and strain of airplane travel:

- ✔ When you're traveling, expect to encounter delays in your air travel plans. Planes are always delayed because of mechanical problems, the weather, or lots of other things that the airlines never tell us about. So prepare for those delays by bringing additional work that you can do on the plane and a list of people to call if you're stuck in the airport. And in case you need to take a break, bring along some magazines, a good book, and your Walkman with your favorite audio cassette.

- ✔ Traffic to the airport is always a bear, especially when you're running late, so always leave yourself some extra commuting time. If you're driving — as opposed to taking public transportation, a taxi, or limo — and you are unfamiliar with the local roads, allow yourself a bit more time because you could get lost.

- ✔ If you're going to leave your car in an airport parking lot, allow extra time to find a parking spot (most of the airports are short of parking). Public transportation, a taxi, or a limo may be an attractive alternative. If you frequently use the same car rental company, you may be able to leave your car in the rental company's parking lot and take their courtesy van to and from the terminal.

- ✔ After you get inside the terminal, anticipate delays at security checkpoints and passenger check-ins. Infrequent fliers always hold up the line.

- ✔ Always arrive at your gate at least 20 minutes before the scheduled departure. If you don't, the airline can bump you and give your seat to someone else, without providing any compensation. (It's a common practice for airlines to overbook their available seats.)

- ✔ When selecting a seat, don't sit in a first-row (bulkhead) seat. Parents traveling with infants are usually seated there. An exit row may be a better option and usually offers more leg room.

- ✔ Always be one of the first people to board the plane. This will guarantee that you'll be able to store your carry-on luggage in one of the overhead bins. Then you can settle in your seat and start working while the latecomers are trying to find a place to put their bags.

- ✔ If you're hungry, bring your own food and beverage. Most airlines are cutting back on their in-flight meals (which weren't very good in the first place) and are only offering peanuts and soft drinks. (If you want to have some fun with the flight attendants, stop at a deli on your way to the airport and pick up a nice fat sandwich; it makes them go crazy.)

- ✔ If you need to confirm the time of an arriving or departing flight, call your airline's automated flight arrival and departure lines for estimated times instead of waiting for a reservations agent.

- ✔ If you know you're going to need a rental car, always call in advance and make a reservation. If you're going to be arriving late, call the car rental company, from the airplane if necessary, to let them know that you're still coming.

If you're tired of listening to annoying and distracting noises while you're flying, try Noise Cancellation Technologies' NoiseBuster. NoiseBuster's "anti-noisewave" technology blocks out the constant drone of the airplane's engines and lots of other unwanted sounds — like screaming children — and enables you to concentrate on your work and hear yourself think. I use NoiseBuster whenever I fly and find that I actually feel relaxed and refreshed after my flight. **NoiseBuster.** Noise Cancellation Technologies, Inc., 800 Summer Street, Stamford, CT 06901, 800-278-3526.

Chapter 20

Ten Tips for Traveling with Your Computer

In This Chapter

▶ Ways to make your computer a tool and not just excess baggage

I know that computers are great, and you can do some amazing things with those three- or four- pound notebooks. But they aren't much good if they run out of juice or you can't connect them to the hotel's telephone. So when you're traveling with a computer, think about your communication needs *before* you leave for the airport. Here are some tips:

- ✔ When you make your hotel reservation, request a modem-ready room. (Most of the major hotel chains have installed modem-ready telephones.)

- ✔ Make sure that your laptop is fully charged when you arrive at the airport. Security personnel may ask you to turn it on to verify that it's a real computer.

- ✔ Always bring along a fully charged replacement battery so that you can continue working after the first one runs out of energy.

- ✔ If you're carrying a brand new, super-duper, fancy-schmancy computer, don't flaunt it. Store it in a plain but sturdy briefcase or traveling bag. This way, it won't be a tempting target for thieves.

- ✔ Bring along a collection of extension cords so that you can use your portable computer comfortably in your hotel room. This would include an extension power cord, an extension phone line cord, and extra in-line and duplex phone jacks. (When you check out in the morning, don't forget to pack everything up and take it with you.)

- ✔ Always travel with a screwdriver and a pocket knife so that you can remove wall plates and strip insulation from phone wires, if necessary. If you really want to be prepared, bring along an acoustic coupler to attach to your phone, alligator clips to attach your modem to phone wires, and a line tester to locate live phone wires.

> ✔ When traveling overseas, check your computer's power adapter. Make sure it can accommodate 110/120 and 220/240 voltages and line frequencies of 50/60 Hz because different voltages are used in different countries. Don't forget to bring along power adapter plugs that fit the electrical outlets of the countries you'll be visiting. An assortment of electrical wall plugs can be found at most computer stores.

I'm a big fan of CompuServe, and here are some ways that CompuServe can help you when you're traveling.

> ✔ If you're in your hotel room and need to print a document, just use CompuServe. If you have faxing software, you can send yourself a fax to the hotel's fax machine. And if you don't, you can send yourself an e-mail message, but instead of sending it as e-mail, send it as a fax to the hotel's fax machine. Then go down to the front desk to pick it up.
>
> ✔ If you need to send a fax back to your office or to someone else, you can use CompuServe instead of the hotel's faxing services. It's much cheaper and will not include any of the hotel's long-distance phone charges.

If you do a lot of international traveling and you're not already a member of CompuServe, you should consider joining. CompuServe is the most international of all the major on-line services and can be reached by a local call in more than 700 cities around the world. **CompuServe.** 5000 Arlington Centre Blvd., Columbus, OH 43220, 800-848-8990. (If you're already a CompuServe member, you can get a list of all of the local access numbers for thousands of locations in the United States, Canada, and countries around the world by typing **GO PHONES.**)

A friend told me that when he was vacationing in Australia, he used CompuServe to send his daughter a fax each day (she is not a CompuServe member so he couldn't send her e-mail). The cost of sending the fax from Australia to the United States was under $1.

Chapter 21

Ten Tips for a Top-Notch Filing System

In This Chapter

▶ Info to help you keep your documents in order

Because my specialty is helping people organize their papers and set up their filing systems, I would be remiss if I didn't include a section on how to set up an easy-to-use filing system. The following tips were taken from my best-selling book, *If You Haven't Got the Time to Do It Right, When Will You Find the Time to Do It Over?*

Use File Folders

Instead of leaving letters, memos, reports, and other papers lying on the top of your desk, put them in file folders. Remember, though, that with time, a folder will get beat up, dog eared, and dirty. When it does, you should replace it. Don't waste your valuable time trying to reuse an old, beat-up file folder that only costs a nickel.

Collate Your File Folders

To make it easy to see the labels on your folders, collate them — left, center, and right — so that you can see three labels at once.

If you have a lot of alphabetical files, make the tabs mean something to you. I like using the $1/3$ cut files, files that have tabs in three positions: left, center, and right. If you set up your filing system in this manner, it makes pulling files from the drawer and refiling them much easier: Put the letters of the alphabet on the file tabs in this order:

Left	Center	Right
A	B	C
D	E	F
G	H, I	J
K	L	M
N	O	P, Q
R	S	T
U, V	W	X, Y, Z

Label Your Files

Always put a label on your files. If you don't, you won't know what's inside them.

Write Your File Labels by Hand

Keep a supply of file folders in your desk drawer, and when you need one, just pull it out and write the label with a fine-tipped pen (pencils smudge and soon become illegible). Don't waste your valuable time trying to type a gummed label with a typewriter.

If you *do* want typed labels, you should go out and purchase a Seiko Smart Label Printer PRO. The SLP Printer Pro attaches to the serial port of your computer and prints labels from a roll, one at a time, instead of from a sheet. I use mine everyday and find that it's a great productivity-improvement tool. **Seiko Smart Label Printer PRO.** Seiko Instruments USA Inc., 1130 Ringwood Court, San Jose, CA 95131, 800-888-0817.

File Labels Should Read Like the Telephone Directory

When you're writing labels for the names of people, they should be written just like you see them in the telephone directory: last name, first name, middle initial.

Get Rid of Your Hanging Folders

Many people use *hanging* folders to keep their manila folders from falling over. In theory, this system is OK, but in practice, it just doesn't work because the hanging folders themselves can take up to a third of the space in an empty drawer. If you find that your file drawers are filled beyond capacity, get rid of the hanging folders and replace them with expandable file pockets.

Use Expandable File Pockets

As an alternative to hanging folders, use expandable file pockets (also called accordion files). I like the pockets that expand to 3 inches. You put the file folders inside the file pockets and put the pockets into your file drawers. They stand up all by themselves.

Organize Your Files

Files that you use all the time should be placed at the front of the drawer so that they're easy to get to. Files you use less frequently can be placed behind them. Other files that you need to keep, but won't look at very often, should be placed in the drawers of your credenza, in other filing cabinets in the office, or in permanent, off-site storage.

Work from Your File Folders

After you set up your filing system, you should get into the habit of working from files so that you can have facts at your fingertips, instead of having to rely on your memory.

The 5th Wave

By Rich Tennant

"Miss Lamont, I'm filling the congregation database under 'SOULS', my sermons under 'GRACE', and the financial contribution spreadsheet under 'AMEN'."

Chapter 22
Ten Tips for Organizing Your Hard Drive

* *

In This Chapter

▶ Ways to keep your hard drive nice and neat

* *

*I*n the last chapter, I gave you some tips on how to organize your files. Now I want to give you some tips on how to organize your hard drive. One of the biggest problems everyone has in working within the DOS and Windows operating environments comes from the system's inability to accept file names that mean something. With DOS, you're limited to an eight-character file name with a three-character extension.

A note for Mac users: You Mac people have it easy. You don't have to worry about file name extensions or eight-character file name limitations. In addition, creating a new folder (or directory, in old-fashioned DOS speak) is as easy as choosing the New Folder command from the File menu in the Finder. Throughout the rest of this chapter, I use DOS/Windows terminology, but you can still pick up a few helpful tips (and see how most of the world has to wrestle with an operating system that's somewhat less elegant than the Mac's). Just remember that a dirtectory is the same as a folder, and most of this chapter will make sense to you.

A Hard Drive Is an Electronic Filing Cabinet

From my perspective, a hard drive is nothing more than an electronic filing cabinet, and I would like to begin by telling you some of the things that you *shouldn't* do, because if you don't organize your computer files, you'll eventually be working in chaos.

Don't put all of your files in your computer's root (C:\ ) directory

In no time at all, you'll have so many files that you won't know what files are there or which programs they belong to.

Don't store your document files with your program files

Don't store your document files in the same directory as your operating system or program files, such as WordPerfect, Lotus 1-2-3, Quicken, ACT!, and so on. If you store files in this manner, you're flirting with disaster. It's too easy to accidentally delete a program or system file because you thought it was an old letter or memo you no longer needed. (How did you know that a file with a *.BAT, *.COM, *.EXE, or *.DLL extension was important?) After you delete such a file, you'll find that your word processor or even your computer won't run — and you won't have the slightest idea why.

Don't make your root directory (C:\ ) your default directory

The default directory is the directory in which every file is automatically saved. Your root directory should be reserved for your program and working file directories and the handful of files that are needed to make your computer run, like the CONFIG.SYS and AUTOEXEC.BAT files. (If you want to know more about AUTOEXEC.BAT and CONFIG.SYS files, pick up the latest edition of *DOS For Dummies*.)

Set Up Separate Directories

I'm also not a big fan of using three character extensions as a method of trying to identify different types of files. For example, many people use extensions such as *.DOC for documents, *.PRO for proposals, *.MEM for memo, and so on. But they're doing this because they've *dumped* everything into one directory.

I think it makes much more sense to set up separate directories and subdirectories that can be used to store similar types of information. When you set up your directories in a logical, systematic manner, you'll save yourself hours of time in the future.

If, for example, you've got a big client who generates a lot of correspondence, set up a separate directory for this person or firm and don't mix these files with any other files. Give the directory a name like BIG_CLNT. Now you'll probably have different kinds of files for this client, so you should have additional directories — that is, subdirectories — named LETTERS, PROPOSAL, SPRD_SHT, or any other topic or category that you feel would be appropriate (see Figure 22-1).

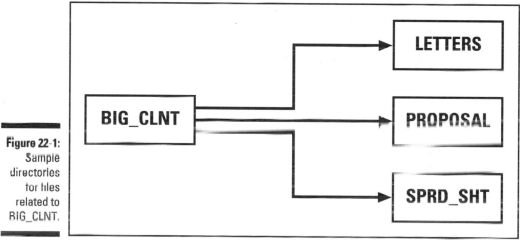

Figure 22-1:
Sample
directories
for files
related to
BIG_CLNT.

Give your files a name that means something. Don't name your files by the creation date. How will you know what's in a file with a name like C:\LETTERS\01-07.DOC? Wouldn't it make more sense to give it a name like C:\LETTERS\SALESCON for a document that was written concerning a sales contract? Or if you have different versions of the contract, start numbering them by using the three character extension: SALESCON.1, SALESCON.2. With this method of organizing and naming your directories and files, you'll be able to locate your files in a matter of moments.

To continue with this example, if you send correspondence to several people on a regular basis, why not create separate "sub-subdirectories" to store their correspondence? As shown in Figure 22-2, if you regularly send letters to John, Sue, and Bill, create separate subdirectories under the LETTERS subdirectory. This way, you can keep all your correspondence organized.

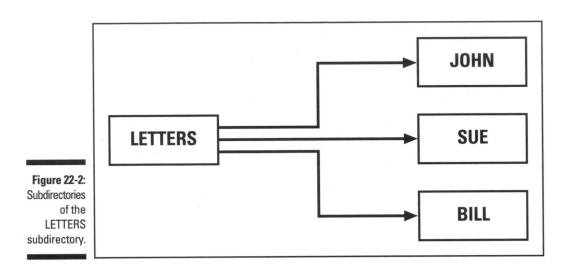

Figure 22-2:
Subdirectories
of the
LETTERS
subdirectory.

When a directory begins to get too large — more than 30 or 40 files — start looking for files that relate to each other or that can be grouped together. Then create a new subdirectory and move those files into it. This way, it's easy to manage your files.

Chapter 23

Ten Ways to Increase Your Computer's Performance

. . . .

In This Chapter

▶ Stuff that will make life with your computer easier

. . . .

*E*very morning, I look at the newspaper and see that the prices for new computers keep on dropping. When I bought my first word processor — a dedicated word processor, not a computer — it cost me almost $2,000, plus another $500 for a sheet feeder. (Yes, that's right.) And that was only in 1988. (I bought my first computer in 1990.) Today, you can buy a Pentium computer with a monitor and a printer for $2,500.

Now don't get nervous. I'm not writing this chapter because I think you should go out and purchase a new computer this very minute. (In the *next* chapter, I'll tell you what bells and whistles I think you should have on your next computer). I'm writing this chapter because there are a lot of things you can do with your present machine to improve it's performance without having to replace it. At some point, you *will* have to replace it, but you may be able to put off the new purchase for a year, and by then, computers will be even cheaper. (If you're wondering why I'm including a chapter on computers in a time-management book, the answer is easy: When you're sitting at your computer and nothing's happening, you're wasting time. And since time is money, you should get the most out of your computer.)

Some of the things I mention in the next few pages are a bit technical. If you're not familiar with the insides and inner workings of a computer, don't try to do any of these things yourself. Just invite your favorite computer guru over for dinner, and then casually ask him or her to help you with a *little* project.

If You're Still Using a 286 or 386, It's Time to Replace It!

OK, I lied. You should get nervous, because if you're still using an old 286 or a not-quite-so-old 386 computer, there's no point in your reading this chapter any further. Your machine is too old to be saved. It just doesn't have the horse-power to take you through the nineties. It's like driving a 1969 Volkswagen, or maybe a 1974 Volkswagen. It may take you where you want to go, but then again, it may not make it. I suggest you immediately turn to the next chapter and read the discussion of what you should look for in a new computer.

Get a Memory Manager

This suggestion is easy: You can do it on almost any PC, and you don't have to take the machine apart. You just install some new software. No matter how much RAM — 4MB, 8MB, 16MB — you have in your computer, a memory manager will improve its performance. (RAM is the stuff that lets you run your word processor, spreadsheet programs, and everything else.) It's only the first 1024K of memory, also called the first megabyte, that's used to run your computer. (This goes back to the original design of the personal computer.) Of this first megabyte of memory, conventional memory takes up the first 640K, and high memory takes up the balance, 384K.

Conventional memory is important because all your important software — your word processor, spreadsheet, solitaire, minesweeper, and so on — run in conventional memory. And when you have more conventional memory available, your programs run better.

Without going into all the gory details, a memory manager takes all the miscellaneous things that your computer had been placing in conventional memory, things that had been using up a good chunk of that 640K, and puts them in high memory. This way, you have more memory for your programs. Quarterdeck Office System's QEMM (QEMM is an an acronym for Quarterdeck Expanded Memory Manager) makes a very powerful memory manager. When I first installed QEMM, several years ago, I was able to increase my available conventional memory from 543K to 619K, an increase of 13 percent. I recently installed Quarterdeck's most recent version and increased my available conventional memory to 634K. Now I'm able to allocate more than 99 percent of my available memory for my software. **QEMM.** Quarterdeck Office Systems, 150 Pico Blvd., Santa Monica, CA 90405, 800-354-3222.

Double the Capacity of Your Hard Drive

There was a time when a 40MB hard drive was sufficient to hold all of your programs. Today, *suites* — packages of programs that often include a word processor, spreadsheet, database, and graphics program — take more than 40MB all by themselves. And with software developers continuing to add more bells and whistles to their programs with each product upgrade, it's easy to run out of disk storage space.

If you're running out of storage space on your hard drive, you do have an alternative if you're not ready to replace your hard drive. You can install a data-compression program that will effectively double the capacity of your hard drive.

A data-compression program does something really neat: It's able to shrink the size of your files. As a general rule, you can compress word processing files to about half their original size. Database and spreadsheet files compress even more. Program files don't compress very much.

After you've compressed your disk drive, you still use your computer just as you did before. When you open a file, the data is decompressed and expands back to its original size for use within your program. When you save the file, it's automatically recompressed to save space. It all happens so quickly that you aren't aware that anything's happening. The only thing you do notice is that you can store twice as much data on your hard drive. Stacker is the leading disk compression program. **Stacker.** Stac Electronics, 5993 Avenida, Encinas, Carlsbad, CA 92008, 800-522-7822.

If You Still Need More Disk Space, Get a New Hard Drive

A data-compression program is a great way to get more out of your current hard drive, but it's only going to buy you some time. Sooner or later, you're going to run out of hard disk space. And when that happens, you have two choices: You can add a second disk drive to your computer if you don't want to replace your original disk drive, or you can go out and replace the old hard drive with one of those new, huge 500MB or 1000MB (gigabyte) disk drives.

There is an important reason why it's in your best interest to replace your old disk drive with a new one, in addition to the fact that the new drives are so much bigger. The new drives read the data on the hard drive much more quickly than the older drives, so your whole system runs faster.

Seagate Technology makes a complete line of hard disk drives. Their newest drive the Decathlon 850 (ST5850A) has a capacity of 850MB. It uses Seagate's fast ATA technology and can transfer data from the hard drive to the computer's central processing unit (CPU) at speeds of up to 16MB/second.

Installing the Seagate drive in my computer was rather easy to do. The instructions that came with the hard drive were very thorough and comprehensive. (Before I do anything with my computer, I *always* call tech support just to see whether there's any additional information I should know. This practice has helped me stay out of trouble.) And when I called the tech support line at Seagate, the person who answered the phone was not only helpful, but she actually walked me through the entire installation process. But once again, if you've never done this kind of thing before, ask your favorite computer guru to come over to help you with a *little* project.

With the new Seagate hard drive, my various programs (WordPerfect, ACT!, and everything else I use on my computer) run faster because the access time — the time it takes to read and write information from the hard drive to the computer's memory — is much faster. (In fact, the Decathlon 850 transfers data so fast that my computer can't keep up with it. I guess it's time to get a Pentium. But that's another story.) The faster your computer runs, the more productive you are. **Seagate Technology.** 920 Disk Drive, Scotts Valley, CA 95066. To find your nearest Seagate dealer, call 800-468-3472.

Add a Cache Controller Card

You've probably never heard of cache controller cards, also known as disk accelerators, but even though you don't know what they do, they can do a lot to make your computer run faster. A cache controller card handles the flow of data from your hard drive to your computer's central processing unit (CPU). On some systems, it's able to reduce the read and write access time from the hard drive to the CPU from 9–12 ms (milliseconds, or thousandths of a second) to 0.1 ms.

After I took the top off my computer, I just pulled out the old controller card, inserted the new one, and reattached the cable that runs from the card to the hard drive. To say it was easy is an understatement. When I turned my computer back on, I could see that everything was running faster. Promise Technologies makes a full line of cache controller cards. **Promise Technologies.** 1460 Koll Circle, San Jose, CA 95112. For a products catalog or for the number of the nearest computer store that carries Products Technologies' cache controller cards, call 800-888-0245.

Get a New Video Card

If you think that all of your programs are running just a bit too slowly, or if you've just gotten into multimedia and CD-ROMs, and everything appears on your screen in slow motion, it may not be your computer that's slowing you down. It may be your video card instead. Even though you just purchased a super-fast computer, the computer manufacturer may have installed last year's video card, one with only 1MB of memory, in order to keep the price down.

Today's video cards can really make your computer fly. I replaced my old video card with a Diamond Stealth 64 with 4MB of memory. When I turned my computer on, I couldn't believe how much faster it ran. I didn't notice too much of a difference when I was working in WordPerfect because the screen doesn't redraw itself that frequently. But when I started using my graphics programs, the images on the screen redrew themselves in just a fraction of a second, with 16 million colors.

I would have to estimate that my graphics programs are now running five to ten times faster than they were before. It's also done the same thing to my CD-ROMs. And, if you're one of those people who likes to play games on your computer, a faster video card will make a world of difference. Diamond Computer Systems makes a full line of video cards. **Diamond Computer Systems.** Diamond Computer Systems, 2880 Junction Avenue, San Jose, CA 95134-1922, 800-468-5846.

Improve Your Vision with a New Monitor

If you're using an old monitor, or your current monitor is smaller than 15 inches, it may be time to give the old one away and buy a new one. A new monitor can make a world of difference to your daily productivity. If you have to over-concentrate to read the words on your monitor because of either low resolution or small screen size, the muscles in your neck and shoulders become tense — and you get tired. With a new 15-, 17-, or 21-inch monitor, there will be such a substantial increase in your productivity that it will pay for itself in a matter of weeks.

When I recently upgraded my computer, I replaced my old monitor with a Nanao 15-inch color monitor. I didn't know what I had been missing until I plugged it into my computer and turned it on. The first things I noticed were the increase in size, clarity, and brightness. And with the flat, non-glare screen, I no longer needed a visor to keep the glare from the lights in my office off my monitor. Furthermore, Nanao's WideView screen provides an edge-to-edge viewing area.

I also didn't realize, until after I changed monitors, how much I was straining to read the text on my screen because of the small screen size and the low resolution. Now I know how people feel when they come back from the eye doctor with a new set of eyeglasses. I can see clearly again. In fact, I no longer need to have the monitor so close to me. **Nanao USA Corporation.** 23535 Telo Avenue, Torrance, CA 90505. Nanao makes a complete line of high- and ultra-high-resolution color monitors from 15 inches to 21 inches in size. For a catalog and a current price list, call 800-800-5202.

Add More Memory

Earlier in this chapter, I mentioned the importance of using a memory manager to make your computer run more efficiently. In the old days, before Windows, you could only run one program at a time, so the amount of memory wasn't a big concern. Today, it's a big deal! One of the beautiful things about Windows is that you can run one, two, three, four, or more programs at once if you've got enough memory. And the more memory you've got, the faster these programs will run.

If your computer has only 4MB of memory, it's time to call your computer guru friend and invite him or her over for dinner. After dessert, you can ask your "guest" to put some more memory into your computer. It's not difficult to do, if you know what you're doing.

Some of the newer programs, like WordPerfect 6.1, need at least 8MB of memory to run properly. (I've heard through the grapevine, that you won't even be able to run Windows 95, Microsoft's next version of Windows, with less than 8MB of memory.)

I recently increased my computer's memory from 8MB to 16MB, and I can see a huge improvement in my computer's performance. My computer programs run faster, and I can have more of them open at the same time. Kingston Technology Corporation makes a complete line of memory upgrade modules that can increase your computer's memory to 8MB, 16MB, 32MB, 64MB, and beyond. **Kingston Technology Corporation,** 17600 Newhope Street, Fountain Valley, CA 92708, 800-835-6575.

Upgrade Your 486 Computer to a Pentium

If you already own a 486 computer but it's a year or two old, you can now upgrade your computer to a Pentium by using one of Intel's new Pentium

OverDrive processors. With more processing power, you'll be able to crunch the numbers on your spreadsheets much more quickly, your multimedia programs will run faster, and you'll have more power to play your games.

To install an OverDrive processor, all you have to do is remove the old computer chip from your computer and insert the new one in it's place. (But once again, if you don't know the ins and outs of computers, invite your computer guru friend over for dinner.) **Intel OverDrive Processor.** Intel Corporation, 2200 Mission College Blvd., Santa Clara, CA 95051, 800-538-3373.

Improve Your Productivity by Upgrading Your Software

Whenever the developer of your favorite program releases a new version, you should go out and buy a copy. (They'll let you know about it because you'll get a postcard in the mail every day for at least six months.) These bells and whistles will help you get your work done more quickly. And that's why we use these machines so much, because we want to produce high-quality work, keep all our clients and customers happy, and then go home for dinner.

Expand Your Horizons with a Modem

If you really want to expand your horizons, increase your knowledge, improve your productivity, and give yourself access to an almost unlimited amount of information, you need to attach a modem to your computer. A modem gives you the opportunity not only to communicate with other people using your computer, but it also gives you the capability to send and receive e-mail messages and computer files, access on-line information services, search thousands of databases, and share information with people who have similar interests on bulletin board services. And best of all, you can use it to dial your phone for you.

Hayes Microcomputer Products has developed and sold more modems and communications software for personal computers than any other company in the world. Their most recognizable and widely implemented technologies has given rise to the phrase "Hayes compatible" that is prevalent in virtually any modem advertisement you see. Hayes makes a number of different modems that are designed specifically for use at home or in the office. **Hayes Modems.** Hayes Microcomputer Products, Inc. P.O. Box 105203, Atlanta, GA 30348. Call 404-840-9200 for a catalog, price list, and the name of your nearest Hayes dealer.

Don't forget that there's a coupon from Hayes at the back of this book.

You Need a Good Printer

With today's super-fast machines and powerful software, you can produce the kinds of letters, documents, presentations, and proposals in hours that used to take a group of people the better part of a day. But the creation of the work inside the computer is only the first part of the process. The second part is getting it to look good on paper. And if you want it to look as good on paper as it does on your computer screen, you've got to have a good printer.

Brother International makes a complete line of printers for the home and the office. Their newest line of laser printers — the HL-630, HL-645, HL-655 — offer high-quality printing at affordable prices. (The first two models have a 16 MHz microprocessor with 512KB and 1MB of RAM, respectively. The HL-655 has a 25 MHz microprocessor with 2MB RAM.) With Brother's *Straight Paper Path* design, you can print on a wide variety of paper stocks and sizes — from 3" x 5" index cards, to letter envelopes, to legal-sized paper. All three printers print at 6 pages per minute.

If you need a high-end laser printer, the HL-1260 is a phenomenal machine! It's designed for the person who needs high-quality text and graphics output, network connectivity, and the capability to handle complex printing tasks easily and effortlessly. The HL-1260 is fast. It prints at the rate of 12 pages per minute at a resolution of 600 DPI (dots per inch). (For graphical output, you can increase the resolution to 1200 DPI.) Printed text and graphics look so good that you would think the printed document was created by a "professional" printer.

The HL-1260 is driven by a super-fast, 32-bit, 20 MHz RISC processor and comes with 2MB RAM that can be easily upgraded to 26MB. It even comes with a 500 sheet, multipurpose paper tray. And if you need a color printer, Brother's HS-1PS has a lot of printing power.

I've been using the same Brother printer for more than five years now, (not the HL-1260; it's brand new) — and have written four books with it. Day after day, it's done what it was designed to do. I turn it on, and it prints, and prints, and prints. The only time it stops is when it's run out of paper or the toner cartridge needs to be replaced. It's been a dependable workhorse.

Brother International makes a complete line of printers for the home and office. **Brother International Corporation.** 200 Cottontail Lane, Somerset, NJ 08875. For the name of your nearest Brother dealer, call 800-284-4357.

Chapter 24

Ten Things to Get When You Buy Your Next Computer

. . . .

In This Chapter

▶ Stuff to spend money on

. . . .

Getting your work done in the quickest amount of time is what business is all about. If we were to assume that the computer you're using today is taking care of your needs, within a year, it'll be "old technology." About two or three times each week I'm asked by my friends and relatives what kind of computer should I buy.

As far as brand names go, there are many good ones. But I believe that the quality of service the manufacturer or computer store offers is of primary importance. (I've been buying all of my computers from a little store on the northwest side of Chicago, Ernie's Office Machines. Rich Barkoff, who owns the place, has always given me great service and has *forgotten* more about computers than I'll ever know.) This is even more meaningful than low price because when you've got a question or have a problem, you want to be able to talk with someone who can help you.

That said, here are the things I would get in a new computer if money weren't an issue. (But since it probably is, you'll just have decide which features are more or less important to you.)

Buy a Super-Fast Computer

Today it's a Pentium or Power PC; tomorrow it'll be the P6. Beyond that, I don't have the slightest idea. You'll never be disappointed when you buy the fastest computer that's currently available.

Add Lots of Memory

Today you need a minimum of 8MB just to get your computer to run. If you want your computer to really hum, get 16MB or even 32MB of memory.

Include a Huge Hard Drive

Five years ago, a 40MB hard drive was satisfactory. Today, you should get at least a 500MB hard drive, and for just a little more money, you can get a 1000MB (1 gigabyte) hard drive.

Put In a Fast Video Card

Get a video card with at least 4MB of memory. Your graphics programs, CD-ROMs, and games will fly across your screen.

Get a Big Monitor

When we started using computers, we had these itty-bitty, black-and-white (or was it green or amber?) monitors. Today, there are 15-, 17-, and 21-inch monitors that display 16 million colors. Treat yourself to either a 17-inch or 21-inch monitor. You'll thank yourself for it.

For Fun, Install a Fast CD-ROM

The first CD-ROMs were slow, and it took a lot of time to transfer information from the CD-ROM to the computer. Then they developed double-speed CD-ROMs, and now they've got triple-speed and quadruple-speed CD-ROM drives. If you plan on using your CD-ROM, get a triple-speed. If you plan on using it a lot, get a quadruple-speed CD-ROM.

Don't Forget a Sound Card with High-Quality Speakers

If you're going to be using your CD-ROM, you need a good sound card and great speakers. Your sound should sound as good as the graphics look.

To Communicate with the Outside World, You Need a High-Speed Modem

Three years ago, we were happy with 2400 bps (bits per second) modems. Last year, 14,400 bps modems were the rage, and now everyone is starting to use 28,800 bps modems. Buy the fastest modem that's available. Your computer is the gateway to the world, and your modem is your key.

Protect Yourself with a Backup Tape Drive

Backing up your hard drive just makes good sense. With an automatic backup system, the whole process is really easy, and should something happen to your computer, you'll be able to restore any lost or damaged files in almost no time at all.

Chapter 25

Ten Timesaving Tips for Getting More out of Technical Support

1 know that computers *never* have glitches, and computer programs aren't shipped from the software vendors with *bugs* in them, so I'm not even sure why I should throw in some tips on how to make dealing with technical support easier. But if a situation *were* to arise in which you had to call tech support, these tips may make your life easier:

✔ Write down the technical support number in the front of the user's manual or highlight the number on the page where it's printed. Either bend a corner of the page or attach a sticky note to it so you can find it quickly. (I put all of my tech support numbers into ACT!.)

✔ Next to the number, write down the product's serial number or your user ID number. This way, when you're asked for this information, you won't have to start hunting around for it.

✔ Every company has a computerized phone system that has many different menus to chose from. To save yourself time, write down the appropriate sequence of numbers to press so that your call can be quickly routed.

✔ If you need to talk with technical support, try to do it first thing in the morning — not where *you're* located but where tech support is located — before everyone else tries to call. Check your user's manual because some software companies' tech support departments are open as early as 7:00 a.m. EST. Remember that the busiest time for technical support is early on Monday morning because everyone was trying to do something with the computer over the weekend and got into trouble.

✔ Don't call tech support during lunch hours — not yours, theirs — which is usually between the hours of 11:30 a.m. and 1:30 p.m. local time. During these hours, departments are generally understaffed, and you'll spend even more time waiting.

✔ If a company has recently started shipping a new product, you can expect the tech support phone lines to be ringing off the hook. There will be thousands of users who have questions or problems. Try calling either very early in the morning or at the end of the day.

✔ As a general rule, you should expect to be placed on hold for at least 10 to 15 minutes before you even talk to a technician, so make it a point to be doing something else while you're waiting on the phone.

✔ If you're calling and continue to get a busy signal, use the redial feature on your phone. On many phones, the telephone will automatically redial a busy number if you turn on the speaker and then press the redial button.

✔ Before you install a new piece of software or do something that changes your system's configuration, read the installation manual. Then call tech support and ask whether there's anything more you should know before you install the software, something that may not have been mentioned in the manual. Many times, the tech support person will even walk you through the whole installation process.

And one final thought: Don't make changes to your computer at a time of day when you can't call tech support for help. What are you going to do if your computer quits working and tech support doesn't open until 8:00 a.m. on Monday, Pacific Standard Time?

Chapter 26

Ten Reasons to Get on the Internet

● ●

In This Chapter

▶ My attempt to convince you to surf the Net

● ●

*U*nless you've been stranded on a desert island for the past few years, you've probably heard of the *Internet*, a.k.a *cyberspace*, the *infobahn*, the *Inay, Cyberia*, or the dubiously conceived and dreadfully overused *information superhighway*. Should you "get on" It? The answer, which is probably not the one you were hoping for, is yes. Sooner or later, you *will* be on It whether you want to be or not, so you may as well take the plunge now and stay one step ahead of the sluggish masses. That way, when the rest of humanily Is finally dragged kicking and screaming out to the electronic frontier, you will already have staked out your own corner of the Net. Swallow your pride, go buy yourself a pocket protector, and get thee to the Net. If you need more reasons than that, continue reading.

Internet E-Mail

E-mail is still the most popular and widely available Internet service. You can use it to communicate with millions of people worldwide, subscribe to mailing lists of all kinds, and it looks really cool on your business card.

Usenet News Groups

The number of news groups available has surpassed 10,000 at some providers. As the world's largest bulletin board, Usenet is the heart and soul of the Internet. Usually, each group maintains a FAQ (a compilation of *frequently asked questions*), which is very helpful. Topics range from everything you can think of to some things you can't.

The Worldwide Web

You use a Web browser program, such as NCSA Mosaic, to "surf" the Web. The Web is the ever-expanding, global collection of hypertext (interconnected/interconnectable documents) residing on the Internet. It's the fastest-growing part of the Net. The Web is full of multimedia and other fun stuff, such as sounds, pictures, free programs (including Web browsers), and movies. You can put your personal or business *home page* on the Web for others to browse. Good browsers are capable of handling some e-mail functions, Usenet news groups, Gopher (see the following paragraph), file transfers, and hypertext.

Gopher

Gopher is an Internet service that reduces much of cyberspace to an endless series of easily navigated menus. You simply follow Gopher links that look interesting until you find the file or text or whatever strikes your fancy, and then you realize it's 2:00 in the morning. Using Gopher, you can find most everything on the Net.

File Transfer Protocol (FTP)

It sounds like the title of some techno-thriller, but all it means is that you can use it to send and retrieve files of all types all over the world from your desktop. If e-mail is like a super-fast postal service, FTP is like a hyper FedEx or UPS.

You Will Become More Valuable to Current or Future Employers

It's true. In this era of downsizing, insecurity, and instability, the one shining example that appears to hold solid promise for the foreseeable future is the Internet. Being able to put your Internet skills on your resume dramatically enhances your value as a potential hire. If you're Internet-savvy, that makes you "forward-thinking," "cutting edge," "hi-tech," and any number of other buzzwords.

Because They Are on It

Your competitors, the credit bureaus, governments, banks, insurance companies, the media — all of them have access to the Internet and use it to the hilt. That puts you at a strategic disadvantage. Sooner or later, you're going to have to take those first baby steps into the datascape. The longer you wait, the more behind you'll be, and the more savvy *they'll* be. It's not fair, but that's how it is in the brave new world.

It's Better for You than TV

Sure, as with the boob tube, in cyberspace you still slouch in front of a screen, but at least on the Net you get to actively participate. Let's face it: The TV model features a zoned-out you, awash in programming and manipulated by unseen, faraway powers. The Internet model features you as an independent actor/explorer using your imagination in an all-new digital landscape. Better to be a mouse potato than a couch potato.

Because then You Won't Feel Like You're Missing Out

You have this sickening feeling that secret, wonderful, and historic events are taking place in this newly discovered country called the Internet, but you've never been there. Even more depressing: No one there knows how clever and wonderful you are, and technophobia is keeping you from joining in. Well, in order to stop having that feeling, you have to just bite the bullet and join the infopocalypse.

You'll Have Something to Talk About at the Next Cocktail Party

Instead of staring mutely at the cheese dip, imagine boldly delivering reports from the digital frontier! What could make you more charming and mysterious than the ability to regale listeners with tales of electronic daredevilry? What topic perks up more ears than the Internet? Someone else at the party is bound to be on the Net, too, and before you know it, you're exchanging e-mail addresses and chatting about your favorite Web sites.

Impress Everyone with Your Business Card

If you're into impressing people, put your Internet address on your business cards right next to the number for your mobile phone, your car phone, your fax number, your home phone, and your home fax number.

To learn more about the Internet, pickup a copy of IDG's *The Internet For Dummies, 2nd Edition.*

Your Pipeline to the Internet

To get onto the Internet, you need to subscribe to an Internet provider. The Pipeline is one provider that offers very powerful and easy-to-use software — and the software's free. The point-and-click program organizes the rough and tumble Net into logical topic groups and integrates its features, including the Web, seamlessly. It provides full access to everything the Internet has to offer: universal electronic mail, 10,000+ discussion groups, and a cornucopia of resources ranging from on-line books to instant storm forecasts to today's Supreme Court opinions to live, real-time conversations with people anywhere in the world.

The Pipeline. 150 Broadway, Suite 610, New York, NY 10038. For information about subscriptions and software, you can reach The Pipeline at 212-267-3636 (voice), 212-267-4380 (fax), or 212-267-8606 (modem — up to 28.8kbps, V.34 — log-in as a guest). To request information about The Pipeline by e-mail, address your e-mail message to info@pipeline.com. Internet users can also "gopher" directly to pipeline.com or "ftp" directly to ftp.pipeline.com.

The Pipeline

File   **Goodbye!**   **Services**   **Internet**   **Bookmarks!**   **Help**

Pathways into the Internet

- The Pipeline: Information, Software, Accounts . . .
- Today's News from the AP and Other Sources
- The Internet: Guides and Tools
- The Reference Desk
- Shopping: The Pipeline Mall
- Arts and Leisure
- Weather Everywhere
- The Government
- Other Gophers and Information Servers

Mail   Write   News   Today   Talk   How

Jan 30 11:50 AM Online 156 mins

Chapter 27

Ten Reasons Why You Should Be on CompuServe

• •

In This Chapter

▶ Compelling reasons to join CompuServe

• •

*I*f you're not ready to face the challenge of the "final frontier" — the Internet — you may want to give CompuServe a try. CompuServe is the oldest and largest of all the commercial on-line services, with almost 3,000,000 members. If there's anything you need or want, you can probably find it on CompuServe. Here are some of the things you can do:

- If you've got a question, you can post it on any of the bulletin boards in the 2,600+ forums. Post your question at 10 p.m. in the evening, and you'll probably have a half-dozen responses by 7 a.m. the next morning, from anywhere in the world.

- If you're doing research, there are a host of databases you can browse through to look for newspaper and magazine articles, all from the comfort of your home or office. When you find something that's of interest to you, just download it into your computer.

- E-mail is a big part of CompuServe. You can send e-mail messages to anyone who is a CompuServe member and to anyone who has an e-mail address anywhere in the world.

- As part of sending e-mail, you can also attach computer files to your e-mail message. This feature enables you to transfer huge amounts of information in just a few moments of time that the recipient can read on his or her own computer. This is much more effective than sending someone a fax.

- If you have technical questions about your computer or your software, almost every vendor in the country is a member of CompuServe. You can go into the vendor's forum and send and receive e-mail messages from other people who use the same hardware or software that you do. And you can often communicate with people from the company's technical support department.

Before you buy your next computer or upgrade your software, go into the vendor's forum or to the user's group and post a message asking how they like [insert brand of computer or name of software]. Within a day, you'll know whether you should or shouldn't make your purchase. It's also a lot of fun reading all the other messages that people have left on the bulletin board. No one's shy on CompuServe.

- ✔ If you're going on a trip and want to know what the weather is like — anywhere in the United States or in the world — just type in the name of the city and then click OK. Within a few moments, you'll be able to read the National Weather Services's local weather forecasts and look at their weather maps.

- ✔ For those of you who are news junkies, you can read the latest stories straight off the Associated Press wire service. You no longer have to wait until the top of the hour to find out what's going on in the world. You can read tomorrow morning's headlines now. (And if you want the latest sports scores, you can get those off the AP also.)

- ✔ If you're selling a product or a service, CompuServe offers you many opportunities to come into contact with potential buyers. And when you're looking for a specific product, there's probably someone on CompuServe who has exactly what you need.

For more information about CompuServe, you can write or call **CompuServe.** 5000 Arlington Centre Blvd., Columbus, OH 43220, 800-848-8990.

I posted a message in several of the CompuServe forums asking people, "How do you use CompuServe to save time?" One person wrote this message back to me, within a day:

> *Where CompuServe really excels, Jeff, is in eliminating the need to "reinvent the wheel." For example, a couple of days ago a TV producer in Seattle posted a message on this forum stating that he was trying to make an underwater housing for a small, lipstick-sized camera. He asked if any forum members had experience or suggestions in such an undertaking. He has already received several replies, and I noticed in the download in which I found your message that a forum member has provided him with step-by-step, inch-by-inch directions. These forums allow us to share a vast pool of experience with many other people, pools into which we can reach with just a few keystrokes. Never before in the history of mankind has it been so easy for so many to work together.*

Index

• I •

• J •

• Q •

Notes

Notes

Notes

Notes

Notes

Notes

Notes

Notes

Notes

Notes

Notes

Notes

Notes

Notes

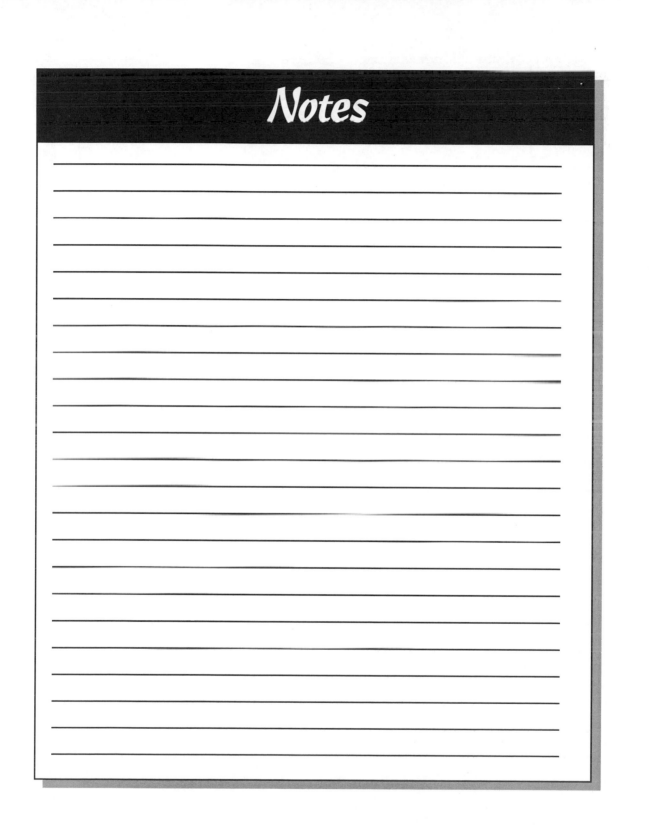

Notes

Notes

Notes

Notes

DUMMIES PRESS

Title	Author	ISBN	Price

12/20/94

INTERNET / COMMUNICATIONS / NETWORKING
CompuServe For Dummies™	by Wallace Wang	1-56884-181-7	$19.95 USA/$26.95 Canada
Modems For Dummies™, 2nd Edition	by Tina Rathbone	1-56884-223-6	$19.99 USA/$26.99 Canada
Modems For Dummies™	by Tina Rathbone	1-56884-001-2	$19.95 USA/$26.95 Canada
MORE Internet For Dummies™	by John R. Levine & Margaret Levine Young	1-56884-164-7	$19.95 USA/$26.95 Canada
NetWare For Dummies™	by Ed Tittel & Deni Connor	1-56884-003-9	$19.95 USA/$26.95 Canada
Networking For Dummies™	by Doug Lowe	1-56884-079-9	$19.95 USA/$26.95 Canada
ProComm Plus 2 For Windows For Dummies™	by Wallace Wang	1-56884-219-8	$19.99 USA/$26.99 Canada
The Internet For Dummies™, 2nd Edition	by John R. Levine & Carol Baroudi	1-56884-222-8	$19.99 USA/$26.99 Canada
The Internet For Macs For Dummies™	by Charles Seiter	1-56884-184-1	$19.95 USA/$26.95 Canada

MACINTOSH
Macs For Dummies®	by David Pogue	1-56884-173-6	$19.95 USA/$26.95 Canada
Macintosh System 7.5 For Dummies™	by Bob LeVitus	1-56884-197-3	$19.95 USA/$26.95 Canada
MORE Macs For Dummies™	by David Pogue	1-56884-087-X	$19.95 USA/$26.95 Canada
PageMaker 5 For Macs For Dummies™	by Galen Gruman	1-56884-178-7	$19.95 USA/$26.95 Canada
QuarkXPress 3.3 For Dummies™	by Galen Gruman & Barbara Assadi	1-56884-217-1	$19.99 USA/$26.99 Canada
Upgrading and Fixing Macs For Dummies™	by Kearney Rietmann & Frank Higgins	1-56884-189-2	$19.95 USA/$26.95 Canada

MULTIMEDIA
| Multimedia & CD-ROMs For Dummies™, Interactive Multimedia Value Pack | by Andy Rathbone | 1-56884-225-2 | $29.95 USA/$39.95 Canada |
| Multimedia & CD-ROMs For Dummies™ | by Andy Rathbone | 1-56884-089-6 | $19.95 USA/$26.95 Canada |

OPERATING SYSTEMS / DOS
MORE DOS For Dummies™	by Dan Gookin	1-56884-046-2	$19.95 USA/$26.95 Canada
S.O.S. For DOS™	by Katherine Murray	1-56884-043-8	$12.95 USA/$16.95 Canada
OS/2 For Dummies™	by Andy Rathbone	1-878058-76-2	$19.95 USA/$26.95 Canada

UNIX
| UNIX For Dummies™ | by John R. Levine & Margaret Levine Young | 1-878058-58-4 | $19.95 USA/$26.95 Canada |

WINDOWS
| S.O.S. For Windows™ | by Katherine Murray | 1-56884-045-4 | $12.95 USA/$16.95 Canada |
| MORE Windows 3.1 For Dummies™, 3rd Edition | by Andy Rathbone | 1-56884-240-6 | $19.99 USA/$26.99 Canada |

PCs / HARDWARE
| Illustrated Computer Dictionary For Dummies™ | by Dan Gookin, Wally Wang, & Chris Van Buren | 1-56884-004-7 | $12.95 USA/$16.95 Canada |
| Upgrading and Fixing PCs For Dummies™ | by Andy Rathbone | 1-56884-002-0 | $19.95 USA/$26.95 Canada |

PRESENTATION / AUTOCAD
| AutoCAD For Dummies™ | by Bud Smith | 1-56884-191-4 | $19.95 USA/$26.95 Canada |
| PowerPoint 4 For Windows For Dummies™ | by Doug Lowe | 1-56884-161-2 | $16.95 USA/$22.95 Canada |

PROGRAMMING
Borland C++ For Dummies™	by Michael Hyman	1-56884-162-0	$19.95 USA/$26.95 Canada
"Borland's New Language Product" For Dummies™	by Neil Rubenking	1-56884-200-7	$19.95 USA/$26.95 Canada
C For Dummies™	by Dan Gookin	1-878058-78-9	$19.95 USA/$26.95 Canada
C++ For Dummies™	by Stephen R. Davis	1-56884-163-9	$19.95 USA/$26.95 Canada
Mac Programming For Dummies™	by Dan Parks Sydow	1-56884-173-6	$19.95 USA/$26.95 Canada
QBasic Programming For Dummies™	by Douglas Hergert	1-56884-093-4	$19.95 USA/$26.95 Canada
Visual Basic "X" For Dummies™, 2nd Edition	by Wallace Wang	1-56884-230-9	$19.99 USA/$26.99 Canada
Visual Basic 3 For Dummies™	by Wallace Wang	1-56884-076-4	$19.95 USA/$26.95 Canada

SPREADSHEET
1-2-3 For Dummies™	by Greg Harvey	1-878058-60-6	$16.95 USA/$21.95 Canada
1-2-3 For Windows 5 For Dummies™, 2nd Edition	by John Walkenbach	1-56884-216-3	$16.95 USA/$21.95 Canada
1-2-3 For Windows For Dummies™	by John Walkenbach	1-56884-052-7	$16.95 USA/$21.95 Canada
Excel 5 For Macs For Dummies™	by Greg Harvey	1-56884-186-8	$19.95 USA/$26.95 Canada
Excel For Dummies™, 2nd Edition	by Greg Harvey	1-56884-050-0	$16.95 USA/$21.95 Canada
MORE Excel 5 For Windows For Dummies™	by Greg Harvey	1-56884-207-4	$19.95 USA/$26.95 Canada
Quattro Pro 6 For Windows For Dummies™	by John Walkenbach	1-56884-174-4	$19.95 USA/$26.95 Canada
Quattro Pro For DOS For Dummies™	by John Walkenbach	1-56884-023-3	$16.95 USA/$21.95 Canada

UTILITIES / VCRs & CAMCORDERS
| Norton Utilities 8 For Dummies™ | by Beth Slick | 1-56884-166-3 | $19.95 USA/$26.95 Canada |
| VCRs & Camcorders For Dummies™ | by Andy Rathbone & Gordon McComb | 1-56884-229-5 | $14.99 USA/$20.99 Canada |

WORD PROCESSING
Ami Pro For Dummies™	by Jim Meade	1-56884-049-7	$19.95 USA/$26.95 Canada
MORE Word For Windows 6 For Dummies™	by Doug Lowe	1-56884-165-5	$19.95 USA/$26.95 Canada
MORE WordPerfect 6 For Windows For Dummies™	by Margaret Levine Young & David C. Kay	1-56884-206-6	$19.95 USA/$26.95 Canada
MORE WordPerfect 6 For DOS For Dummies™	by Wallace Wang, edited by Dan Gookin	1-56884-047-0	$19.95 USA/$26.95 Canada
S.O.S. For WordPerfect™	by Katherine Murray	1-56884-053-5	$12.95 USA/$16.95 Canada
Word 6 For Macs For Dummies™	by Dan Gookin	1-56884-190-6	$19.95 USA/$26.95 Canada
Word For Windows 6 For Dummies™	by Dan Gookin	1-56884-075-6	$16.95 USA/$21.95 Canada
Word For Windows For Dummies™	by Dan Gookin	1-878058-86-X	$16.95 USA/$21.95 Canada
WordPerfect 6 For Dummies™	by Dan Gookin	1-878058-77-0	$16.95 USA/$21.95 Canada
WordPerfect For Dummies™	by Dan Gookin	1-878058-52-5	$16.95 USA/$21.95 Canada
WordPerfect For Windows For Dummies™	by Margaret Levine Young & David C. Kay	1-56884-032-2	$16.95 USA/$21.95 Canada

1/26/95

Fun, Fast, & Cheap!

CorelDRAW! 5 For Dummies™ Quick Reference
by Raymond E. Werner

ISBN: 1-56884-952-4
$9.99 USA/$12.99 Canada

Windows "X" For Dummies™ Quick Reference, 3rd Edition
by Greg Harvey

ISBN: 1-56884-964-8
$9.99 USA/$12.99 Canada

Word For Windows 6 For Dummies™ Quick Reference
by George Lynch

ISBN: 1-56884-095-0
$8.95 USA/$12.95 Canada

WordPerfect For DOS For Dummies™ Quick Reference
by Greg Harvey

ISBN: 1-56884-009-8
$8.95 USA/$11.95 Canada

Title	Author	ISBN	Price
DATABASE			
Access 2 For Dummies™ Quick Reference	by Stuart A. Stuple	1-56884-167-1	$9.95 USA/$11.95 Canada
dBASE 5 For DOS For Dummies Quick Reference	by Barry Sosinsky	1-56884-954-0	$9.99 USA/$12.99 Canada
dBASE 5 For Windows For Dummies™ Quick Reference	by Stuart J. Stuple	1-56884-953-2	$9.99 USA/$12.99 Canada
Paradox 5 For Windows For Dummies™ Quick Reference	by Scott Palmer	1-56884-960-5	$9.99 USA/$12.99 Canada
DESKTOP PUBLISHING / ILLUSTRATION/GRAPHICS			
Harvard Graphics 3 For Windows For Dummies™ Quick Reference	by Raymond E. Werner	1-56884-962-1	$9.99 USA/$12.99 Canada
FINANCE / PERSONAL FINANCE			
Quicken 4 For Windows For Dummies™ Quick Reference	by Stephen L. Nelson	1-56884-950-8	$9.95 USA/$12.95 Canada
GROUPWARE / INTEGRATED			
Microsoft Office 4 For Windows For Dummies™ Quick Reference	by Doug Lowe	1-56884-958-3	$9.99 USA/$12.99 Canada
Microsoft Works For Windows 3 For Dummies™ Quick Reference	by Michael Partington	1-56884-959-1	$9.99 USA/$12.99 Canada
INTERNET / COMMUNICATIONS / NETWORKING			
The Internet For Dummies™ Quick Reference	by John R. Levine	1-56884-168-X	$8.95 USA/$11.95 Canada
MACINTOSH			
Macintosh System 7.5 For Dummies™ Quick Reference	by Stuart J. Stuple	1-56884-956-7	$9.99 USA/$12.99 Canada
OPERATING SYSTEMS / DOS			
DOS For Dummies® Quick Reference	by Greg Harvey	1-56884-007-1	$8.95 USA/$11.95 Canada
UNIX			
UNIX For Dummies™ Quick Reference	by Margaret Levine Young & John R. Levine	1-56884-094-2	$8.95 USA/$11.95 Canada
WINDOWS			
Windows 3.1 For Dummies™ Quick Reference, 2nd Edition	by Greg Harvey	1-56884-951-6	$8.95 USA/$11.95 Canada
PRESENTATION / AUTOCAD			
AutoCAD For Dummies™ Quick Reference	by Ellen Finkelstein	1-56884-198-1	$9.95 USA/$12.95 Canada
SPREADSHEET			
1-2-3 For Dummies™ Quick Reference	by John Walkenbach	1-56884-027-6	$8.95 USA/$11.95 Canada
1-2-3 For Windows 5 For Dummies™ Quick Reference	by John Walkenbach	1-56884-957-5	$9.95 USA/$12.95 Canada
Excel For Windows For Dummies™ Quick Reference, 2nd Edition	by John Walkenbach	1-56884-096-9	$8.95 USA/$11.95 Canada
Quattro Pro 6 For Windows For Dummies™ Quick Reference	by Stuart A. Stuple	1-56884-172-8	$9.95 USA/$12.95 Canada
WORD PROCESSING			
Word For Windows 6 For Dummies™ Quick Reference	by George Lynch	1-56884-095-0	$8.95 USA/$11.95 Canada
WordPerfect For Windows For Dummies™ Quick Reference	by Greg Harvey	1-56884-039-X	$8.95 USA/$11.95 Canada

FOR MORE INFORMATION OR TO ORDER, PLEASE CALL ▶ 800. 762. 2974

For volume discounts & special orders please call
Tony Real, Special Sales, at 415. 655. 3048

Macworld QuarkXPress 3.2/3.3 Bible
by Barbara Assadi & Galen Gruman

ISBN: 1-878058-85-1
$39.95 USA/$52.95 Canada

Includes disk with QuarkXPress XTensions and scripts.

Macworld PageMaker 5 Bible
by Craig Danuloff

ISBN: 1-878058-84-3
$39.95 USA/$52.95 Canada

Includes 2 disks with Pagemaker utilities, clip art, and more.

Macworld FileMaker Pro 2.0/2.1 Bible
by Steven A. Schwartz

ISBN: 1-56884-201-5
$34.95 USA/$46.95 Canada

Includes disk with ready-to-run databases.

Macworld Word 6 Companion, 2nd Edition
by Jim Heid

ISBN: 1-56884-082-9
$24.95 USA/$34.95 Canada

Macworld Guide To Microsoft Word 5/5.1
by Jim Heid

ISBN: 1-878058-39-8
$22.95 USA/$29.95 Canada

Macworld ClarisWorks 2.0/2.1 Companion, 2nd Edition
by Steven A. Schwartz

ISBN: 1-56884-180-9
$24.95 USA/$34.95 Canada

Macworld Guide To Microsoft Works 3
by Barrie Sosinsky

ISBN: 1-878058-42-8
$22.95 USA/$29.95 Canada

Macworld Excel 5 Companion, 2nd Edition
by Chris Van Buren & David Maguiness

ISBN: 1-56884-081-0
$24.95 USA/$34.95 Canada

Macworld Guide To Microsoft Excel 4
by David Maguiness

ISBN: 1-878058-40-1
$22.95 USA/$29.95 Canada

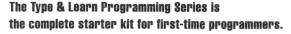

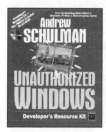
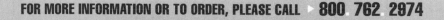

ORDER FORM

HIGHLAND TOWNSHIP LIBRARY

Order Center: **(800) 762-2974** *(8 a.m.–6 p.m., EST, weekdays)*

12/20/94

Quantity	ISBN	Title	Price	Total

Shipping & Handling Charges

	Description	First book	Each additional book	Total
Domestic	Normal	$4.50	$1.50	$
	Two Day Air	$8.50	$2.50	$
	Overnight	$18.00	$3.00	$
International	Surface	$8.00	$8.00	$
	Airmail	$16.00	$16.00	$
	DHL Air	$17.00	$17.00	$

*For large quantities call for shipping & handling charges.
**Prices are subject to change without notice.

Ship to:

Name _____

Company _____

Address _____

City/State/Zip _____

Daytime Phone _____

Payment: ☐ Check to IDG Books (US Funds Only)

   ☐ VISA   ☐ MasterCard   ☐ American Express

Card # _____ Expires _____

Signature _____

Subtotal _____

CA residents add
applicable sales tax _____

IN, MA, and MD
residents add
5% sales tax _____

IL residents add
6.25% sales tax _____

RI residents add
7% sales tax _____

TX residents add
8.25% sales tax _____

Shipping _____

Total _____

Please send this order form to:

IDG Books Worldwide
7260 Shadeland Station, Suite 100
Indianapolis, IN 46256

Allow up to 3 weeks for delivery.
Thank you!

IDG BOOKS WORLDWIDE REGISTRATION CARD

RETURN THIS REGISTRATION CARD FOR FREE CATALOG

Title of this book: Time Management For Dummies

My overall rating of this book: ❏ Very good [1] ❏ Good [2] ❏ Satisfactory [3] ❏ Fair [4] ❏ Poor [5]

How I first heard about this book:

❏ Found in bookstore; name: [6] _____   ❏ Book review: [7]

❏ Advertisement: [8]   ❏ Catalog: [9]

❏ Word of mouth; heard about book from friend, co-worker, etc.: [10]   ❏ Other: [11]

What I liked most about this book:

_____

_____

What I would change, add, delete, etc., in future editions of this book:

_____

_____

Other comments:

_____

Number of computer books I purchase in a year: ❏ 1 [12] ❏ 2-5 [13] ❏ 6-10 [14] ❏ More than 10 [15]

I would characterize my computer skills as: ❏ Beginner [16] ❏ Intermediate [17] ❏ Advanced [18] ❏ Professional [19]

I use ❏ DOS [20] ❏ Windows [21] ❏ OS/2 [22] ❏ Unix [23] ❏ Macintosh [24] ❏ Other: [25] _____
(please specify)

I would be interested in new books on the following subjects:
(please check all that apply, and use the spaces provided to identify specific software)

❏ Word processing: [26] _____   ❏ Spreadsheets: [27]

❏ Data bases: [28]   ❏ Desktop publishing: [29]

❏ File Utilities: [30]   ❏ Money management: [31]

❏ Networking: [32]   ❏ Programming languages: [33]

❏ Other: [34]

I use a PC at (please check all that apply): ❏ home [35] ❏ work [36] ❏ school [37] ❏ other: [38] _____

The disks I prefer to use are ❏ 5.25 [39] ❏ 3.5 [40] ❏ other: [41] _____

I have a CD ROM: ❏ yes [42] ❏ no [43]

I plan to buy or upgrade computer hardware this year: ❏ yes [44] ❏ no [45]

I plan to buy or upgrade computer software this year: ❏ yes [46] ❏ no [47]

Name: _____   Business title: [48] _____   Type of Business: [49] _____

Address (❏ home [50] ❏ work [51] /Company name: _____)

Street/Suite# _____

City [52] /State [53] /Zipcode [54]: _____   Country [55] _____

❏ **I liked this book!** You may quote me by name in future
IDG Books Worldwide promotional materials.

My daytime phone number is _____

IDG BOOKS

THE WORLD OF
COMPUTER
KNOWLEDGE

❑ YES!

Please keep me informed about IDG's World of Computer Knowledge.
Send me the latest IDG Books catalog.

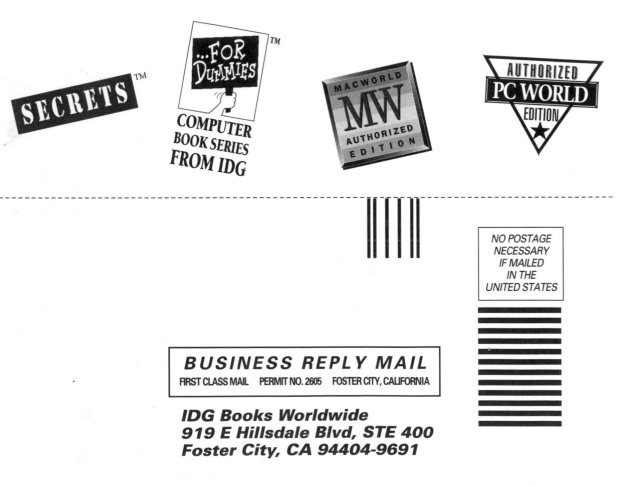

SECRETS™

...FOR DUMMIES™
COMPUTER BOOK SERIES FROM IDG

MACWORLD MW AUTHORIZED EDITION

AUTHORIZED PC WORLD EDITION

NO POSTAGE
NECESSARY
IF MAILED
IN THE
UNITED STATES

BUSINESS REPLY MAIL
FIRST CLASS MAIL   PERMIT NO. 2605   FOSTER CITY, CALIFORNIA

IDG Books Worldwide
919 E Hillsdale Blvd, STE 400
Foster City, CA 94404-9691